SHIRLEY BOOTH

SHIRLEY BOOTH

A Biography and Career Record

David C. Tucker

McFarland & Company, Inc., Publishers

Jefferson, North Carolina, and London

Frontispiece: Shirley Booth, circa 1957,
in a Paramount Pictures publicity photograph.

LIBRARY OF CONGRESS CATALOGUING-IN-PUBLICATION DATA

Tucker, David C., 1962–
Shirley Booth : a biography and career record /
David C. Tucker.
p.   cm.
Includes bibliographical references and index.

ISBN 978-0-7864-3600-2
softcover : 50# alkaline paper ∞

1. Booth, Shirley.   2. Actors—United States—Biography.   I. Title.
PN2287.B6374T83   2008   791.4302'8092—dc22 [B]   2008001072

British Library cataloguing data are available

Cover photograph: Shirley in one of her favorite movie roles—
as Dolly Levi in *The Matchmaker* (Paramount, 1958)

Manufactured in the United States of America

*McFarland & Company, Inc., Publishers
Box 611, Jefferson, North Carolina 28640
www.mcfarlandpub.com*

To the memory of my sister,
Donna Tucker Sassone
(1960–2006),
a great lady in her own right

Acknowledgments

The next time I write a biography, I only hope there are as many Van Pattens available to answer questions as there were for this one. Joyce Van Patten not only gave me one of my first interviews for this book, sharing her recollections of working with Shirley Booth in two Broadway shows, but also put me in contact with other friends and colleagues. One of them was her brother, Dick, who worked with Shirley on *Duffy's Tavern*, and went out of his way to provide some great stories. Both were a delight to interview. I am grateful to them and to everyone who took the time to share recollections.

Another strong contributor to this book is Michael D. Strain, of Indianapolis, who kindly loaned a number of rare Shirley Booth photographs from his personal collection. Michael's generosity substantially enhanced the look of this book, and his eagerness to read the finished product helped keep me motivated and at my desk. Speaking of people I've never met, Old Time Radio expert *extraordinaire* Jim Cox wrote the first published review of my earlier book *The Women Who Made Television Funny: Ten Stars of 1950s Sitcoms* (McFarland, 2007), and it was the kind of review a writer always hopes to get. I hope he likes this book as well, and I thank him for the encouragement he gave a newcomer. The support and aid of two other fellow scribblers, Lynn Kear and James Robert Parish, is gratefully acknowledged as well.

Librarians who kindly responded to research queries, and provided valuable information, include Amy Andreasson of the Eldredge Public Library (Chatham, MA), Eileen Colletti of the Hartford (CT) Public Library, Cynthia Franco of the DeGolyer Library at Southern Methodist University, and Joy Holland of the Brooklyn (NY) Public Library. I also made extensive use of materials held by the University of Georgia libraries, and the Woodruff Library at Emory University.

Closer to home, my DeKalb County (GA) Public Library colleagues Barbara Kelly and Susan Williams were helpful with genealogical and interlibrary loan assistance, respectively, while Ken McCullers was an excellent proofreader, and provider of moral support. To my family and friends, who have been sorely neglected of late while I pursue my "hobby" of writing books, thanks for everything you do to keep me going.

Table of Contents

Introduction

When I told people I was writing a book about Shirley Booth, some did not immediately recognize the name of the distinguished actress who won an Oscar, two Emmys, and three Tony Awards. But if I mentioned that she played the title role on television's *Hazel,* they usually made the connection — and smiled.

This is, surprisingly, the first full-length biography of one of the great actresses of the American theater, one whose accomplishments also encompassed television, radio, and films. It covers her life and career from her debut in a stock theater company circa 1918, through 32 Broadway shows between 1925 and 1970, her heyday as a movie star in the 1950s, her Academy Award for Best Actress for her debut film *Come Back, Little Sheba,* and finally her starring roles in two television comedy series.

Shirley Booth was, in more ways than one, an Everywoman. She was never one of those actresses who attract notice primarily for their beauty, and whose careers fade with their looks. Shirley was an attractive woman of average good looks, with a normal mature woman's figure, whose career only escalated as she grew into middle age and beyond. (She was 54 years old when she won her Oscar; 63 when *Hazel* debuted.) What was exceptional about her was always the wide-ranging talent that allowed her to play a plethora of interesting and varied characters. Unlike some actresses who were convincing only as intelligent, well-bred women, or who were best-suited to either dramatic or comedic roles, Shirley could do it all. Literate Broadway drama by William Inge, or saucy maid in a television sitcom, she was always convincing, and always captivating.

Because she made it look so easy, reviewers and audiences sometimes fell into the trap of believing that she *was* the character she played — whichever one it happened to be at the time. But as Brooks Atkinson astutely noted in 1954, reviewing her Broadway musical *By the Beautiful Sea,* it was a fallacy to assume that she just happened to land so many roles to which she was perfectly suited. "Everything she appears in seems to be just right for her. The slatternly housewife in *Come Back, Little Sheba,* the romantic tourist in *Time of the Cuckoo,* the careless trollop in *A Tree Grows in Brooklyn,* the cynical secretary in *Goodbye, My Fancy,* and the race-track moll in *Three Men on a Horse* were also just right for Miss Booth. Some of these parts were small ones. But they seemed to suit Miss Booth down to the ground because she acted them with such technical resourcefulness and with so much sincerity. Everything suits a thoroughly experienced actor who has personal magnetism."[1]

Like many others, I first knew Shirley Booth as the goodhearted but interfering maid in the hit television comedy series *Hazel,* which originally aired from 1961 to 1966. Viewing reruns of the show in the 1970s, I wasn't familiar with the leading lady's illustrious career, and therefore didn't grasp why the name SHIRLEY BOOTH was emblazoned so prominently above the show's title. I never saw any of her Broadway shows, and wouldn't have understood the television critic who said that having Miss Booth play Hazel was roughly equivalent to casting the great John Barrymore as Henry Aldrich. In fact, many of Shirley's colleagues were startled when she accepted the lead in a TV series, thinking it a huge step down for someone of her credentials. To her credit, she never denigrated the role, or the medium, happily banked her sizable paychecks, and was quick to tell anyone who asked that she thoroughly enjoyed playing Hazel.

It may be only fair to warn readers that this is not the type of biography that details the odd, traumatic, or sexually adventurous life of its subject. Shirley Booth, to the best of my knowledge, had no crippling addictions or scandalous secrets, and will never go down in history as the star most likely to throw a tantrum at work. However, I choose to believe that we can, and should, admire Shirley Booth for the amazing length and breadth of her career, and for the uniformly fine quality of her performances. These accomplishments make her eminently worthy of a biography and career record. I also, from the time I first began researching this book, found her consistently intriguing, quotable, and interesting as a person. Reading profiles of her in dog-eared, musty-smelling copies of 1950s popular magazines like Life and Collier's, I found myself drawn to her, and understood why audiences were as well. Interviewing several of her friends and colleagues only enhanced the portrait of a many-faceted woman.

If there is, in fact, no smoking gun in her personal life, there were nonetheless, in the course of her ninety-plus years, the same types of ups and downs that most of us experience. She was raised by a strict and dictatorial father who forbade her to pursue a stage career, and she would forever after have a troubled relationship with him, so much so that they eventually stopped speaking. After her first marriage, to radio comedian Ed Gardner of Duffy's Tavern fame, ended unhappily, she married again, only to find herself widowed a few years later.

An introvert by nature, Shirley Booth came vividly to life onstage, claimed she never suffered from stage fright, and was perfectly capable of taking a nap before the curtain rose. In her performances there was almost always a nakedly human and vulnerable quality, often tinged with a hint of sadness, making audiences and critics alike fall in love with her over and over again. In her off hours she often preferred solitude, usually accompanied by the animals she loved best. She was attracted to the starring role in Hazel because she herself had experienced loss in her life, and liked the idea of playing a woman who finds satisfaction in becoming part of a family.

This book covers in full her accomplishments in theater, radio, film, and television. Supplementing the biographical chapters, the appendices include an annotated list of her Broadway shows, a log of her radio work, a filmography, the most detailed guide ever compiled to the 154 episodes of her hit television series Hazel, and a guide to its short-lived follow-up, 1973's A Touch of Grace. The book describes not only her featured role in Duffy's Tavern, one of the most fondly remembered comedy shows of its era, but also her lesser-known shows Hogan's Daughter and Strictly Business, and the show that might have been, Our Miss Brooks.

Film historian Bernard F. Dick has said, and rightly so, that Shirley Booth's career "can never be as well documented as it should be, because [she] belonged to an age when memory, not technology, was the keeper of the flame."[2] Nevertheless, I hope that this book will do its share in acquainting readers with her legacy, and appreciating the remnants of her work that we are still able to enjoy.

1. Thelma Takes Stock

When she was awarded a Best Actress Oscar for her performance in *Come Back, Little Sheba* (Paramount, 1952), Shirley Booth joined a select company of performers who won Academy Awards for their first appearance in a feature film. It was neither the first nor the last accolade that Shirley would rack up in the course of a long and much-honored career — she already had to her credit a Tony Award, her second, for the same role, and would later add two Emmys, a Golden Globe, and a third Tony to her trophy shelf.

Her appearance on the cover of *Time* magazine in the summer of 1953, newly acknowledged as a full-fledged star in her mid-fifties, was the culmination of thirty-five years of work in the theater, and in radio. There had been any number of setbacks and disappointments along the way, and in the 1940s Shirley would take comfort in some words of encouragement that came from her first husband, radio comedian Ed Gardner: "Ed said, 'Shirley, people envy me my success, but they all hope you'll make it to the top one of these days. They say, good ol' Shirley, she's been pluggin' away a long time.'"[1]

When she did make it big, she didn't do so as many actresses do, by capitalizing on her youth and beauty. She later said that she had known full well from an early age that she was not destined to be one of the great beauties of her time.

"As soon as I was old enough to understand," Shirley said, "my mother consoled me for not being beautiful with this quotation, 'What you are is so much louder than what you say that I cannot hear you.'"[2]

She took that advice to heart. Still, atypical a star as she may have been, there was one thing she had in common with many Hollywood glamour girls (and boys), then and now — a birth date of her own choosing, and a life story told largely on her own terms.

The journalists eager to profile Shirley in the wake of her Oscar win relied mostly on her own account of her youth and early career, beginning with her birth in New York's Morningside Heights on August 30, 1907. Occasionally, an even later date would be offered — as in a 1951 *Collier's* profile, which gave her age as forty, born in 1911. (In 1942, profiling Shirley in the wake of her success in Broadway's *My Sister Eileen*, the editors of the generally authoritative *Current Biography* simply threw up their hands where Shirley's age was concerned, saying, "The date is a secret."[3]) Not until her death in 1992 did her true age and date of birth — August 30, 1898 — become widely known. It was Shirley's surviving sister, Jean, who provided that late correction to the record.

Shirley's first easily verifiable professional credit was an ingénue role on Broadway in January 1925, appearing opposite a juvenile lead named Humphrey Bogart in an unmemorable comedy called *Hell's Bells*. Surprisingly, few journalists stopped to match this fact against the reported birth date of 1907, and wonder how she had attained such a toehold before reaching the age of eighteen. When the subject did come up, Shirley, who readily acknowledged that she had trained for the theater in a succession of stock companies before graduating to Broadway, simply explained that she had dropped out of school and gone onstage at the age of twelve! Combined with her oft-given account of the disapproval with which her father regarded her stage ambitions, this might conceivably have raised a red flag with biographers, but most accepted her account as given. Perhaps they, like audiences over a period of more than 50 years, had fallen victim to the Booth charm.

The baby born in 1898 to Virginia Wright Ford and her husband, Albert James Ford, would be named Thelma; "Shirley" came later. Mr. and Mrs. Ford were young, still in their early twenties, and had been married for less than a year when Thelma, their firstborn child, arrived. The family was then living in the Morningside Heights district of New York City.

Morningside Heights was going through a renaissance—an article published a few years earlier in the *New York Times* had described it as "the most attractive part of the city to anybody who is seeking a home that is somewhat suburban in its characteristics."[4] The completion of a subway route provided ready access to and from the neighborhood, and the establishment of Columbia University nearby gave it prestige.

Baby Thelma was baptized at the historic Trinity Church in Manhattan, where father Albert at one time served as leading soloist in the church choir. "I did not inherit the mantle of his voice," the adult Shirley said, "but I loved to sing in Sunday school, when I was six or so."[5] She would follow the Episcopalian faith for the rest of her life.

Though there was little in the background of the Ford family to suggest they had given birth to a future Oscar winner, young Thelma found from a very early age that she enjoyed performing. As a toddler, she found herself onstage in a Sunday school program, singing "In the Good Ole Summertime." It was an exciting experience, and the sound of audience applause intrigued her. She would later say that it was during this performance that she first experienced the sensation of ambition.

"That was my first experience with applause, and I was gone," she said years later. "No one could convince me that I was not going on the stage. And I figured I'd be pretty darn good, too."[6]

Having no siblings for playmates (sister Jean didn't come along until 1914), Thelma was a solitary child who learned to entertain herself with her imagination, along with clothes she borrowed from her mother's closet. Another childhood divertissement was a game she called "Talking Balkan." Riding on streetcars with her mother, Thelma would separate herself from her mother momentarily, and then reappear, chattering away in a phony but identifiably "foreign" language that never failed to catch the ears of fellow passengers. The attention this drew from her fellow passengers Thelma found gratifying.

It was also evident early on that the future Shirley Booth was a people watcher, a trait that would later serve her well as an actress. In particular, Thelma had an affinity for older people. "When my mother would lose me," she later said, "she'd look for an old man with a white beard. If there was one in the area, there I'd be, hanging around admiring him."[7]

By the time she was ready to attend school, the Ford family had left Morningside Heights, relocating to Brooklyn. As an adult, she remembered living "on the corner of Ocean Avenue and Newkirk,"[8] in Flatbush. Enrolled in P.S. 152, Thelma initially was uncomfortable, stricken with shyness. Coming home one afternoon after a bad day at school, the little girl sought out her mother Virginia and said, "Nobody likes me."

Virginia, always in Shirley's corner, advised her daughter to show an interest in her classmates, and to look for whatever special qualities she could find in each little boy or girl. "If you like them enough," Virginia told her daughter, "they'll like you."[9] Shirley could still recall that advice nearly fifty years later, and recognized that her ability to relate to other people, and to be *simpatico* with their feelings, had served her well as an actress.

Gradually, Thelma began to emerge from her shell. It was her gift for performing that ultimately broke the ice with her classmates. A talented mimic, she regaled her classmates with impersonations of the teacher while that lady was out of the room. When she wrote an essay, "Autobiography of a Thanksgiving Turkey," that was chosen to be read aloud in the school auditorium, Thelma once again basked in the glow of applause.

If young Thelma Ford was hungry for attention and acclaim, it was likely the result of her father's chilly nature. A bright and precocious child, bursting with energy, she wanted badly to please her father, but in that aim she was inevitably disappointed. "He was the sort of man," Shirley later explained, "you'd run up to breathless and happy and he'd say, 'Your hands are dirty.'"[10]

As noted previously, most of the available information about Shirley's childhood comes from the recollections she shared with journalists many years later. Though her account varied little in the numerous interviews she gave, surviving records sometimes call into question her version of events. The decision to shave nine years off her date of birth occasionally resulted in inconsistencies, notably the statement that she left home at the age of twelve. In a similar vein, Shirley told journalists her father had been a sales manager with IBM when she was growing up; however, International Business Machines did not exist under that name until 1924, by which time she was no longer living at home.

In 1910, the year Thelma Ford would turn twelve, the family was still living in Brooklyn. In April, a United States Census taker recorded young Thelma at home with her parents on 75th Street. Her father was said to be employed in sales in the tobacco industry.

In later years, Shirley would tell reporters that her infatuation with show business had resulted in her dropping out of high school to pursue her career, but this does not appear to be the case. Historians of Brooklyn's Erasmus Hall High School describe her as an alumna, class of 1916, but school records from that period have not survived to verify whether or not she graduated. Even as early as the 1910s, Erasmus Hall, which would later play host to Barbra Streisand, Beverly Sills, and other noted performers, took pride in its dramatic instruction.

"There is no need to mention," declared a 1911 history of the school, "the long list of actors and actresses who obtained their initial training in the Garrick [Dramatic Club] at school, for theatre-goers have become familiar with the good work of our alumni...."[11] Drama was considered an important aspect of the liberal arts education that Erasmus Hall students received, as the same publication noted: "The ability to sink one's own individuality, and to assume other characters, is bound to develop any boy or girl, and to be able to stand on one's feet and talk to an audience is what this training will do for them."[12] While Shirley likely would have concurred with the sentiment, she never cited Erasmus Hall as the place where she was struck with the acting bug.

Though it is apparently true that Thelma Ford did not complete her high school education at Erasmus Hall, she was not really a dropout in the usual sense of that term. In the mid to late 1910s, Albert Ford and his family left Brooklyn. Along the way, there was a brief stay in Philadelphia, where Mr. Ford had a short-term job assignment. It was in Philly that

Shirley's alma mater, Brooklyn's Erasmus Hall High School, pictured in 1912.

the future Shirley Booth had a prophetic meeting with a man who would, intentionally or not, steer her in the direction of an acting career.

As recounted in a 1952 *Life* magazine profile of Shirley, "the Fords were living at a family hotel, Mr. Ford's assignment being only a temporary one, and another resident was J. Hammond Daly [sic; Dailey], a nice young man employed in a local stock [theater] company. Daly was lonesome and was attracted to what must have seemed a charming family group, and asked if he could sit at their table for meals."[13] (*Life*'s account, based on Shirley's then-generally accepted birth date of 1907, said this took place when she was seven years old, implying that it occurred circa 1914).

It was from John Hammond Dailey that young Thelma first realized that some adults made their living playacting for a paying audience, and she was fascinated by his stories of stage life. Sensing her interest, Dailey felt it only fair to warn the girl that acting in a stock company was hard work, much less glamorous than it might seem. It didn't matter.

After a short stay in Pennsylvania, Albert Ford ultimately settled his wife and children (including Shirley's new young sister Jean) in the Hartford, Connecticut area. A review of city directories for the Hartford area shows the Fords in place by 1914, the year that Jean was born. A 1952 newspaper profile of Shirley, summarizing the highlights of her life and career more accurately than many articles would do, disregarded the usual story of dropping out of Erasmus Hall High School, stating, "Continued schooling in Hartford, Conn., where family moved because of father's work."[14]

Whether in Brooklyn, Philadelphia, or Hartford, however, there was no escaping the tensions that existed in the Ford household. Looking back on her childhood and youth, Shirley Booth's loyalties were crystal clear. She adored and idolized her mother, while her relationship with her father was so troubled that they would later simply break off communications altogether. Albert and Virginia Ford were apparently seriously mismatched, so much so that this was readily apparent to their daughter. It was Shirley's opinion, then and later, that her father was to blame for the unhappiness in the Ford household.

"He was a martinet," she said, "an autocrat, a real dictator, the kind who believed that children should be seen and not heard. He expected absolute obedience—from his children, his wife and his dog. And he usually got it."[15] More than fifty years later, the adult Shirley felt that her father's stern demeanor had done much to squelch the happiness of her gentler, more emotionally open mother.

The West Hartford community, where the Fords eventually took up residence on Arnoldale Road, was an upper middle class enclave that represented a step up in the family's fortunes. According to the *Hartford Courant,* Mr. Ford "was the manager of the Dayton Scales Co. at 190 Pearl Street,"[16] which sold "computing scales and sliders, new and second-hand."[17] Dayton Scales were a product of the Computing Scale Company, which was one of the firms merged in 1911 to form the Computing-Tabulating-Recording Company, predecessor to IBM, so this appears to be the point at which Shirley's father took up the career she attributed to him as an adult.

Not long after the family settled in Hartford, Thelma was delighted to learn that John Hammond Dailey was engaged with the local Poli Players stock company, housed on Main Street in downtown Hartford. She entreated her mother to invite Mr. Dailey to dinner, and renew the acquaintance. "Before the poor fellow had finished his soup," Shirley recalled laughingly, "I had wormed a promise out of him to introduce me to the company manager. I wanted to be an actress."[18]

Nicely reared young ladies from good families were by no means expected to go on the stage in the 1910s, and Mr. Ford, given his pragmatic and dictatorial nature, did not approve of any such activity for his child. Given how he supposedly ran roughshod over his household, this should have been a brick wall young Thelma couldn't overcome. But as Shirley later explained, "Mother and I fought back with the ferocity that only the meek and timid can muster when they have their back to the wall."[19] With Mrs. Ford backing her daughter's case, Thelma's father grudgingly allowed his daughter to dabble in acting as a hobby, thinking it would cure her of any silly notions about a career as a professional performer. Needless to say, he guessed wrong.

However, on one point Mr. Ford put his foot down—under no circumstances was young Thelma to dirty the family name by using it onstage. Whatever acting she did was not be under the name of Thelma Ford. For the time being, Thelma retained her given first name, playing her first roles as "Miss Thelma Booth."

As an adult, Shirley said her first stage experience came when Mr. Dailey helped her obtain a role in his stock company's production of *Mother Carey's Chickens,* in which she played one of the children. Again, this bumps up against chronological inconsistencies. Kate Douglas Wiggin's novel for children was published in 1911 (a follow-up to her better-remembered *Rebecca of Sunnybrook Farm*), and the play based on it (which Wiggin co-wrote with Rachel Crothers) was first produced on Broadway in the fall of 1917, when Shirley was already nineteen years old.

However, an appearance in this play was indeed one of Shirley's first successes with the Poli Players. According to a 1929 article in the Fords' hometown newspaper, the *Hartford Courant,* "Miss Booth has gone far in the theater since Frances Williams, who proudly claims that she 'discovered' Shirley, selected her to play the eccentric comedy role of Lally Joy in *Mother Carey's Chickens* when it was produced by the old Poli Players at the Palace

Theatre several years ago."[20] Lally Joy is a neighbor of the Carey family, who has a crush on teenage son Gilbert.

In 1953, when Shirley Booth won her Academy Award, *Courant* columnist Bob Zaiman polled current Hartford residents for their recollections of the young Thelma Ford. He recounted her stage beginnings thusly: "Way back in 1921 [sic], a beautiful young West Hartford girl walked into the Palace Theatre on Main Street where the Poli Players were rehearsing a comedy called *Mother Carey's Chickens* and asked for an audition. Her name was Thelma Ford, she told James Thatcher, general manager of the company, and she had no stage experience whatsoever. But she insisted that she was a capable actress and begged for a trial. Always on the lookout for new talent, Thatcher gave her the audition and was so impressed that he immediately engaged her...."[21] Leading lady Frances Williams, who was also Mrs. Thatcher, supposedly took charge of the 20-year-old newcomer, and taught her the rudiments of stage acting.

Actor J. Hammond Dailey, pictured in 1925, was an early mentor to Shirley, helping her gain a toehold in the Poli Players stock theater company.

The Poli Players' production of *Mother Carey's Chickens* premiered on November 25, 1918. It was favorably reviewed in the *Courant,* which termed it "delightful," noting, "It is not a play for the sophisticated but rather for those people who prefer the milder and more wholesome type of entertainment."[22] Thelma Booth was one of several featured performers mentioned as having "added their share" to the production.

However, while this was one of Shirley's first acting jobs, she had in fact appeared in at least one of the Players' previous productions that season. A surviving program from the Palace Theater for the week of November 4, 1918, finds the Poli Players mounting a production of *Daddy Long Legs.* The play, adapted by Jean Webster from her 1912 novel, tells the story of an impoverished young orphan, Jerusha Abbott, nicknamed Judy. Miss Abbott's college education is unexpectedly financed by an anonymous older man she has never met, but to whom she writes regular letters describing her experi-

A November 1918 playbill from the Palace Theatre shows "Miss Thelma Booth," as she was then known, in the cast of *Daddy Long Legs.*

ences at school. Because she knows nothing about her benefactor except for a quick glimpse she once had of him from behind, she nicknames him "Dear Daddy-Long-Legs." Webster's play had been a hit on Broadway during the 1914-15 season, with Ruth Chatterton starring as Judy, and much later became the basis for the 1955 film with Fred Astaire and Leslie Caron.

Eleventh-billed in the playbill for this production, Thelma Booth was cast not as the heroine, Judy, but as Julia Pendleton, while her friend J. Hammond Dailey enjoyed a larger role as Walters. Julia Rutledge Pendleton is, in the novel, a well-bred college classmate of heroine Judy, who describes her thusly: "She never makes the slightest effort to be amiable ... Julia and I were born to be enemies."[23]

Daddy Long Legs was expected to be one of the high points of the Poli season, as evidenced by a breathless article that appeared in the *Courant* just prior to opening night. The feature story, which read more like a press release, stated, "It is the dramatic gem of the season and the patrons of the Poli Players may anticipate an event of the utmost pleasure and enjoyment without the slightest prospect of being disappointed."[24] It was further noted that the sets for this production were unusually ambitious, and that the theater manager had paid the highest royalties of the company's history for this show. Performances were held at 8:15 P.M., with daily matinees at 2:15 P.M.

Though Thelma was not mentioned by name in this article, it was reported that the acting company of *Daddy Long Legs* would include "six which will be played by local children, adding a touch of local color to the play."[25] The child actors would play some of the orphans who were residents at the John Grier Home. The *Courant's* review a couple of nights later again failed to mention her specifically, but did point out that "several new and very competent players did well."[26]

Once she had gotten her foot in the door of the Palace Theatre, Thelma progressed rapidly. Only a few weeks after her run in *Mother Carey's Chickens,* Thelma had an unexpected opportunity to step into the spotlight, in one of those episodes that is usually believed to happen only in productions of *42nd Street.* A few days before Christmas, 1918, the *Courant* reported that Thelma was, unexpectedly, playing the lead role of Ruth Thorne in the Poli Players' production of *Lavender and Old Lace.* Based on a 1902 novel by Myrtle Reed that had supposedly sold more than 500,000 copies, *Lavender and Old Lace,* was described as a "fine drama of New England life,"[27] with Shirley playing a magazine writer who visits her spinster aunt, and becomes romantically involved with a local newspaperman.

Shirley stepped into the role on only about 24 hours' notice, after the company's established ingénue Faith Avery fell ill with pneumonia just prior to opening night. During curtain calls at the conclusion of her first performance, Thelma was presented with a bouquet of flowers by company manager Sylvester Poli, for having kept the show afloat. Having proved her worth, Thelma would be taken more seriously as a company member for the remainder of the season.

It was quickly becoming evident that acting was, for the future Shirley Booth, far more than a passing preoccupation. "By the time I was a teen-ager," she said almost fifty years later, "nothing other than acting seemed worthwhile. And that wasn't because acting seemed to be the road to great wealth. I merely wanted to act."[28]

From the beginning, the work was fascinating to her. "I wanted to 'explain' people—make them understandable and readily recognizable to others. I've never swerved from this objective. Creating understanding among people is a wonderful accomplishment. It has also taught me much. From age 17 until the present, every play that I have appeared in has broadened me."[29]

What had begun as a hobby for Thelma was quickly becoming something more, and her name would pop up often in accounts of the Poli Players' 1918-19 season at the Palace Theatre. In April 1919, newspaper advertisements trumpeted "an elaborate revival of the greatest American comedy since Rip Van Winkle"—*Sis Hopkins.* The stage show arrived in Hartford on the heels of the just-released silent film version that starred Mabel Normand. Poli's leading lady Florence Rittenhouse (also the wife of Thelma's friend and mentor J. Hammond Dailey) assumed the lead role of the naïve farm girl who longs for "schoolin,'" and ads for the show promised theatergoers "one week of mirth and happiness."[30] *Sis Hopkins* furnished opportunities to hear several Poli company members sing, among them Thelma Booth, whose number would be "How Are You Goin' to Keep 'Em Down on the Farm?" The *Courant's* review was kind to the production, allotting most of its praise to Miss Rittenhouse, but also noting that Thelma "contributed her share, attired in a striking costume of a flaring orange shade,"[31] and sang well.

Not all of her time in 1918 and 1919 was spent onstage, however. Hartford resident Paul McCoy, employed as a fitter of belts and trusses at G. Fox and Company, later said of the former Thelma Ford, "She used to be my girlfriend. I was still in high school and playing football for Hartford High at the time. I guess I courted her for about a year while she was playing with the Poli company in Hartford and New Britain. I used to borrow an old Maxwell car to take her out on dates. She was a wonderful girl."[32]

According to Shirley, she and younger sister Jean operated under a strict moral code that she attributed mostly to her mother. "Her ideas on morality were right out of church," Shirley said of Mrs. Ford. "Any woman who drank or smoked was definitely a loose woman to her, and she warned us never to kiss a boy or even to sit alone with one on a couch."[33]

By the spring of 1919, Thelma's work with the Poli Players had become extremely important to her. In just a few months, she had gone from neophyte to featured player, holding her own with a company of experienced professionals. It was a great arrangement — until the manager of the Palace Theater, James P. Clancy, announced that he was making a format change. The Poli Players' engagement at the Palace was coming to an end, having lasted for about a year, and manager Clancy would be bringing in vaudeville acts instead. The change, reported the *Courant*, "was absolutely necessary, largely owing to the scarcity of plays available. Rather than decrease the quality of the offerings he said it had been decided to close the stock season."[34]

On the evening of May 17, after the Players' evening performance, members of the company, including Thelma, were called onstage to take a final bow, and receive a bouquet of flowers. "Again and again the audience called the players forward and each time there was a fresh volley of hand-clapping," said the *Courant*.[35] The next morning, the company's baggage and equipment would be shipped to Springfield, where the Poli Players would begin a new engagement, after a one-week vacation.

The loss of ready acting opportunities at the Palace Theater was a turning point in the life of "Thelma Booth." If her father had regarded her performances with the Poli Players as not much more than a pastime, it soon became evident that it represented much more to Thelma. She was now dead set on a career as an actress, and it was at this point that she and her father truly locked horns.

With opportunities in Hartford at a standstill, Thelma announced her intention to go to New York in search of work. Mrs. Ford arranged for Thelma to stay with her "Aunt Della," a family friend, in New York, much to the displeasure of Shirley's father. Ironically, Shirley Booth would say in later years that she owed her career to Albert Ford.

"It was my father who made an actress, which was the last thing in the world he wanted," she later said. "I was so dominated by him that I felt shadowy. I didn't have any identity. So I escaped to the one place where I could be a definite personality — on the stage. I still feel that way. To me, I'm a shadowy person — I take on a part as protective coloring.... The character *has* to be a real person because it's the only way I can have any feelings that I'm real."[36]

In the 1920s, when she was an unknown struggling to establish herself as an actress, Shirley would gird herself with the conviction that she *had* to be a success — otherwise, she would lose face with her father. A few years later, when Shirley's career was on the rise after a long apprenticeship, Shirley and her father concluded that they simply did not understand each other, and probably never would. After the death of her mother in the mid–1930s, they stopped speaking. At the height of her fame, in the early 1950s, she confirmed that they had not spoken for many years, and there seemed little reason to expect a change.

Thelma's professional stock career began with a $25 a week job as the ingénue of Sylvester Poli's company in New Haven, Connecticut. It was James Thatcher, who'd given her her first audition in Hartford, who put her on the payroll, in what was originally supposed to be only a temporary assignment. Not only was the salary meager, but the burgeoning actress was expected to furnish her own costumes. Nervously aware that she was inexperienced, Shirley spent the first few weeks fearful that she would be fired at any moment.

Actor Ralph Bellamy, later a friend and co-star of Shirley's, also learned his craft doing stock theater, and gave an excellent explanation of how things worked in his memoirs: "In the twenties, before radio and talking pictures and television, almost every city of fifty thousand or over had at least one resident stock company.... The larger cities sometimes had two or three.... The plays were recent Broadway successes."[37] Operating the company were a director, a stage manager, and someone who did simple scenery, along with a group of about ten actors.

The result was, in some ways, the television of its day — straightforward, unpretentious entertainment for the masses, as B movies would be in the 1930s and 1940s. Rather than taking a single play on tour, the members of a resident stock company settled into a local theater, and offered its steady customers a new show every week. It was impractical to bring in new actors for each production — every week, one show was being performed while the next was being rehearsed with the same players.

As Bellamy pointed out, "The actors were all good. They had to be. They did ten performances a week — seven nights and Wednesday, Saturday, and Sunday matinees."[38]

Each actor was engaged in one of the stock world's standard classifications. Among the ten actors who formed a repertory company were a leading man and leading lady, a juvenile (male) and ingénue, as well as comedians, character people, and those who could play whatever small parts remained. If each play was to be performed by the same small group of people, it stood to reason that the actors often played roles to which they weren't perfectly suited. Actors learned to make choices quickly, be self-sufficient and reliable, and tackle whatever type of part they were handed. The experience would not only stand Shirley in good stead as a professional actress, but leave her somewhat mystified when producers and directors tried to slot her into a "type," or expressed surprise that she was able to go comfortably between comedy and drama, radio and film.

Stock company productions were enormously popular in those days. As one theater historian noted of the Poli companies: "The theater is packed at every performance; hundreds buy a weekly subscription ticket, retaining the same seats for the season; and it would be difficult to over-estimate the amount of pleasure that has been added to the lives of many persons, who look forward to the subscription day with unfeigned delight." Still, the same observer noted that the schedule was grueling for cast members — "I wonder when the actors find time to sleep."[39]

When the actors weren't actually onstage, there was always a script for next week to be learned. Actresses were likely to be found busily ironing costumes, while simultaneously studying lines on a page laid out in front of their work. And for actresses, in particular, costumes were an ongoing issue. As Shirley's mentor from the Poli Players, Frances Williams, explained, "Clothes are a very big question in stock, especially with the women of the company. While the men can buy a dress suit that can be worn in several plays without being out of place, with an actress the dress she is to wear is the one thing which must be decided immediately after her part for the coming week has been assigned. Color is very important here, as it is quite essential that each of the ladies have a different shade of dress."[40] As the ingénue, Shirley often got last choice in these matters, after the leading lady and others had picked out the costumes that suited them. Twenty-five years later, as a successful Broadway actress, Shirley would be one of the regular contributors to a charity that provided second-hand costumes for aspiring performers. Clearly she hadn't forgotten her early stock experience.

Shirley would later enjoy recalling an incident that demonstrated what could happen when the members of a stock company were worn to a frazzle. The leading man in one production fell victim to exhaustion, thanks to the eight-performance-a-week schedule, and found himself unable to remember his lines onstage. Looking offstage, he was alarmed to see that the designated prompter had dozed off. "What's the line?" hissed the embarrassed actor.

Jerking himself awake, the stagehand muttered, "What's the play?"[41]

This was the world that Thelma Ford entered in the early 1920s. Had her father been correct that her interest in performing was a passing whim, the tough schedule of a stock company should have put a stop to it. It didn't.

As Shirley admitted later in life, she never had any formal schooling as an actress. Her training came solely from her years in stock theater, and from her keen observation of the world around her. "I was never in a dramatic school in my life but I watch people always—how they look and talk and behave. When the time comes and with theatrical license, of course, I draw on that stock."[42]

Learning her craft the hard way, Thelma Booth became a well-known name in stock theater during the first half of the 1920s. In 1922, she cast off the last vestiges of her childhood name when she played a character named Shirley in a show called *The Lion and the Mouse.* She'd never been wild about the name Thelma anyway, and from then on she was known professionally as Shirley Booth.

Interestingly, despite her father's professed disdain for the stage, and unhappiness that his daughter had entered a profession he did not respect, Shirley's theatrical achievements continued to be publicized in the pages of the *Hartford Courant.* In April 1922, a column item noted that she had finished her engagement with the Union Hill Players, and would next be seen with a company called the Proctor Players, in Albany, New York. Though she was by then acting under the name Shirley Booth, the *Courant* made a point of noting that this was only her stage name, and explaining to its readers that she was in fact the daughter of the Ford family of West Hartford.

That summer, she was back home on Arnoldale Road with Mr. and Mrs. Ford, and frequently onstage at the Palace Theatre. Although the Poli Players had left Hartford in 1919, the move was not a permanent one, and by the early 1920s another Poli company had been installed at their old home, the Palace. Shirley played a key role in the new Poli Players' production of a musical comedy, *Oh, Lady, Lady,* co-authored by P.G. Wodehouse. The production, explained a newspaper write-up, "differs from the average musical comedy in that it has a well defined plot which holds interest through[ou]t the play and the book calls for an augmented cast and chorus."[43] Audiences heard Shirley sing "You Found Me and I Found You," and "Moon Song."

A few weeks later, she was seen in *Off to Paris,* described in Palace Theatre ads as "a rip-roaring musical farce in 3 acts." Shirley played Fifi, a French maid, and sang a duet, "You Play with Me," with co-star Russell Fillmore. *The Hartford Courant* announced that the original play, written by Ann Colby and Leon De Costa, was being eyed for a possible Broadway production, and that "several New York producers to whom the musical comedy has been submitted will be on hand to see it visualized."[44]

In September 1922, Shirley was the subject of another write-up in the *Courant,* when she was named the winner of a Norma Talmadge lookalike contest. Talmadge was a popular movie actress in the early 1920s who also owned her own production company. Shirley was awarded a pearl necklace from a local merchant, Wise, Smith, and Company, and again the names and home address of her parents on Arnoldale Road were noted.

That fall, Shirley auditioned for and was cast in a touring production of John Willard's mystery play *The Cat and the Canary.* Shirley would play the lead role of Annabelle West, which Florence Eldredge originated in the 1922 Broadway production. *The Cat and the Canary* was the granddaddy of many, many movies and television shows about potential heirs to a fortune who must prove their bravery by spending the night in the spooky house of their eccentric late relative. (Among them was a 1927 film adaptation that starred Laura La Plante, as well as a later, comedic version with Bob Hope). When Annabelle is named the sole heir of her uncle's estate, her conniving kin subject her to a terror-filled night in the old mansion in the hopes of driving her insane, and thus causing her to forfeit the inheritance.

One company was already touring in the popular melodrama, and the road tour for which Shirley was hired would play what was known as the "subway circuit." In April, Shirley was pictured in the local newspaper of Salamanca, New York, which proudly noted that the production then playing the town's Andrews Theatre featured the same professional cast seen in cities like Rochester and Buffalo. A few days later, the show's imminent arrival was noted in the pages of the *Coshocton Tribune.* "The thrillingest of all thrillers,"[45] said the advertisements for the May 1, 1923, opening at the Sixth Street Theatre. Among Shirley's co-stars, according to the announcement, would be W. Lee Tracy and Alma Kruger.

Life on the road with a touring production wasn't easy, Shirley admitted, but theatergoers in the towns they visited usually made them feel appreciated. "Audiences in some parts of the country are slow to warm up," she said, "but lots of people bring you cakes and pieces of tatting, and mother you. 'I'm sure you'd appreciate a home-cooked meal,' they say, and you do. Not *all* home-cooked meals, of course."[46]

Now a respected professional in the world of stock theaters, Shirley was gearing up to explore the next phase of her career. In the fall of 1923, after another visit home, she signed to spend the season as the leading lady of the Warburton Players, based in Yonkers, New York. On Labor Day, she opened in a show called "It's a Boy." In 1924, she worked with Stuart Walker's well-regarded company in Cincinnati.

For a stage actor, however, the ultimate goal was usually to appear on Broadway, and for Shirley, at the age of twenty-five, that landmark was just around the corner.

2. Opening Nights

In the fall of 1924, Shirley took a step up in her career, when she was signed to play the young female lead in a Broadway-bound comedy called *Hell's Bells*.

The show recounted the adventures of two old prospectors visiting a small New England town, who are wrongly believed by its residents to be millionaires. Playing the lead roles were two names little known to modern-day audiences, Eddie Garvie and Tom H. Walsh. More familiar was the juvenile cast to play the romantic interest to Shirley's character — another young newcomer by the name of Humphrey Bogart. In his late twenties, Bogart was still a fairly inexperienced actor, but had been in four previous Broadway shows, the most successful of them a 1923–24 comedy called *Meet the Wife*.

The production came together under the auspices of producer Herman Gantvoort, who'd previously acted under the stage name Bill Holland. Acquiring the rights to a comedy called *The Desert Rat*, written by Barry Conners, Gantvoort took the show on tour to polish it up. Philadelphia and Stamford, Connecticut, were among the places it played. Along the way, rewrites led to title changes — first to *Fool's Gold*, since the plot dealt with prospectors. In mid–January, it was announced in the *New York Times* as *The Hide-Behinds*. Ultimately, the producers settled for calling the show *Hell's Bells*.

Upon its January 26, 1925, opening at Broadway's Wallack's Theatre, *Hell's Bells* received lukewarm reviews from New York critics. Ironically, given Shirley's background, *Variety*'s reviewer thought the play better suited to production by stock companies than Broadway. Still, the play did just enough business to survive its first few week, with *Variety* predicting that producers would not be able to keep it afloat long without cutting ticket prices. It was obvious that the show was just hanging by a thread, until a dramatic offstage incident generated a ream of publicity.

Drawing more attention than the play being enacted onstage was an incident that made newspapers around the country in February, when it was reported that Shirley's co-star Eddie Garvie accidentally shot actor Clinton Self during a scene, "with a pistol that he did not know was loaded."

According to the *New York Times*' account of the events of February 11, 1925, "When the shot was fired and Self fell to the floor, Shirley Booth, the leading lady, who was waiting in the wings for a cue, fainted and dropped on the stage in view of the audience. The curtain was lowered and for some time the people in front remained in mystified discomfort."[1] After a short delay, said the *Times*, Shirley was revived, Self was found not to be seriously wounded, and the performance resumed, with Garvie later facing police charges. The story was picked up by wire services, and appeared in newspapers nationwide, as well as in *Time* magazine.

Many years later, Shirley admitted that this entire incident was a hoax, although not one of her making. The show's press agent had dreamed up the entire stunt, arranging for a bullet to be carefully fired into the scenery beforehand, and actor Self's arm prepped with a doctor's lance. Not wanting Shirley to get her costume dirty in her dramatic fall to the floor, the theater manager provided a clean sheet onto which she could collapse.

Shirley played the scene beautifully — enough so that a co-star rushed to her aid.

"I shall never forget how kind Humphrey Bogart — who wasn't in on the plot — was," she said years later. "He was even going to throw water on me when the manager hurriedly acted — again to save that costume."[2]

The publicity stunt had audiences flocking to see *Hell's Bells* for a few more weeks, but producers ultimately closed the show in late spring, after a respectable run of 120 performances. Though the play never blossomed into a full-fledged success, either artistically or financially, it was a noteworthy credit for Shirley's resume, and she was no longer a novice in the eyes of Broadway producers.

Having attracted favorable notice in one lightweight comedy, Shirley soon landed another such role, in a show that placed her front and center among a little-known cast. *Laff That Off*, which opened in the fall of 1925, was produced by Earl Carroll, whose *Vanities* revues were the delight of girl-watchers in the 1920s.

Though Shirley would claim later in life that she had never been particularly pretty, her casting as the ingénue in *Hell's Bells*, and now in *Laff That Off*, suggested otherwise. As one observer summarized the show, "*Laff That Off* tells the story of a stranded would-be actress who is adopted quite philanthropically into the bachelor ménage of three young men. All of them fall in love with her, of course. She returns in the third act as a successful movie queen, adjusts a misunderstanding and gives her hand to the proper suitor."[3] Shirley's leading man was actor Alan Bunce, who would later play the male lead in the popular radio and television comedy *Ethel and Albert*.

Producer Carroll bought the rights to *Laff That Off* after it had toured the provinces with only limited success. Seeing something more in the innocuous comedy script than most Broadway observers, Carroll installed the show at Wallack's Theatre, and proceeded to back his hunch with an expensive advertising campaign when initial ticket sales were sluggish.

As *The New York Times* reported, "There were virtually no results — the box-office patronage continued to be negligible. But for the fact that at the time he was busy with the arrangements for a new edition of the *Vanities*, Carroll would certainly have ordered *Laff That Off* closed and contracted for a new show to occupy the theatre."[4] By the time he was ready to do so, an unexpected thing had happened — *Laff That Off*, with about 100 performances under its belt, had somehow turned a corner, and was enjoying respectable business.

Despite a distinct lack of critical raves, *Laff That Off* would ultimately manage to stay afloat for more than 250 performances, keeping Shirley gainfully employed throughout the 1925–26 season. Commenting on the surprising phenomenon of the show's sleeper success in the summer of 1926, critic George Jean Nathan professed himself stumped as to what the attraction was. The show, he reported, "is not only dull stuff, one would think even from a boob point of view, but it [has] not in its cast at the moment a single actor with an ounce of drawing-power on his own ... I have never so much as heard of any one of them," he

Shirley co-starred with Thomas W. Ross in the unexpectedly successful *Laff That Off.*

harrumphed of Shirley and her co-stars.[5] (By the time Nathan died in 1958, he had had ample opportunity to familiarize himself with Shirley's work, and wrote more favorably about her later efforts).

Summarizing the season in his annual *Best Plays* yearbook, Burns Mantle thought there was a simple explanation for the success of *Laff That Off* (though he certainly didn't rank it among the year's best): "There is a large public that has a way of finding out the substantial comedy entertainment that amuses it without reference to what any of the bored experts may have thought of it."[6]

Still, even lead roles in frivolous comedies were not a surefire ticket to success, as Shirley's next Broadway outing demonstrated. In the fall of 1926, she was cast in her third Broadway comedy, *Buy, Buy, Baby,* which starred Laura Hope Crews and Alison Skipworth. The play's story revolved around a competition among a well-to-do family's younger generation, to see which couple can earn Aunt Esmeralda's inheritance by producing an heir. During its pre–Broadway tour, the show was known by the punning title of *Pay to Bearer.* By the prevailing standards of the late 1920s, the show's subject matter was risqué, and a disapproving reviewer in Chicago described Shirley's role thusly: "She's acting the role of the demure secretary who wins for self and husband a million by being the first of her family to qualify as a parent in [this] lewd and obstetrical farce."[7]

Reviews of the comedy were decent upon its Broadway bow in October 1926, and since the play's authors had done very well with a similar comedy, *Cradle Snatchers,* during the previous season, many observers assumed that *Buy, Buy, Baby* would be similarly well-received by theatergoers. However, ticket sales were disappointing, and the show quickly folded — Shirley's first real flop on the Great White Way.

In retrospect, it seems as if Shirley's early career on Broadway was as successful as a newcomer could probably have expected. Between 1925 and 1928, she opened every fall in a new show. However, there were nonetheless times when she would grow discouraged with her efforts to conquer Broadway, or disheartened when a show for which she had spent weeks in rehearsal crashed and burned as quickly as *Buy, Buy, Baby* did. As she readily admitted, she never mastered the tricks of schmoozing, or actively promoting her own career — for her, the work stood for itself. When things looked particularly grim, she was apt to leave New York, and accept a stint with a stock theater company out of town.

"I was big in stock," she later explained of this period. "I had a reputation and a public. I could have hung around New York and taken my chances, but I had to go where people believed in me and I had to keep acting so I could believe in myself."[8] She would later estimate that she had played more than 600 different roles in stock productions of the 1920s and early 1930s, naming the part of Sadie Thompson in *Rain* as one of her all-time favorites.

But sooner or later she would head back to Gotham, as she did in the fall of 1927, when her latest Broadway comedy, *High Gear,* opened to lukewarm reviews. This show, too, was short-lived — though it would later be sent out on road tours with a more provocative title, *Mary's Other Husband* — and after 20 performances the actress was again unemployed.

The erratic fortunes of stage work meant that Shirley's finances were often dicey as well. For a time in the 1920s, she saved expenses by living at the Rehearsal Club, the women-only theatrical boardinghouse that had been founded in 1913 by an Episcopalian deaconess, Mary Harriss Hall. The Club would later be immortalized as the Footlights Club in *Stage Door.* At various times, the Rehearsal Club, which stayed in business until the 1970s, when it lost its tax-exempt status, would house everyone from Margaret Sullavan (who later starred in the play *Stage Door*) to Carol Burnett.

Still, money was tight, and Shirley would never forget an unfortunate incident that occurred when a friend loaned her a copy of John Dos Passos' then-hot novel about New York City life, *Manhattan Transfer.* She was fifty pages into the book when she had to hurry out one morning to attend an audition.

When she came home, Shirley was dismayed to see that her dog Towser had consumed some two hundred and fifty pages of the borrowed book in her absence. Not only had she not gotten the role for which she'd read, she would now have to pay the price of replacing her friend's book, an expense she could ill afford at that moment. As her friend, press agent Richard Maney, recounted the episode: "Armed with a new copy, Shirley felt she should finish the story. Another phone call. Another fruitless search for a job. No dog to ignore a coincidence, Towser went through *Manhattan Transfer* once more, cover to cover. Shirley has never read a line of Dos Passos since."[9]

In the summer of 1928, Shirley landed a featured role in George Jessel's new play, *The War Song.* Shirley was cast as the star's kid sister, Emily, who, to the family's shame, becomes pregnant though unmarried. In Act Two, Jessel's character, Eddie, learns that one of his fellow soldiers is responsible for his sister's condition, leading to a confrontation. *The War Song* grew out of a one-act play by Commodore Richard Shayer, *Private Jones,* expanded and revised by Jessel in collaboration with the famed playwrights Sam and Bella Spewack, whose later hits would include *Kiss Me, Kate* and *Boy Meets Girl.* The show began a two-week tryout in Philadelphia just after Labor Day, in anticipation of a late September bow at Broadway's National Theatre.

Back in the spotlight, Shirley was featured in a September article in the *Hartford Courant,* which focused on the novelty of well-placed young women from society pursuing their acting ambitions. "They are forsaking the tennis courts, the golf links, and the bridge tables for that magic world of make-believe behind the footlights," reported the *Courant,* "and finding there the careers they profess they have always wanted."[10] Shirley's inclusion in this group certainly implied that the Ford family had come up in the world since their days living on 75th Street in Flatbush.

Among the other young debutantes profiled alongside Shirley in the *Courant* feature was "Miss Katharine Houghton Hepburn." If the two young actresses' paths hadn't yet crossed, they would a few years down the road. Meanwhile, Hepburn was just another aspiring Broadway performer, whose November 1928 show, *These Days,* lasted for only eight of them.

A featured role in a Jessel show, his first since his smash hit *The Jazz Singer,* should have been money in the bank, but *The War Song* was surprisingly not a success on Broadway. Actor-playwright Jessel, in retrospect, thought the show confused audiences with its mix of comedy and tragedy, but also noted, "the Spewacks, being young and new to the theatre, listened to everybody's advice about changes, as did I."[11] Though critical reviews were decent—the reviewer for the *New York Times* described it as a cross between *Abie's Irish Rose* and *What Price Glory?*—ticket sales kept the show going for only a disappointing 80 performances, throwing the cast out of work just as the Christmas holidays approached.

Still, given Jessel's ongoing popularity, there was money to be made on the road, and *The War Song* enjoyed a successful tour of Chicago and other cities after its abrupt departure from Broadway. Aside from Shirley, the tour gave employment to some other newcomers who would rise to prominence onstage or in films, among them Lola Lane, Gene Raymond, and William Gargan.

Back in New York once the tour concluded, Shirley continued to pursue her stage career, but there was a new wrinkle in her life. Invited to a party at the home of producer J. Augustus Pitou, a friend with whom she'd worked in stock, Shirley caught the eye of another guest, one who shared her show business aspirations.

The man who would be known professionally as Ed Gardner was, in 1929, still using his real name, Eddie Poggenburg. Employed as a piano salesman, he had nonetheless long been intrigued by show business, and had dreams of making it his career. A high school dropout, his main credentials in the world of sales were his gift for gab, and an ability to size up people. Eddie took a liking to the pretty young actress and decided to make her acquaintance.

Sidling up to Shirley, Ed said, "Little girl, you need awakening."

Unmoved, she promptly retorted, "You need sleep."[12] Not one to be brushed off lightly, Ed continued to chat her up nonetheless. They were, from the beginning, an unlikely pair. Gardner was gregarious, a hearty drinker, and loved parties. Shirley, who'd never given a party in her life, and often turned down the chance to attend one, was nonetheless intrigued by this brash, fun-loving man. He was certainly 360 degrees removed from her cold and authoritarian father, and perhaps that was part of the attraction that drew her to Ed.

By the fall of 1929, their relationship had become serious, and Ed was proposing marriage to Shirley. For the time being, she put him off while she concentrated on her next acting job, a small part in a show originally announced as *Undertow*. It concerned the adventures of a young woman who relocated with her husband from a small town to New York City, and the tragedies that arose when she fell in with the wrong crowd.

The new show was tried out in Hartford, where hometown girl Shirley was still newsworthy despite her meager assignment. "Isn't it just terrible that I should come back here in such a small part?" she said cheerfully to local columnist Albert J. Duffy. "Don't you dare to take your eyes off the stage when you see the play or you'll miss me completely. You see, originally, there was only one woman in the play and, just my luck, she had to be a blonde. But after they went into rehearsal they cut out two male parts and combined them into make this second woman — and that's me."[13]

By the time the show opened on Broadway, it had been retitled *Claire Adams*. Perhaps Shirley didn't feel this show was her finest moment onstage, or was just trying to signal a change from her recent appearances in light comedies. At any rate, she opted to be billed in *Claire Adams* by a name she had otherwise long ago abandoned, "Thelma Booth." If she was attempting to maintain a low profile, her instinct may have been correct, because *Claire Adams* netted terrible reviews. Among them was the one from *The New Yorker*'s Robert Benchley, who noted that the somber melodrama had a regrettable tendency to make an audience snicker.

Even had the play been a better one, all was not well along the Great White Way. The burgeoning Depression was already having its impact on the theater world, as it was every other aspect of American life in late 1929. *Variety* reported in November that "Broadway is considerably under normal in the number of attractions"[14]; fifteen theaters were vacant, with the number expected to rise in weeks to come. While the biggest shows were still doing adequate business, there was very little room for error, "angels" who wanted to finance Broadway shows were scarce, and "amusements are expected to be depressed for months to come," *Variety* predicted.[15]

Given the current state of Broadway's health, *Claire Adams* was inevitably a goner, and went belly-up in less than a week. On November 23, 1929, the day her show closed its doors, Shirley married Eddie Poggenburg.

Shirley's new husband had been born Friedrich Poggenburg on June 29, 1901. He grew up in Astoria, Queens, the son of a semi-professional baseball player. Eddie's neighbors in the modest, predominantly German-Irish community had included the Zimmermann family, whose daughter Ethel Agnes was found to have a phenomenal singing voice. In the

1920s, Ethel shortened her family name, which was too long (and, perhaps, too ethnic) to fit well on a theater marquee, to Merman. That was the name by which she would subsequently become a major Broadway star. Eddie Poggenburg, in turn, would later decide that he wanted a more euphonious name, and liked the sound of Gardner, the maiden name of Ethel's mother.

Gardner, as he would become in the mid–1930s, dropped out of school at the age of sixteen. "The family thought I was pretty well educated by that time," he later explained, "and judging by the standards of the neighborhood I was."[16]

With his formal schooling behind him, Gardner took a job as a musician in O'Bryon's Café, a neighborhood saloon frequented by his uncle Henry, a carpenter. "They'd have pig roasts on Saturday nights, and I used to play the piano, a fellow named Freddy Vopat the drums, and a guy called Theodore Smith the violin. We were the band and we were rotten. It was a nice place, though, and everybody had a good time."[17] The atmosphere of the unpretentious neighborhood bar (which, in a different interview, Gardner described as "a fairly rough dive"[18]), made an impression on the teenager, and may have helped inspire *Duffy's Tavern* a quarter-century later. When his mother learned of the teenager's new gig, however, she strongly disapproved, and, as Gardner's colleague Abe Burrows later remarked, "This was one of few jobs which Ed ever left without being dismissed, and this wasn't exactly under his own motivation."[19]

By the time he and Shirley met, Ed Gardner had held all sorts of jobs. He'd worked as a prize fight manager, and even had an unsuccessful stint as a dispatcher with the Pennsylvania Railroad, but marrying Shirley gave him the opportunity to look in on the world he found so captivating.

During the summer of 1930, the new Mr. and Mrs. Gardner were in Springfield, Massachusetts, where Shirley had been engaged in a stock company. Since the company manager didn't want it known that his leading lady was married, Shirley and Ed were forced to keep their relationship under wraps. Ed was still employed in sales, by then hawking miniature golf courses, but the hand-to-mouth realities of the early 1930s made it impossible to earn a living peddling such luxury items.

With neither Mr. nor Mrs. Gardner yet established professionally, they tackled the Broadway world together. For all their youthful energy, they could hardly have found a more difficult time to achieve their dreams. The Great Depression, which had begun with the stock market crash in late 1929, had left countless people merely struggling to survive. Attending the theater was hardly seen as a priority when times were this hard.

During the 1929–30 season, 233 new shows had been mounted on the Great White Way; the following season, that number would drop to 187. Vaudeville and stock companies were similarly affected. By the end of the 1930s, stock theaters of the kind that had been Shirley's mainstay were falling by the wayside, thanks to the economic conditions as well as the increased competition from radio and from sound movies.

In the early 1930s, Ed Gardner began to find his way into work in the professional theater. For several months, he worked as a publicist for producer Crosby Gaige. (Gaige's shows of this period included the short-lived *The House Beautiful*, which the acerbic Dorothy Parker famously dubbed "the play lousy.") Whenever an opportunity arose, Gardner took work as a casting director, script typist, understudy — anything that would build his resume of theatrical experience. At one point, both Shirley and Ed toiled in the Federal Works Project Administration's Theater project, one of the few paying jobs available to denizens of the theater at the height of these economic hard times.

Now that Shirley was married, she wanted to stay in New York and be near Ed, rather than continuing to tour with stock companies and WPA shows, but the pickings were slim for an actress not yet a star. In April 1931, she played a featured role in *School for Virtue*, an amateurish comedy with a no-name cast that opened and closed in less than a week. That fall, she resurfaced in *The Camels Are Coming*, another flop, which racked up only 11 performances before giving up the ghost.

Shirley and Ed decided to take matters into their own hands. Even though *The Camels Are Coming* hadn't been a success, its author, Donn Mullaly, had another script ready for production, with a lead female role for Shirley. Gardner had been eager to launch his own theatrical career, tired of working for others, and cast himself as the producer of this new venture. He did not allow himself to be dissuaded by the distinct lack of available capital.

As his latter-day radio colleague Abe Burrows explained, "There are two ways to produce a play, both more or less unpredictable. One is to find an angel, which is Broadway for an individual who wants to back a stage production badly enough to put up the cash. Ed tried the other way; one in which everything from the star's salary to rent of bill poster space is paid in percentages of box office receipts—if any."[20] Even hotel space for the actors was bartered in exchange for profit participation in what came to be called *Coastwise*. Opening in late 1931, Mr. and Mrs. Gardner's joint venture was met by discouraging reviews and ticket sales, and Shirley was soon unemployed again.

Not until the spring of 1933 did Shirley resurface on Broadway, landing a small role (and understudying a larger one) in the Theatre Guild production of *The Mask and the Face*. The star of the show was Judith Anderson; also featured was Shirley's first Broadway co-star, Humphrey Bogart. The play, which was adapted by Somerset Maugham, was not well-received, and went under quickly. However, the entrée into the Theatre Guild would later prove to be valuable to Shirley. In the meantime, she drew at least one compliment from a critic who found her role as a "mildly sinful siren ... convincingly provocative."[21]

That summer, Ed assembled a stock company in Upper Montclair, New Jersey, with Shirley as its leading lady. Oscar Wilde's *The Importance of Being Earnest* was among the shows presented that season. By early August, the company had moved on to Caldwell, New Jersey, and was staging Noël Coward's *Private Lives*. With Shirley's help, Ed was slowly building a resume of show business credentials that would help him build a career as a producer and director.

In the fall of 1933, Shirley nearly returned to Broadway in a show called *Haywire*, written by Kennon Jewett. Producers Richard Aldrich and Alfred de Liagre, Jr., announced a cast for the comedy that included Tom Powers, Harold Vermilyea, and Shirley, with de Liagre to direct. According to the *New York Times,* the show had undergone a title

Coastwise (1931) cast Shirley as a seductive bad girl, but the play was short-lived.

The show that never was: Shirley (at left), with Tom Powers and Elizabeth Love in the trouble-plagued *Haywire.*

change, from *North of Broadway,* after its initial tryouts. After originally announcing a November 28, 1933 opening at the Bijou Theatre, however, *Haywire* proceeded to go haywire. The next column blurb in the *Times* promised a November 30 opening. By the time that day had rolled around, however, the show's formal opening had been "indefinitely postponed,"[22] though a performance of sorts was held that evening for those who had already purchased advance tickets. A week or so later, the show was back to being called *North of Broadway,* destined for a different theater and with some cast changes. By any name, the play seems to have finally died of improvements, and never opened on Broadway, with or without Shirley.

Back in New York once the summer season wound down, Shirley was reading — Dorothy Parker's newly published short story collection *After Such Pleasures.* She was so taken with the author's wit that she found herself reading choice passages aloud to Ed. Since Shirley was having a difficult time finding stage roles that showcased her properly, Ed proposed an idea. Why not rent a theater, and adapt Miss Parker's comic stories into a series of skits in which Shirley could star? Miss Parker's witty stories, which often revolved around male-female relationships, offered standout roles for an actress. Ed obtained the rights to the book, transformed it into a theater script, and cast himself in the role of Shirley's director. The skits would be enacted by an ensemble company that featured mostly little-known players, though one of them was actress Enid Markey (one of the first actresses to play Edgar Rice Burroughs' Jane onscreen, in a silent Tarzan movie, and much later a Hollywood character actress).

In January 1934, *After Such Pleasures* was tried out in a smaller theater before gearing up for its Broadway debut. Opening in February 1934, *After Such Pleasures* represented a new level of ambition for the Gardner-Booth team, and they went into opening night feeling hopeful.

But as Gardner later recalled, "I thought I'd arrived. But through a lack of rehearsals or a weakness for remembering faces, the spotlight man couldn't find the actors on opening night. Everything happened; even the flats tried to fall on our leading man." With a shrug, Gardner added, "I didn't wait to see the reviews."[23]

In fact, the reviews weren't completely negative, most of them finding at least some things to like about *After Such Pleasures*. The reviewer for *The New York Times* praised Ed's work as writer-producer ("Mr. Gardner has done pretty well by Mrs. Parker"), and singled out Shirley's appearance as a young bride "who begins her marriage by putting the bridegroom in the wrong and keeping him there — probably for the run of the contract."[24] Nonetheless, it was not a hit, running only a few weeks and making no real money for Ed and Shirley. Even so, the show propelled husband and wife toward new opportunities. Ed, who was slowly building up his show business credentials, was hired by the J. Walter Thompson advertising agency, where his job would entail working with Thompson clients in the increasingly popular medium of radio.

Money was still tight for the young couple, and after the show closed Shirley and Ed happily accepted an offer to join a troupe of performers who put on weekly variety shows at the Barbizon-Plaza Hotel, called "Sunday Nights at Nine." The lure for participating in the revue was the free room and board that Barbizon-Plaza management gave to company members. Shirley was able to draw on some of the material from *After Such Pleasures* in her weekly appearances. The *New York Times* favorably reviewed the March 4, 1934, opening night of the newly updated revue, noting Shirley as one of the cast members, and commented, "A friendly audience greeted the performance warmly."[25]

The weekly exposure Shirley received in "Sunday Nights at Nine" opened the door to more work. That summer, Shirley was among the cast members in a tryout of J.C. Nugent's play *The Dream Child*, at Lawrence Langner's Westport Country Playhouse. Nugent, a former vaudevillian, cast himself in the lead of the show, and also found roles for his daughter and son-in-law. By the time *The Dream Child* arrived on Broadway that fall, however, Shirley was no longer associated with the production — no great loss, as it drew unenthusiastic reviews, and closed after 24 performances.

She also had a brief engagement at the Locust Valley Playhouse on Long Island, playing the title role in a new comedy called *The Nude in Washington Square*. Actually, the latter part of the title better described Shirley, a self-professed square who certainly didn't appear unclothed in the play. She was, however, cast as blonde artists' model Patsy Smith, whose nude portrait hangs in a New York art gallery, much to the horror of her fiancé's blue-blooded parents. A *New York Times* reviewer, recognizing Shirley from her run in *After Such Pleasures*, said she played Patsy "as amusingly as she did the Dorothy Parker sketches."[26]

Not long afterwards, however, Shirley landed a far more significant gig, thanks again to "Sunday Nights at Nine." In the hotel audience one Sunday night were producer-director George Abbott, and John Cecil Holm, author of a new comedy called *Three Men on a*

Horse. The play concerned some small time crooks who stumble upon a meek, suburban husband who works as a greeting card writer, but has an uncanny knack for picking the winners in horse races. One of the featured characters in *Three Men on a Horse* was Mabel, featherbrained ex-showgirl lady friend of a minor league bad guy. Years later, playwright Holm had not forgotten his first glimpse of Shirley Booth at work: "Two girls came out

Shirley (center) is flanked by Edith Van Cleve (left) and Joyce Apling, original cast members of the Broadway hit *Three Men on a Horse.*

and sat at a table, had a soda, and they talked about men and life and, I think, Brooklyn. Shirley was the blonde girl; every so often I wonder who the other girl was."[27] After the show, Abbott and Holm were invited upstairs to the hotel room that Shirley shared with Ed, whom Holm remembered being addressed by the nickname "Poggie," to discuss the possibility of casting her in *Three Men on a Horse.*

Though George Abbott would become one of the best-known and most respected names in the American theatre, he had not yet had the full-fledged successes that would win him that acclaim. His early career trajectory, in fact, had not been unlike Shirley's. He went into the theater as an actor in the latter part of the 1910s, just as Shirley was getting her feet wet in stock companies. He would spend most of the late 1920s and early 1930s directing, though mostly plays that would enjoy only brief runs. After directing actors for most of the past decade, however, Abbott was quick to see Shirley's potential, and offered her the role of Mabel.

The play opened in January 1935 and was a smash. It would run for more than two years, and make Shirley a well-known commodity in the theatrical community. It was also the first of many Shirley Booth stage roles that would be adapted to film, with another actress assuming her part. Joan Blondell was cast as Mabel in the movie version of *Three Men on a Horse,* released by Warners in 1936. (Ironically, Shirley's Broadway understudy as Mabel was Blondell's lesser-known actress sister Gloria). The success of *Three Men on a Horse* meant that Shirley would no longer have to seek out-of-town work in stock companies, many of which were going by the wayside anyway.

Playwright Holm credited Shirley with giving her characterization as Mabel more depth than most actresses might have. "This could have been a surface smooth, flashy, sexy, dumb dame. But there was more to the role than that and Shirley sensed it at once. Day by day the role developed in rehearsal until, when she opened in New York, she had given the role a sort of pre–Cineramic treatment."[28] After working with Shirley in *Three Men on a Horse* in the mid–1930s, Holm claimed that it came as no surprise to him fifteen years later when the actress had become one of the premier stars of the Broadway stage.

During the show's original run, the theme of horse racing, which was so central to the plot, reportedly affected the cast as well. Seeing that there was a real-life racehorse who shared the name of "Brass Monkey," the horse named in the script, the actors placed bets on the contestant and won. Spurred on by that success, Shirley placed $50 on an entrant named "Shirley B.," and was again victorious. Commented a reporter, "By this time the Broadway bookmakers were going around muttering to themselves, and were being very ungracious about accepting bets from the cast of *Three Men on a Horse.*"[29]

The success of the show led to new opportunities for Shirley. In January 1936, she made a guest appearance, along with film star Edward G. Robinson and comedian Frank Fay, on the NBC radio show *Rudy Vallee's Variety Hour.* It was one of her first forays into radio, a medium that would become increasingly important to her career by the early 1940s.

Radio was also Ed's main source of income, as he was now employed as a producer-director with the J. Walter Thompson agency, responsible for a number of network radio series. Among Ed's assignments during the 1930s were producing the shows of George Burns and Gracie Allen, and directing NBC's *Good News of 1938.* Perhaps his most felicitous assignment was to produce the radio version of the popular "Ripley's Believe It or Not" column. His Thompson colleagues considered this a perfect fit for him, as he was not at all taken aback by the never-ending parade of eccentrics he met in the course of producing the show.

In November 1936, after more than 700 performances, *Three Men on a Horse* switched theaters, moving from the Playhouse to the Fulton, and had its sets refurbished. Several of the original cast members had by then moved on to other projects, but Shirley continued in the role of Mabel. Only a two-week vacation in the summer of 1936 had interrupted her lengthy run in the hit comedy. She and co-star William Lynn were rewarded with improved billing during the show's last few months of life, acknowledging their contributions to its phenomenal success.

Shortly after *Horse* closed in January 1937, Shirley was signed to another strong featured role, in the comedy *Excursion*. The show cast Shirley as an unfaithful married woman with a child. She, her lover, and the little girl are among the passengers on a Coney Island ferry whose captain unexpectedly goes off course during his farewell voyage. Also in the cast was a man whose support had meant much to her in the past—actor J. Hammond Dailey, who'd been instrumental in getting Shirley her first career break two decades before.

Excursion presented what must have been an appealing fantasy to many in New York, and elsewhere. As one commentator put it, "The skipper ... knows

Publicity photograph marking the first-year anniversary of *Three Men on a Horse,* with Shirley featured as Mabel.

that this one trip down the bay has given his passengers no real escape from life's troubles and discomforts.... So Skipper Rich does what every one must have day dreamed of doing some time, he steers his ship for the open sea and an untroubled island near Trinidad, and every one on board, when the time comes, votes to follow this leader in rebellion."[30]

The comedy script, by newcomer Victor Wolfson, was considered quite strong, and it was widely assumed that a hit was in the making. Even before the show had been tested, movie rights to *Excursion* sold to MGM for a hefty price tag. Backstage, however, there was a power struggle brewing between Wolfson and director Worthington Miner.

Attending a rehearsal one day, Wolfson flew into a rage at the way in which the actors were playing a scene. As Miner told it, Wolfson yelled for a break, saying, "This is not my play!... I've never seen such desecration. It's criminal what you've done, Tony Miner!"[31]

Caught in the middle of the dispute, producer Jack Wilson eventually decreed that some of the changes Miner had made would be dropped, returning to the script as Wolfson had submitted it. "The end result," Miner said, "was a beautiful first act, an adequate second, and a bummer for last act."[32]

When the play opened in April, critics were enthusiastic, and a long run was predicted. However, according to Miner, "There was much that was charmingly written, much that was brilliantly played, enough to make an opening night cheer. It took a while for the public to discern that the play, itself, was a cold fish."[33] In this disruptive environment, the production gradually fell off track. *Excursion* closed in July, after only 116 performances.

Even though it had not enjoyed the lengthy run some expected, *Excursion* was nonetheless chosen for inclusion in Burns Mantle's *Best Plays* for the 1936–37 season. "This is a comedy," stated the introduction to the printed play, "that happily possesses a majority of the virtues looked for in a popular success— including those of novelty of idea, an incisive genuineness in characterization, frank audience appeal in story, an abundance of honest humor, and a touch of propaganda."[34]

Now thought of as a comic actress, Shirley surprised critics that fall when she returned to work with a drama called *Too Many Heroes,* adapted by playwright Dore Schary from a real-life lynching case. Shirley was cast as the bitter widow of the lynching victim, a far cry from her recent comedy roles. The experience was a satisfying one for Shirley, who became friendly with Schary and his wife. Audiences didn't flock to see a show about small-town prejudice and persecution in the 1930s, and *Too Many Heroes* didn't last long, but critics applauded Shirley's dramatic performance.

With no new play on the horizon, Shirley relocated to the West Coast in 1938, where Ed's radio career had taken him. After making a few attempts to break into Hollywood, and meeting with little success, she decided to stay home for a while, spend more time with her husband, and be a housewife while her spouse became the breadwinner. That this plan did not meet with complete success is perhaps explained by the memories of comedy writer Carroll Carroll, another longtime Thompson employee.

Carroll made it plain that, despite his marriage to Shirley, Ed was well known to his colleagues as a womanizer. He observed an incident one day in which Ed's boss, John Reber, invited him home to dinner to continue an important business discussion. Said Ed, "Gee, John, I'd like to, but Shirley's expecting me home." When Reber offered to call Shirley and explain why her husband would be late, however, Ed too quickly said, "No! No! Don't do that."[35] It was obvious to everyone present that it wasn't really Shirley whom he was hurrying to meet.

3. Mr. Gardner and Miss Duffy

With ten years of marriage behind them, Shirley and Ed were at a turning point, personally and professionally. Both members of the two-career household were on the upswing professionally. Ed was well-regarded as a radio producer, primarily of comedy and variety programs, while Shirley was now firmly established as a Broadway actress. Yet there would always be uncertainty in their lives, as was the norm for show business people. In the late 1930s, and early 1940s, they juggled a variety of projects, in both New York and Los Angeles. Shirley, rapidly being recognized as one of Broadway's best actresses, was trying to find the right balance between work and home, between her burgeoning career and her marriage to a man who grew to resent her increased fame.

In early 1939, she signed to play a featured role in Philip Barry's comedy *The Philadelphia Story*, which would star Katharine Hepburn. The production was unusually important both to the debt-ridden Theatre Guild, which had mounted a few too many "significant" plays that didn't ring the bell at the box office, and to Hepburn herself. On the outs in Hollywood after being declared "box office poison," Hepburn wanted to fulfill her dream of starring in a hit Broadway show, something that had eluded her in the late 1920s and early 1930s. She knew, though, that New York critics typically looked down on film actors, setting the stakes high for *The Philadelphia Story*. She, and the show, would have to be awfully good to survive. A powerhouse cast, including Joseph Cotten and Van Heflin, certainly helped.

The Philadelphia Story won critical plaudits upon its debut in late March, and was a box office hit, enjoying a one-year run. Its success was thanks in part to Shirley's assured performance as magazine photographer Liz Imbrie. For Shirley, the play helped establish her in another type of role she would essay frequently in her career: the smart, witty career woman. It was a complete turnaround from the role she'd done so skillfully in *Three Men on a Horse,* but audiences and critics were beginning to learn that Miss Booth was unusually versatile.

Journalist Mel Heimer, who became a lifelong Shirley Booth fan, thought her performance integral to the success of *The Philadelphia Story.* Reported her smitten admirer, "I had eyes then only for Kate in that candy-striped blouse and those diaphanous gowns, but when I had come out into the clear, cold night air I realized that while I had yearned for the Hepburn for three hours, I had seen a quietly spectacular piece of acting by Miss Booth. Kate was the showpiece. Shirley was the actress."[1]

What a drag! Shirley shares costuming and makeup tips with three husky Harvard students prepping for a campus show. Whether this publicity photograph sold any tickets for *The Philadelphia Story* is questionable (Michael D. Strain collection).

Ed, meanwhile, had been assigned to produce a CBS radio show, *This Is New York.* The show's star was Deems Taylor, a cultural critic who introduced listeners to Gotham's sophistication and urbanity. Among its early guests, in January 1939, was Shirley. Then, unexpectedly, Ed himself had a turn at the microphone.

As counterpoint to the cultured and erudite Taylor, producer Gardner wanted for one segment a typical lower-middle-class New York type to engage in repartee with the star. He auditioned a number of seasoned radio actors, but none of them could reproduce the sound to his satisfaction. In frustration, with airtime only a short time away, he grabbed the script himself and began doing a reading to demonstrate what he needed. His own reading made everyone around him laugh, and the answer to the problem was obvious: Gardner himself assumed the role in the broadcast. In that moment, the character that became Ed Gardner's bread and butter for the next two decades was born.

Ed continued to appear periodically on *This Is New York,* and the small taste of fame that this brought him only whetted his appetite. For all his success behind the scenes as a producer-director, he craved the kind of high profile attention his wife was receiving. He later admitted that he hadn't handled Shirley's success well. When Mr. and Mrs. Gardner encountered a gushing Shirley Booth fan one day, Ed went mostly unnoticed, until the lady inquired if he was *Mister* Booth. "Yes," he retorted, "John Wilkes."[2]

This Is New York was short-lived, never attracting a viable sponsor, but from the ashes of the project Ed and writer Abe Burrows began developing a new show. They proposed to take Gardner's deeze-dem-and-doze barkeeper character and place him in a typical New York dive called *Duffy's Tavern*. But the idea would take more than a year to come to fruition. Meanwhile, with Shirley busy playing out *The Philadelphia Story*'s run, Ed took up residence in California, where he'd been assigned to produce CBS' *Texaco Star Theatre* for the 1939–40 season. His primary responsibility was for the show's variety elements, which originated from Hollywood with Ken Murray as emcee.

Thinking that Ed's career would require him to settle in California, Shirley was prepared to do so as well, once she'd completed her commitment to the Hepburn play. Not long before she was scheduled to leave for the West Coast, Shirley was enjoying an evening out with friends. She was wearing a new fur coat, which she had bought with her earnings from *The Philadelphia Story,* along with a cash gift from Ed. At the end of the evening out, her coat, valued at $2,500, turned up missing from the checkroom of a mid-town hotel. The staff members on duty told her regretfully that someone had reached behind the counter and snatched it.

She was appalled when the company that operated the checkroom told her that their insurance covered losses only up to a maximum of $75.00, meaning she would not be properly reimbursed for the theft. The story made the New York newspapers, eventually resulting in a lawsuit. In the meantime, Shirley postponed her trip to California while she tried to resolve the matter. The move to the West Coast became a moot point a few weeks later, when Ed's job on *Texaco Star Theatre* came to a close, and he returned to New York in search of a new gig.

That summer, Shirley had her first continuing role in a network radio series, though details are scarce. She was featured alongside Peggy Conklin and Lawson Zerbe in *Strictly Business,* heard Fridays at 8 P.M. on the NBC Blue network. Shirley played the assistant to a press agent in what was described in newspaper listings as a comedy show, though *Variety* pegged it as a serial, saying it would have been better suited to daytime airing. What documentation has survived on *Strictly Business* does not include character names or plot details, and there appear to be no surviving episodes to hear today.

Variety's June review gave a little insight into the show's basic setup: "Center of the serial's pother is a nightclub press agent, flip in speech and breezy in his treatment of the dames. If he isn't on the make for one, another's on the make for him. Lawson Zerbe does a stock characterization of this Don Juan figment. Shirley Booth makes the best of her assignment as a hard-headed damsel who succumbs anyway while Peggy Conklin likewise puts her talents to minor use in the part of the heiress whose more calculating style proves tough competition."[3] Broadcast live, *Strictly Business* was a sustaining (unsponsored) show that came to a close after a brief summer run.

Ed too had his eyes on a network radio spot that summer, and snagged an on-air tryout from CBS for his *Duffy's Tavern* concept. The sample episode, heard on the July 29, 1940, broadcast of the series *Forecast*, didn't yet feature Miss Duffy, or some of the other recurring characters who would become its mainstays. It centered on manager Archie's efforts to hire a suitable Irish tenor for the bar. As would become the norm during the regular series, the unheard owner Duffy called every few minutes throughout the broadcast, complaining about the talent heard and urging Archie to try someone else. From that opening show, it was clear that Duffy's was no high-class establishment. When local cop on the beat Officer Clancy threatens to shut down the tavern, Archie has a ready reply: "You can't close us up. We ain't got a license."

At the end of the 30-minute show, listeners were told to contact CBS if they wanted

Was it a comedy or was it a serial? Peggy Conklin (left), Lawson Zerbe, and Shirley were the stars of the NBC radio series *Strictly Business*.

to hear more of Archie and his cohorts. Though the sample broadcast was well-received, network executives were skeptical about turning it into a weekly series. The show might play fine for urban audiences, but would listeners in small town America get the joke? For the time being, *Duffy's Tavern* went on the back burner, and Ed instead accepted a job as producer-director of NBC radio's *The Rudy Vallee Sealtest Show*.

In that capacity, Gardner would be credited with shoring up Vallee's sagging ratings with an unusual gimmick — one that the sponsor initially resisted. He signed an aging and addicted John Barrymore to the cast, for a starting salary of $1,500 per week. The premise involved presenting "The Great Profile" in a series of self-mocking skits that lampooned his heavy drinking and subsequent career backslide. Some among Barrymore's friends and supporters found the concept in poor taste, and Barrymore himself later told a friend, "I am doing the work of a whore.... There is nothing as sad in all the world as an *old* prostitute."[4] But radio audiences, not knowing that Barrymore truly was so alcohol-impaired that his ability to perform was never taken for granted, mostly found Barrymore's appearances hilarious, and Gardner brought *The Rudy Vallee-Sealtest Show* to new heights of popularity.

Meanwhile, Shirley received a call inviting her to audition for producer George S. Kaufman's new show, the comedy *My Sister Eileen*. Based on the popular *New Yorker* stories by Ruth McKenney, *Eileen* told the story of a young aspiring writer who moves to New York City with her beautiful, naïve sister. The two women move into a noisy, problem-ridden basement apartment in Greenwich Village, where they encounter a wide variety of

Mr. Appopolous (Morris Carnovsky) ushers Eileen (Jo Ann Sayers, left) and Ruth (Shirley) into their new Greenwich Village apartment in *My Sister Eileen*.

oddball New Yorkers in their pursuit of success and romantic encounters. The original script, by Joseph Fields and Jerome Chodorov, was then reworked by Kaufman.

Shirley auditioned for the role of Ruth at the suggestion of co-author Chodorov, and despite some reservations from Kaufman and his colleagues as to whether she was right for the part. Having absorbed the script overnight, and noted that the character of Ruth was supposed to be sturdily built, Shirley decided to improve her prospects by looking the part from Day One. "In the morning, I put on a tweed suit that I didn't like because it made me look too plump, and when I met Mr. Kaufman I stood up so that he would get the widest view of me."[5] It was more likely her reading than her costuming that did the trick, but Kaufman and his colleagues agreed that Shirley should play Ruth.

Shirley's co-star Jo Ann Sayers, in the title role, was a blonde newcomer cast more for her looks than for her experience, which was restricted to a couple of college plays. Early in rehearsals, Kaufman sized up Shirley and realized she could take care of herself onstage, concentrating instead on intense coaching of the neophyte Sayers. The two actresses became friendly. "[Shirley] is so simple and direct and she knows so much," Sayers said, "but she lets you alone unless you ask for advice."[6]

Since there had been no out-of-town tour before *Eileen* hit Broadway (a confident Kaufman having deemed it unnecessary), no one knew what to expect of the show, which would open on December 26, 1940. Advance ticket sales for the unknown quantity were modest. Just days before the show was set to open, the company's mood was seriously disturbed by the sudden death of the real-life Eileen McKenney. The former Miss McKenney, who'd married writer Nathanael West (*Day of the Locust*) a few months earlier, was returning from a hunting trip in Mexico with her husband on Sunday, December 22. West was at the wheel, driving near El Centro, California, when their car collided head-on with another vehicle. Mrs. West died at the scene; West, who'd run a stop sign, survived only a few hours longer. The tragedy left many members of the *My Sister Eileen* company uncertain they should proceed with opening night as planned.

Ultimately, in the spirit of "the show must go on," the cast and producers decided not to postpone the play. Few could have predicted that *My Sister Eileen* would keep Shirley gainfully employed until 1943, breaking records for the length of its Broadway run. No longer was she supporting Hepburn or some other star; this was Shirley's show, and she made the most of it.

Though Shirley had previously been best-known to theatergoers for *Three Men on a Horse*, playing a character with limited smarts, the role of Ruth was closer to her characterization of Liz Imbrie in *The Philadelphia Story*. Ruth was a type that Shirley would play more frequently in the future—the smart and assertive career woman, quick with a wisecrack. When lovely Eileen comes home and tells her she met a man that day, Ruth retorts, "Only one? What's the matter? Were you stuck in an elevator?" Noticing that a garish painting done by their landlord Mr. Appopolous has vanished from the wall of their apartment, Ruth comments, "There must be an idiot sneak-thief in the neighborhood."

Ed, too, scored a big break, when he and partner Abe Burrows finally managed to sell *Duffy's Tavern* as a weekly series. It premiered on March 1, 1941, joining CBS' Thursday night schedule under the sponsorship of Schick. As *Duffy's Tavern* came together, Gardner and Burrows added new characters. New additions to the cast included African-American actor Eddie Green, as deadpan waiter Eddie. (Asked in one episode how they can make the joint a little classier, Eddie looks around at the bar's regulars and suggests, "Get these people outta here.") The dumbbell of the group was Clifton Finnegan (the name thought to be Ed's jab at Clifton Fadiman), who prefaced every statement out of his mouth with a "Duh...." Remembered one longtime *Duffy's Tavern* fan, "Finnegan's claim to fame was his brother at Harvard Medical School—who is forever shrined there in a jar of alcohol. And the picture of Finnegan himself once appeared in a medical journal—with a question mark under it."[7]

Ed and his partner also had a part for Shirley. They worked into the format Shirley's well-honed girl-from-Flatbush routine, for which she'd had little use in her recent stage assignments. She played the owner's waitress daughter, Miss Duffy, a loud, brash young lady who was preoccupied with men, and her prospects of getting married — according to one of the show's jokes, she was the possessor of a ready-made marriage license made out to herself and "To Whom It May Concern." During the war years, Archie would characterize Miss Duffy as "a dame that hangs around draft boards waiting for rejects." (When she asks huffily what's so terrible about a guy with flat feet, he replies, "Nothing. Except our country's standards are higher than yours."[8])

Abe Burrows, who knew Shirley offstage as a classy, soft-spoken lady, was surprised by her innate ability to inhabit this character. "Shirley Booth was an amazing Miss Duffy," he said. "Here was an elegant actress who came from Hartford, Connecticut [sic], doing the best New York accent I have ever heard. If you aren't born in New York, it's very hard to fake this sound. Through the years I auditioned people for *Duffy's Tavern*. They would often step up and say they were New Yorkers, but after two minutes I'd know they were faking it. Shirley Booth really had the right sound. Her ear was perfect."[9]

As for Ed's character, one writer described Archie thusly: "He is a braggart, and a bit of a dope. His silences, when he doesn't quite understand something, are eloquent. When he talks, which is generally, he commits assault and battery upon the King's English, but, on the other hand, he refuses to be feazed [sic] by the eminent guest stars who are occasionally honored by invitations to the Tavern. He is the sidewalk humor New York, casual and impudent...."[10] He was also, according to most of Ed Gardner's working colleagues, just an extension of the star himself.

Though never seen, Duffy himself was richly characterized through others' descriptions. We know from Eddie the waiter that Duffy is a cheapskate, and doesn't pay his staff well. ("Sometimes a man needs a few of the luxuries of life," Eddie complains on one occasion. "A nickel for the subway ... new cardboard for his shoes." [11])

Perhaps the closest modern-day equivalent to *Duffy's Tavern* is the much-acclaimed NBC sitcom *Cheers* (1982–93), set among the working-class denizens of a Boston bar. That show, in fact, had a direct lineage from Ed Gardner, since *Cheers'* Emmy-winning director James Burrows is the son of *Duffy's* Abe Burrows. Other fans of *Duffy's Tavern* found the *All in the Family* spinoff *Archie Bunker's Place* (CBS, 1979–83) reminiscent of the radio classic — Carroll O'Connor's Archie shared not only

CBS publicity photograph for Shirley's role as Miss Duffy in the hit radio comedy series *Duffy's Tavern*.

the first name of Gardner's character, but also the finely tuned ability to mangle the English language.

From the outset, *Duffy's Tavern* was both a critical and popular success, quickly making Ed Gardner a top radio star. (As was standard for the period, Gardner was the only regular who received on-air billing by his own name; Shirley and the other members of the company were uncredited). Ratings surveys showed that seven million listeners tuned in for the weekly broadcast. During the show's first year, Gardner was named Outstanding New Radio Comedian by *Movie-Radio Guide*.

Contrary to the network's initial fears that it was too much of a New York in-joke, the show attracted high ratings nationwide, and a broad range of listeners. It was popular with everyday listeners, but also admired by more sophisticated types, who otherwise disavowed much of the popular comedy heard on radio. For a time, its title was shortened to simply *Duffy's,* after a new sponsor decided that the image of a roughhouse tavern was unseemly. Soon the original title was restored, however, as it became apparent that listeners liked the show just fine.

By 1942, it was a show business status symbol to appear as a guest star on the program, and be insulted by Archie. The show's not-particularly-logical premise allowed for stars like Susan Hayward to somehow show up at Duffy's as part of a normal evening's entertainment. Among those who stepped up and played along were name stars like Charles Laughton, Tallulah Bankhead, Gene Tierney, and John Garfield.

The male guest stars were usually subject to a once-over from man-hungry Miss Duffy. When it's announced that the intellectual Clifton Fadiman, host of the brainy quiz show *Information Please,* will be paying a visit, Miss Duffy immediately begins reading Dostoevsky in hopes of attracting his attention. When Fadiman arrives, however, she tries a less subtle approach. When the two are introduced, the first words out of Miss Duffy's mouth are, "Plaza 5–9970" (her phone number). Chided by Archie, she explains to Fadiman, "Well, you're always asking questions, so I thought I'd give you the answer first." (Shirley also appeared on Fadiman's show, acquitting herself well in the quiz, and impressing listeners who thought she shared Miss Duffy's distinctly limited smarts).

Among the other comic highlights of the show were the occasional musical numbers Shirley screeched in Miss Duffy's adenoidal tones. Hearing her rendition of "Chant of the Jungle" in the 3/23/43 broadcast, guest star Frank Buck (of *Bring 'Em Back Alive*) fame cracks, "I would never bring *her* back alive!"

For Shirley, one of the key challenges of her radio success was timing. Radio shows in the early 1940s were performed live, usually twice during an evening—once for the East Coast audience, and then again a few hours later for listeners out West. In 1942, *Duffy's Tavern* was heard Tuesday evenings at 8:30 P.M., on the Blue Network. All well and good, except that Shirley was also expected to be on hand when the curtain rose on that evening's performance of *My Sister Eileen*.

Since she appeared in the opening scene, toting her typewriter as she and Eileen arrive at their New York apartment, the curtain could not rise until Shirley was ready. At five minutes until nine, when the radio program was coming to a close, a car was waiting outside for her. Shirley made a mad dash for the theater, and within minutes, as soon as she'd caught her breath, switched gears from Miss Duffy to Ruth McKenney. Later that evening, she was back in the radio studio, playing Miss Duffy a second time for its West Coast broadcast.

Though the success of *Duffy's Tavern* made both Gardner and Shirley well-known, and afforded them an opportunity to work together, their offstage relationship had some rocky patches. Living and working together only served to bring their differences into high relief. Ed was a partier, gambler and drinker, and not by nature a monogamous man. During the years of their marriage, they'd endured a number of separations. Sometimes work kept them apart, but there were also times when Shirley rebelled against Ed's behavior, and considered ending the marriage. The success of *Duffy's Tavern* only fed Gardner's ego, and gave him the power needed to step up his womanizing.

According to writer Parke Levy, Gardner's two avocations in life were his radio show, and his sex life. "Anything that walked— if it breathed, he'd go for it. Gardner was a real cocksman," Levy said. Despite Gardner's status as the husband of a prominent Broadway actress, Levy said, "Ed cheated like mad. But it never bothered him."[12] His J. Walter Thompson colleague Carroll Carroll confirmed that success only served to free Gardner of what few inhibitions he may have possessed. Later, after the show relocated to

Ed Gardner in his star-making role as bartender Archie in *Duffy's Tavern*.

California, *Duffy's Tavern* writers often found themselves summoned to a script session poolside at Gardner's lavish house, where they were apt to find their boss hosting a pool party with several female guests, and not a swimsuit in sight.

Columnist C.B. Driscoll, paying a visit to the studio during a *Duffy's Tavern* broadcast, thought Shirley and Ed complemented each other nicely, though it was evident that they "are of such varying temperaments ... Ed is about as high-strung and nervous as anybody you can find in this nervous town. Shirley is calm, pleasant, always carrying off her part with an easygoing informality. But if either drops the ball in the course of the show, the other picks it up and keeps the play going."[13]

However, actor Dick Van Patten, who appeared on *Duffy's Tavern* while still a teenager, saw a less pleasant side of the Gardner-Booth relationship. "She was a wonderful wife, but Ed Gardner did not treat her that well," Van Patten says. "Very chauvinistic— he yelled at her, screamed at her, and she just obeyed him. She was that kind of a wife." Abe Burrows wrote a recurring role for Van Patten as numbskull Clifton Finnegan's genius little brother, Wilford, and the actor still has fond memories today of the time he spent with Shirley, who "taught me to play gin rummy."[14]

Ed Gardner worked long hours on *Duffy's Tavern*. He was a perfectionist who was rarely satisfied with the scripts his writers prepared, and demanded much rewriting. Abe Burrows later said that it was Gardner who introduced him to Benzedrine, then the "upper" of choice for the writer facing a deadline, and expected to somehow stay up 48 or more hours straight before the broadcast.

Another writer who got his start with Ed was Larry Gelbart, later known for *M*A*S*H* and *Tootsie*, among his many high profile projects. Gelbart, a teenager when he was recruited for *Duffy's Tavern*, recalled, "Owner of the program, able to hire and fire, Ed Gardner did a good deal of both. He was most mercurial, to say the least, in his selection of writers. When under the influence, which is where he spent eighty to ninety proof of his time, he went from mercurial to maniacal, creating a virtual revolving door through which writers went after he paid each as near to a pittance as he could manage."[15]

Somehow, from all the pandemonium came a good show every week. But when the broadcasts were complete, Ed wasn't content to wind down by staying quietly at home with his wife. He'd enjoyed any number of insignificant flings while married to Shirley, but in 1942 a woman came along whose relationship with Ed quickly turned into something more. One night, Ed came backstage after *My Sister Eileen* and blurted out the truth: he had fallen in love with this woman, and wanted Shirley to give him a divorce.

In 1942, Shirley traveled to Reno and obtained her divorce from Ed Gardner. Not long afterwards, he married actress Simone Hegeman, a Frenchwoman. The second marriage

Ed and Shirley, showing few signs of wedded bliss (Michael D. Strain collection).

was apparently a successful one, lasting the rest of Gardner's life and producing two sons for the new Mr. and Mrs. Gardner. Meanwhile, Shirley, once again a bachelor girl, took an apartment alone on East 61st Street in Manhattan.

To her credit, Shirley's public statements regarding her ex-husband would be uniformly gracious and discreet for the rest of her life. Though Gardner's carousing and womanizing were poorly kept secrets in the New York show business community, she generally depicted their breakup as a mutual one due to incompatibility. "I just couldn't keep up with Ed," she said in 1954. "He loves gaiety and parties and I'm too much of an introvert. I can't bear being around people too long at a time."[16]

Years later, after Ed had passed away, Shirley was a bit more open about the rift that developed between them. "I took good care of him," she said thoughtfully. "I saw that he didn't drink too much and that he husbanded his strength. Maybe I took too good care of him. The concentration you need for acting ... it isn't always good in private life. Having been alone part of the time, you dedicate yourself to marriage. You get sold on the idea so much you want to be with them more than they want to be with you."[17]

Though their personal relationship had come to a difficult and painful end, professionally it would take longer for Ed and Shirley to split up. Surprisingly, Gardner seems not to have considered that asking Shirley for a divorce would make their professional collaboration awkward. Perhaps he assumed that no actress would willingly give up a well-paid job in a hit radio series, but there was no longer any pleasure involved with *Duffy's Tavern* for Shirley.

When *Duffy's Tavern* began a new season in September 1942, Shirley resumed her role as Miss Duffy alongside her soon-to-be ex-husband. But changes were in the air. In December, she announced that she would leave the cast of the still-popular *My Sister Eileen,* after a two-year run. Betty Furness stepped into the role of Ruth McKenney, but the gig was a brief one. Without Shirley, *Eileen* closed in January 1943, having clocked well over 800 performances.

Its remarkable staying power earned it a spot on the list of longest-running Broadway comedies, but also led to a hit movie, with Rosalind Russell assuming Shirley's role as Ruth. *Eileen* would be revived in multiple other incarnations in years to come — as a motion picture again in 1955, as the Broadway musical *Wonderful Town,* and ultimately as an unsuccessful television sitcom in 1960–61. But for Shirley, after such a lengthy run playing the same character, it was time for something new. She was ready for a new challenge on Broadway, and had serious misgivings about continuing her radio role as Miss Duffy.

With the show at its height of popularity and attention, Ed pressed her to continue, not wanting to tinker with success. Compounding the importance of keeping Shirley in the cast was another deal Ed had on the fire — he had begun negotiating for a movie version of *Duffy's Tavern.* In the spring and summer of 1943, Ed Gardner was close to a highly lucrative deal to sell the movie rights to *Duffy's Tavern.* Though he himself, as bartender Archie, would be the principal carryover from the radio cast, he also wanted to deliver the other key actors who had made it a hit. But given the acrimony that had passed between Shirley and her philandering ex-husband, she was not inclined to prolong their professional association.

In April, syndicated columnist Hedda Hopper reported that Gardner and Booth would team for the film, and "play their same roles on the screen."[18] Gardner, in the midst of negotiations with film studios, was undoubtedly the source of that information. A few weeks later, however, Shirley told the *New York Times* that she was giving up the role of

Miss Duffy, and would not return to the radio cast for the 1943–44 season. Citing her divorce from Gardner as one of the reasons she did not wish to continue, Shirley also said, without providing any specifics, that the role had become "sort of a Frankenstein"[19] to her. On June 29, 1943, Shirley made her last *Duffy's Tavern* appearance, opposite guest star Ray Milland.

Not surprisingly, the loss of Shirley's talent, and unique voice, was a blow to *Duffy's Tavern.* Although Ed Gardner was still able to close a deal for the film rights in August, contracting the property with Paramount Pictures, he was forced to go forward without Shirley. Gardner's contract to star in the film, and assist in its production, netted him a $150,000 windfall, and provided lucrative options for Paramount to follow it up , if desired, with a series of *Duffy's Tavern* films over a five-year period.

Nevertheless, Shirley declined the studio's offer of $50,000 to play Miss Duffy onscreen. Ultimately, the film, released in 1945 with Ann Thomas cast in Shirley's old role, leaned heavily on cameos from Paramount players— Bing Crosby, Betty Hutton, Alan Ladd — rather than the original source material, and was widely panned. After the tepid response to the initial film, there would be no further discussion of sequels.

Their professional divorce also left Gardner to begin the new radio season trying to find another actress who could approximate the sound and flavor his ex-wife had given to the key character of Miss Duffy. Gardner auditioned countless actresses, but wasn't satisfied with any of them. Eventually the search was expanded, allowing potential Miss Duffys from all over the country to send in recorded auditions, or to be given a quick hearing by telephone. Finally, Gardner awarded the role to Florence Halop. The younger sister of "Dead End Kid" Billy Halop, the 20-year-old would later be featured in the 1950s TV sitcom *Meet Millie,* and, at the end of her long career, as bailiff Florence on TV's *Night Court.* Halop's audition reportedly was good enough that Gardner's wife Simone, listening to the record, thought she was hearing Shirley's voice.

A few weeks later, NBC's Blue network broadcast the season opener of *Duffy's Tavern,* with Florence Halop stepping into the role of Miss Duffy. With Shirley gone from the cast, Ed Gardner had opted to relocate production to Hollywood, giving him easier access to the star names he sought as guests. Though Halop's debut as Miss Duffy was generally well-received by critics, some noted that the part of Miss Duffy seemed to have been diminished. *Variety*'s reviewer thought Gardner hogged the show himself, and shortchanged both guest star Veronica Lake and supporting players like Halop, failing to "give her something substantial to do."[20]

Over the next several years, Gardner would try numerous women, including highly regarded radio actresses like Doris Singleton and Sandra Gould, in the role, but never be completely satisfied with whoever took Shirley's place. By late 1947, Gardner was closing on Miss Duffy #10, with Margie Liszt the current incumbent, but whoever played the role existed in Shirley's shadow.

The squabbles with Gardner, plus the pain of seeing her marriage collapse, took their toll on Shirley. Even before *Eileen* closed, when she made Gardner aware that she was thinking of leaving *Duffy's Tavern,* the situation quickly became tense. When he was unable to dissuade her from quitting, things grew ugly. According to her friend and frequent co-star Max Showalter, "Ed was constantly inundating her with accusing and blasphemous phone calls and letters. She would arrive at the theater tense and shaken."[21]

4. G.I. Bill

Given her three-year run in *My Sister Eileen*, Shirley was immediately offered roles in other Broadway comedies once its run had concluded. Instead, she surprised her colleagues by auditioning for a dramatic lead in *Tomorrow the World*, a new play about the dangers of Nazism in wartime America. *Tomorrow the World* centered on a 12-year-old boy who, after being raised in a pro-Nazi environment overseas, is brought to America by his uncle, a college professor. Film actor Ralph Bellamy, who had learned his craft in stock theater companies just as Shirley had, would be the top-billed star.

The role Shirley wanted was that of Leona Richards, the professor's fiancée, a school principal whose Jewish heritage would clash with the anti–Semitism that had been so deeply imbedded in the child. Producer Theron Bamberger certainly knew Shirley's work, and was impressed by her audition, but had reservations about casting an actress so associated with comedy.

"The public is used to thinking you're funny," he told her. "You might get laughs in our play in spite of yourself."

Shirley wasn't buying it. "Getting laughs isn't quite that easy," she explained, having spent roughly a quarter-century perfecting the art. Bamberger relented, and the part of Leona was hers.[1]

Tomorrow the World opens as the Frame family awaits the arrival of Emil Bruckner, an orphan after his father was killed by the Nazis. Ready to open their hearts to a troubled child, the Frames are shocked instead by the poised and seemingly self–possessed young newcomer who proudly wears a Nazi uniform and declares his loyalty to his native country, saying, "I am a German, and I shall always be a German ... The American blood stream is a mixture of the scum of the earth."

Emil is particularly disturbed to learn that his Uncle Michael has just proposed marriage to a woman who is Jewish. Still loyal to the Nazi cause, young Emil plots to steal his uncle's chemistry research for the benefit of the enemy, and nearly kills his young cousin Patricia when she catches him breaking into her father's lab.

It is Shirley's character, Leona, who is the first to realize how successfully Emil has been tainted with racial hatred, and concludes that the transformation he allows his uncle to think he is undergoing is merely a ruse to assuage the enemy. Emil finds an unexpected ally in Michael's elder sister Jessie, who doesn't share his anti–Semitism, but has devoted much of her life to making a home for her brother and his family, and fears the prospect of Michael remarrying.

Shirley co-starred with film actor Ralph Bellamy (at right), and 12-year-old discovery Skippy Homeier, in the 1943 Broadway hit *Tomorrow the World*.

In the show's second act, Leona penetrates Emil's façade, confronting Emil about some ugly words he wrote about her on the sidewalk until he bursts out, "It's a lie! A Jewish lie! ... A Jewish lie from a Jewish whore!"

When Emil's attack on young Patricia forces Michael to see his nephew as he truly is, the professor despairs of his attempts to rehabilitate the boy. Leona urges him to press on, saying, "But don't you see, Mike. If you and I can't turn one little boy into a human being — then God help the world when this war is won, and we have to deal with twelve million of them!"

Aside from the performances of Shirley and Ralph Bellamy, much of the interest in *Tomorrow the World* arose from the strong featured performances by two child actors— twelve-year-old Skippy Homeier, who played Emil, and nine-year-old Joyce Van Patten, in her third Broadway show, cast as Patricia. Homeier, according to one story circulated at the time, actually registered a complaint against Shirley with their union, Equity, complaining that the slap she delivered to his face every night during their second act confrontation didn't need to be quite *that* realistic.

Young Miss Patten, part of an acting family that also included brother Dick (later star of the *Eight Is Enough* TV series), would remember Shirley more benignly. "Shirley Booth was like a mother to me," the former child actress later told syndicated columnist Earl Wilson. "I remember sitting on her lap."[2]

According to Joyce Van Patten, she was originally signed only to understudy the role of Patricia, but was pressed into service during the road tour. Director Elliott Nugent had assigned his own daughter, Nancy, the role of Patricia, but the girl was sick when the show opened in New Haven, so Van Patten went on. In Boston, with Nancy still under the weather, Joyce Van Patten again played Patricia, and both she and Skippy Homeier received "wonderful reviews"[3] — so much so that Nugent ultimately found himself in the untenable position of firing his own daughter. Officially, Nancy Nugent continued as an alternate, appearing at occasional matinees, but was overshadowed by Van Patten.

On opening night, it was clear that audiences found the drama absorbing, and had no trouble accepting Shirley in a dramatic role. She was amused, but flattered, when an opening night patron rushed up to her after the curtain fell and said, "Miss Booth, I always have loved you as a comedienne and now I am thrilled to find that you are a really good actress too."[4] Another audience member was seen thumbing through her playbill, and asking her companion if the lady who played Leona was really the same one who was in *My Sister Eileen.*

Tomorrow the World should have been a happy experience for Shirley. Her leading man Ralph Bellamy and his wife Alice became her lifelong friends. Critical notices were excellent upon the show's April opening at the Ethel Barrymore Theatre. As her colleagues recognized, however, Shirley was still in a fragile state. She would later say that she had little recollection of the time she spent in rehearsals for *Tomorrow the World,* or of its early weeks before audiences.

Co-star Ralph Bellamy vividly remembered the condition his leading lady was in: "On stage she was perfect. Then she'd make an exit — and literally walk into a brick wall. We'd lead her by the hand to her dressing room, put her on a couch, and give her a sedative. When it came time for her next entrance we'd lead her to the stage and push her on. The minute those lights hit her she'd start performing — and exit right into a brick wall again when the scene ended. This went on for three months."[5] Producer Bamberger corroborated Bellamy's story, noting only that the couch in Shirley's dressing room was an afterthought — initially they just laid her out on the floor between scenes.

The show's stage manager encouraged Shirley to see a chiropractor. As it turned out, the doctor treated more than her physical ails. "He was a psychoanalytically oriented chiropractor," Shirley explained. "He told me to lie down and let my mind wander back to early memories. Just to say whatever came into my mind. Then he said that next time I should bring a bathing suit. His idea was that he could tell a lot about your mental tensions by watching your body movements while you talked.

"And sure enough, I'd find my arms writhing around like a pair of snakes when I'd get on some subjects. So I'd come every day and get into my bathing suit ... and lie down and start talking. His theory was that mental troubles are sort of like little bubbles in the head like, and you can talk them out to the surface and they break — no more bubbles. I don't know, but it helped me."[6]

Though the chiropractic treatments seemed to ease some of her strain, both physical and emotional, a more lasting cure to her problems was soon to appear on the horizon. Once the worst of her traumas were over, Shirley began to make her way back toward a normal life. She was charmed by child actor Joyce Van Patten, who in turn was fascinated by Shirley's large and lavish dressing room, plastered with pictures and memorabilia from her earlier shows. During the run of the show, Joyce was occasionally allowed to spend Saturdays and Sundays at Shirley's apartment, which impressed the little girl as being very

Busy Shirley, pictured in May 1943, has just completed the radio broadcast of *Duffy's Tavern*. Now she must hurry, if she's to make her curtain call in *Tomorrow the World*.

glamorous. "I think she loved that," Van Patten says today of the maternal role Shirley played in her life during the show's run.[7]

Shirley also took an interest in war work, becoming one of numerous Broadway stars who helped to staff the Stage Door Canteen. Housed on 44th Street, the Canteen was a night-club founded by members of the theatrical community to entertain servicemen visiting New

Shirley's jitterbug routines with "Killer Joe" Piro were a popular attraction at the American Theatre Wing's Stage Door Canteen.

York. It provided food and entertainment at no cost to soldiers, giving them a welcome respite from their wartime strains. (Bette Davis and John Garfield later developed a similar organization on the West Coast, which they called the Hollywood Canteen).

Shirley became a semi-regular at the New York Canteen, being noted especially for her dancing. Her frequent dancing partner was Frank "Killer Joe" Piro, a professional dance instructor so nicknamed for his incredible stamina, which few of his partners could match. He and Shirley became the jitterbug champions of the Stage Door Canteen, a welcome diversion from the brooding that had occupied much of her time in recent months. She also entertained the servicemen with songs, both comic and dramatic. In 1942 and 1943, CBS broadcast a *Stage Door Canteen* radio series, and Shirley appeared in several of the broadcasts.

Though they didn't meet at the Canteen, it was also a soldier who would bring an abrupt change to Shirley's life in 1943. Unexpectedly, a real-life gentleman caller came into her world. While Shirley was still married to Gardner, they had met William H. Baker, Junior during a Nantucket vacation. When Bill learned, a few years later, that Shirley was now divorced, he paid a call on the newly single actress, and romance quickly bloomed.

William Hogg Baker, Junior was, in mid–1943, a corporal in the United States Army, but his peacetime career had been that of investment banker, with a company called Loomis–Sayles, Incorporated. He came from a well-placed family based in Montclair, New Jersey. Bill's father was the president of the Merritt-Chapman and Scott Corporation, a marine salvage and construction company, while his mother, Catherine Elizabeth Baker, had been a piano and violin concert artist in the United States and abroad prior to her marriage in 1906.

The Baker family, residents of Montclair since the late 1910s, was sufficiently prominent socially that their activities were frequently noted on the society pages of the *New York Times*. According to newspaper accounts, Baker was born in Hannibal, Missouri before the family settled in New Jersey. He had graduated from Princeton University in 1929, a few months before Shirley met and married Eddie Poggenburg. That same year, Bill was in attendance at a debutante ball given in honor of his sister Jane's debut in society. The weddings of Bill's sisters Jane (in August 1937) and Edith (in January 1938), as well as several related social functions commemorating them, were covered at some length on the society pages as well.

Less favorable publicity for the family came shortly after the death of Bill's father in May 1932, when several insurance companies filed suit claiming they had been defrauded. The life of the late Mr. Baker had been insured for more than $700,000 in the summer of 1931, with policies purchased from a number of insurance companies. The crux of the lawsuit was the claim that the senior Mr. Baker had failed to disclose, in seeking the insurance coverage, his treatment "for vertigo, high blood pressure and heart ailments"[8] just weeks earlier, which had resulted in a stay at the Battle Creek Sanitarium. The suit was withdrawn a few months later, with no details made public except that it had been amicably settled. In 1934, while still in his twenties, Bill was named a director of Merritt-Chapman and Scott, the company of which his father had served as president.

The fast-developing romance with Bill Baker did wonders for Shirley's self–esteem and happiness. Younger than she, Baker was cut from a completely different cloth than her boisterous, attention-seeking ex-husband. Like Shirley, he was somewhat shy socially. They discovered that both enjoyed quiet pursuits at home. This was a man completely satisfied to enjoy a quiet evening at home with a book and Shirley's companionship. Bill was an accomplished amateur painter, shared her love of animals, and had dreams of living on a farm someday. By the end of the summer, syndicated columnist Dorothy Kilgallen told her readers that the recently divorced Shirley was "on the verge of an aisle waltz with a wealthy Southern lad."[9]

On September 5, 1943, as *Duffy's Tavern* was gearing up for a rocky new season of broadcasts without Shirley, the *New York Times* published the announcement of her forthcoming marriage to Corporal Baker. Inducted into the Army in late 1942, he was at the time of the wedding announcement in training with the 100th Division. The announcement was made only days after Shirley celebrated her 45th birthday.

Dining alone at Sardi's a few days after the announcement was made, Shirley's glow of pleasure was obvious to all who saw her. Actress Florence Reed, seated at a nearby table, sent her a note: "You'll have to move, darling. You're so happy it gets in my eyes."[10] Shirley would cherish the memory of this period for the rest of her life.

Shirley became Mrs. William H. Baker, Jr. on September 24, 1943. The wedding ceremony took place at the East End Avenue home of Bill's aunt, Mrs. Franklin Baker, Jr., with the Reverend Norris L. Tibbetts of the Riverside Church officiating. Shirley took a brief leave from *Tomorrow the World,* with understudy Mildred Todd assuming the role of Leona, while she and Bill honeymooned.

Shirley continued with *Tomorrow the World* until it closed in 1944, even after Bellamy had left the show and been replaced by actor Conrad Nagel. Once it concluded, however, she didn't immediately seek a new professional engagement. Bill was still in the Army, and she spent much of her time for the next several months following him from camp to camp, keeping him company as he fulfilled his duties.

While Bill was stationed at Fort Bragg, in North Carolina, she decided to make her husband breakfast in bed. Never mind that they were staying in a hotel room with no kitchen facilities. Quick-witted Mrs. Baker plugged in her electric iron, turned it upside down, and found it just the thing to cook bacon and eggs, provided you had your umbrella at hand to catch the drippings.

That summer, Shirley was heard on NBC's *Cavalcade of America,* starring in a patriotically themed play called "The Gals They Left Behind." Shirley played Jo Sullivan, plucky wife of an Army corporal, who goes from a New York apartment to temporary residence at her great-aunt's rundown farm in Maine while her husband serves overseas. Over the course of the 30-minute broadcast, Jo and a friend gamely cope with the challenges of farm life, all the while writing cheerful letters to keep up her husband Bill's spirits. It was apropos casting for Shirley, whose own Bill would soon be receiving his Army discharge.

Once Bill's stint in the Army was done, he and Shirley happily made plans for their new life together. Though he had been a successful businessman, he had a longing for a simpler life, and shared with Shirley his dream of living on a farm. Though a born-and-bred city girl, Shirley too found the notion appealing, and they began searching for a new home away from the grime and noise of New York City.

They fell in love with a property called Wind Race Estate, in Bucks County, Pennsylvania, an area that had become popular with New York show people wanting a country retreat. After the difficulties of the war years, the remodeled stone farmhouse represented a welcome serenity to both, and they pooled their savings to purchase the property. They would be taking over a working 64-acre cattle farm, and Bill proposed to become a gentleman farmer, while Shirley happily assumed the role of housewife.

For a time, Shirley's stage career was of secondary importance to her. In fact, columnist Dorothy Kilgallen reported sorrowfully in the spring of 1944 that Shirley was "retiring for the duration."[11] While that proved to be an overstatement, Shirley did in fact put her stage career on the back burner for the next several months.

Given her priorities during this period, radio was an attractive option, requiring a substantially smaller time commitment than an ongoing Broadway role. In the fall of 1944,

Shirley introduced to Sunday night listeners of CBS' *The Kate Smith Hour* a new character that some found strongly reminiscent of her old one from *Duffy's Tavern*. Dottie Mahoney was a 27-year-old single girl from Brooklyn who was eager to get married. As Dottie said in her first appearance, reading aloud from her diary: "Papa says he knows a lotta girls of 27 who are already married. Mama says how come Papa knows so many girls who are 27?" Marking her birthday with a party, Dottie says she "sent invitations to all the boys I know but he called up and said he'd rather play pool."[12]

Shirley would be heard frequently as Dottie on *The Kate Smith Hour,* and took the character to other shows as well. If she was no longer playing Miss Duffy, she was playing a character similar enough that one journalist observed that she seemed to have won custody of Miss Duffy in the divorce from Gardner. At least in these appearances, she finally received billing under her own name, and was described by Smith to her listeners as "not only a great dramatic actress, but also a fine comedienne."[13]

In 1944 and 1945, Shirley also made several appearances on CBS radio's *Theater of Romance,* a series that provided abridged versions of popular movies and plays. In "Bachelor Mother" (11/21/44), based on the 1939 comedy that had starred Ginger Rogers, Shirley played department store clerk Polly Parish, who takes temporary custody of an abandoned baby she finds on the doorstep of a foundling home. She returned to the show for its January 23, 1945 broadcast, assuming the Barbara Stanwyck role in "Ball of Fire." Shirley also headlined an adaptation of her own *My Sister Eileen,* heard that August. Her appearances on the show soon ceased, as *Theater of Romance* relocated its base of operations to California for the 1945–46 season so as to have access to more movie players.

In the mid–to late 1940s, she would appear only sporadically on Broadway. In early 1945, longtime mentor George S. Kaufman wanted her for a featured role in his musical comedy, *Hollywood Pinafore.* A modern reworking of Gilbert and Sullivan's *Pinafore,* the musical transplanted the action to a Hollywood movie studio. The role being offered Shirley was the showy part of Louhedda Hopsons, a caricature of Hollywood's two best-known gossip columnists. Louhedda is described by her peers as "Miss Butter-Up."

Shirley later said that it was only at the urging of her husband that she accepted the gig. Bill told her, "You're a great actress; you should not deprive the stage." Though she was pleased that he was so supportive of her career, she commented, "I've often wondered whether I was that great an actress or that bad a housewife!"[14]

In early March, with rehearsals for *Pinafore* getting underway, Shirley spent an evening taking part in a third-anniversary party for the Stage Door Canteen. The event was commemorated with a birthday cake four feet high, weighing 300 pounds, as well as entertainment from Shirley, Bill "Bojangles" Robinson, and members of the *Up in Central Park* stage company. Warrant Officer Stephen J. Morello, the first serviceman to visit the Canteen on its opening night in 1942, was on hand as well, and told the *New York Times,* "You'll find the seven lively arts right here."[15]

Despite the substantial talent involved, *Hollywood Pinafore* received lukewarm notices from critics upon its opening Memorial Day weekend, and lasted only a few weeks. Though the show itself was largely panned, critics did take notice of the fact that Shirley could sing, something she had not done in previous roles. In the 1950s, musical comedies would become yet another genre in which the actress could comfortably work.

Though *Hollywood Pinafore* gave up the ghost quickly, Shirley took part in another Gilbert and Sullivan parody in November 1945, when she was a guest on Fred Allen's radio show. She was paired with baseball's Leo Durocher for a skit called "Brooklyn Pinafore," assuming the role of a Dottie Mahoney-ish sports fan, "Little Bobby-Socks," who flirted with Durocher. Shirley would become a favorite guest of Allen's literate comedy show, ultimately making 10 appearances during the mid–to late 1940s.

In the summer of 1946, Shirley was onstage at the Berkshire Playhouse in Stockbridge, Massachusetts, trying out a new comedy called *Off the Air*. The script by Knowles Entrikin and Howard Breslin mined the world of radio soap opera, casting Shirley as a successful serial queen troubled by the suddenly falling ratings of her once-popular show. (In real life, aside from her own experience with radio acting, Shirley was a friend of longtime soap writer Elaine Carrington, creator of serials such as *Pepper Young's Family* and *When a Girl Marries*). The show itself drew lukewarm reviews, but Shirley's work was praised in the local newspaper. "Miss Booth is properly ethereal when approaching her sacred mission of portraying Life for America's housewives, and properly cunning when dealing with the sordid business of making a living."[16]

Her only Broadway show of 1946 was a drama called *Land's End*, based on the novel *Dawn in Lyonesse* by Mary Ellen Chase, which came and went with embarrassing abruptness in December 1946. The drama centered on a young working-class couple in Cornwall, England, whose stormy romance seems to parallel the legend of Tristam and Iseult. Shirley was cast as barmaid Susan Pengilly, best friend of the heroine, whose seduction of her friend's fiancée leads to tragedy.

For someone used to Broadway runs as long as *My Sister Eileen* had enjoyed, the failure of *Land's End*, which closed after less than a week, was a bit of a shock to Shirley. *The New York Times'* Sam Zolotow, announcing the producers' decision to pull the plug after only a handful of performances, commented that much attention had been paid to various aspects of the production, notably some impressive scenic design recreating Cornwall. "One essential ingredient, unfortunately, was overlooked amidst the intensive concentration— the play itself," Zolotow wrote.[17]

She was not seen at all on Broadway in 1947, though she did do some stage acting. In February and March, she was immersed in what playwright Arthur Laurents would later call "a three-city tour of hell,"[18] playing a featured role in the comedy-drama *Heartsong*. Laurents' script detailed the marital problems of young Joe and Kate Bannion, brought into sharp focus by the revelation of a long-ago abortion. Producer Irene Mayer Selznick, in her maiden voyage as a theatrical producer, thought Laurents' script had possibilities but needed work. Laurents was happy to have his script optioned, but eventually resisted the amount of rewriting that his producer wanted. On one thing, though, they both agreed — the featured role of alcoholic Malloy was the strongest element of the show, and a perfect fit for Shirley's wit and comic timing.

Opening in New Haven with Shirley supporting Lloyd Bridges and Nancy Coleman, *Heartsong* was in chaos. Shirley's role was one of the few elements that remained constant as *Heartsong* careened from city to city, with cast and script in constant upheaval. "Shirley Booth was superb," said producer Irene Mayer Selznick. "Her scenes played so brilliantly they could almost carry the show."[19] Almost, but not quite.

Finally, in Philadelphia, long after both Bridges and Coleman had bailed out, Selznick called it quits on the Broadway-bound production, absorbing a $75,000 loss. The experience would be important to Shirley mainly because it introduced her to Laurents, who would later write her hit play *The Time of the Cuckoo*. Producer Selznick would later say resentfully that Laurents plundered the *Heartsong* script, incorporating Shirley's basic characterization and most memorable lines of dialogue for *Cuckoo*.

Back home in Pennsylvania, she became involved with the local Bucks County Play-house. Theron Bamberger, her Broadway producer from *Tomorrow the World,* was also active in the theater company, and in the summer of 1947 they mounted a revival of *My Sister Eileen* for their friends and neighbors. It was a powerhouse show for a summer the-ater, with George S. Kaufman directing, and Jo Ann Sayers reprising her role from the orig-inal Broadway company as Eileen.

Staying close to home was becoming increasingly important to Shirley. Not only was it a long and tiring five-hour commute into the city and back, but Bill's health was show-ing signs of strain under the heavy work of operating a cattle farm.

"He loved the farm," Shirley explained. "He'd seen so much devastation during the wear that he wanted to make things grow. But he did too much. He always did the heavy work while his helper drove the tractor. He didn't know he had a heart condition."[20] Only in his forties, Bill suffered a heart attack, and he and Shirley endured months of worry and stress over his recovery.

The Men We Marry, which opened at the Mansfield Theatre in January 1948, would set an all-time record as Shirley's biggest Broadway flop. The script cast Shirley as well-to-do Maggie Welch, a successful novelist whose daughter Mary, a war widow, has fallen in love with a penniless young medical student. When Maggie invites two old school friends to stay at her Maryland estate, the three women, cynical from their own experiences with men, decide that Mary would be better off marrying a comfortably fixed older man, and create chaos by meddling in the romance.

Ferocious reviews greeted *The Men We Marry,* the first solo effort of neophyte 22-year-old producer Edgar Luckenbach. What was intended to be a sophisticated light comedy was characterized by critics as boring, shallow, and phony, and the play dimmed its lights after only three performances. Critics mostly absolved Shirley and her co–stars, simply saying that this talented ensemble had somehow signed up for a really wretched play.

In fact, the ill-fated show boasted quite a strong cast, featuring well-regarded British actors Neil Hamilton (later Commissioner Gordon on TV's *Batman*) and John Williams (best-remembered today for his many Hitchcock appearances), as well as comic actress Margaret Hamilton from *The Wizard of Oz.* The production was not an inexpensive one — *Variety* noted that the well-fixed young producer, heir to family wealth earned in the steamship industry, "has provided a rich interior and is said to be paying goodly salaries to the fairly well-knowns in the cast," but added that "the kid got the wrong steer from an agent, unless he selected the script himself."[21] (The experience apparently cured Lucken-bach of his Broadway aspirations; he produced no further shows, but later enjoyed a much more successful tenure as a business executive, serving as CEO of the family company).

According to columnist Bill Henry, the inevitable results of those scorching reviews didn't take long to happen. "The backers read the sour reviews Saturday morning, and dis-covered by Saturday night that the general public had also read them and, by Sunday morn-ing they had nailed the door shut and shipped the scenery off to Cain's Warehouse. That's how quickly a frost can nip you in this town."[22]

With that show behind her, Shirley turned her attentions to radio. In early 1948, she signed an agreement with CBS to develop a radio situation comedy vehicle. The project, to be under the supervision of network vice-president Hubbell Robinson, would intention-ally avoid replicating a Miss Duffy or Dottie Mahoney characterization for its star. Instead, "the actress will take the part of a schoolteacher."[23]

What developed from that initial idea would ultimately become one of radio's most

Shirley's most notorious Broadway flop was the comedy *The Men We Marry,* which closed after three performances. Here she's flanked by co-stars Doris Dalton (left) and Marta Linden.

popular and enduring comedies—but not with Shirley at the helm. The show, in fact, was *Our Miss Brooks.* On April 9, 1948, CBS listeners heard an audition show for the proposed series.

The audition show varied in some significant ways from the series that would ultimately emerge. As Eve Arden would later do, Shirley played unmarried high school teacher Connie Brooks, who shared a home with landlady Mrs. Davis while nursing a crush on biology teacher Mr. Boynton.

In the opener, however, the school was not Madison High but South High. Stuffy Osgood Conklin, Miss Brooks' memorable adversary, was not the school's principal but the president of the local school board. Mrs. Davis, an elderly widow with no children in the subsequent series, here had a teenaged daughter named Ruth, who was the love interest for Connie's student Walter Denton.

There was one other critical difference between Shirley's audition show and the popular series that would later come together—in this incarnation, *Our Miss Brooks* wasn't particularly funny. Hubbell Robinson would later lay some of the blame for this at Shirley's feet—Shirley, he said, wasn't able to find the humor in Miss Brooks' predicaments in the same way that Eve Arden later would.

But it would be fairer to note that the audition show, as scripted by Ed Jurist and Norman Tokar, was simply a flawed effort. Shirley's clunker of a first line introduced her to the radio audience with the statement: "You know, it's a funny thing. I'm always careful about standing in a draft. But no matter how careful I am, I always get a pain in the neck teaching English Two." This was greeted by pretty much a dead silence in the studio, probably while listeners scratched their heads and tried to figure out what the hell the line meant.

Even the announcer didn't make the show sound like much fun: "Our Miss Brooks! Have you met her yet? Maybe you think a schoolteacher's life is dull. Well, it is. But there are moments when even Miss Brooks' life can be as romantic and glamorous as a movie star's. It's when she's dreaming, and especially when she's dreaming about Mr. Boynton, the biology teacher..."

Now that we've established that our heroine's life is dull when she's awake, it's all downhill from there. Shirley gets one decent laugh in the opening scene, when Mrs. Davis breaks into her dream to warn her it's time to go to school. "Oh, no, Mr. Boynton," she responds in her dream-fogged state. "I don't have to go to school for *this*. This comes naturally!"

The ensuing plot depicts Miss Brooks as making a poor first impression on the school board president, having been a passenger in Walter Denton's car when he sideswipes Mr. Conklin in a fender-bender. Later, in a plot uncomfortably reminiscent of newspaper headlines fifty years later, Mr. Conklin mistakenly believes that Miss Brooks is carrying on a romantic assignation with one of her teenage students.

By June, *Variety* reported that "the Shirley Booth deal curdled,"[24] and that that version of *Brooks* was a goner. But there was still life in the project, as it turned out. *Our Miss Brooks* resurfaced a couple of months later, with production relocated to Hollywood and Warner Brothers contract player Eve Arden stepping into the lead role. (In the interim between Shirley and Eve Arden, the property had also been offered to Lucille Ball, who declined). Arden, too, said no initially, unimpressed with the script. In mid–summer, however, she okayed a substantially rewritten version of the same script that Shirley had used, but with the jokes sharpened considerably. The series sold, and became a hit for Arden within weeks of its debut.

The critics weren't the only ones that found Shirley's audition show less than pleasing. Also paying close attention was a screenwriter named Don Ettlinger, whose credits included *I Was a Male War Bride* (1949). Ettlinger had submitted to CBS a radio script called "Our Miss Booth," and been turned down flat. When he heard *Brooks* on the airwaves that summer, he promptly filed a lawsuit against the network, and eventually collected a reported $50,000 settlement from CBS.

Shirley, meanwhile, having put *Brooks* behind her, went back onstage that summer. In July, she was seen at the Chapel Playhouse in Guildford, Connecticut, in a production of Ring Lardner and George S. Kaufman's 1929 comedy *June Moon*. Playing Lucille Sears, the songwriter's wife, Shirley made a strong impression on the reviewer from the *Hartford Courant*: "Miss Booth might easily have made Lucille a nag and a bore, but instead she portrays her as a thoroughly likeable character, one who hasn't lost her sense of humor although she has lost all her grand illusions of a happy marriage. And when she tells off her thoughtless mate in the last act, she does it not with bravura, but with a sincerity that comes only from one who has loved and lost. This reviewer, for one, cheered her inaudibly."[25]

In the fall of 1948, Shirley launched another long Broadway run, with her featured role in the comedy *Goodbye, My Fancy*. Fay Kanin's politically oriented comedy starred film actress Madeleine Carroll as Agatha Reed, a congresswoman returning to her alma mater after many years to receive an honorary degree, and rekindling an old romance with the man who is now the school's president. Shirley, a last-minute addition to the cast, had a strong featured role as "Woody," Agatha's pragmatic and witty secretary. Woody, who must struggle to adjust schedules when her boss decides to make the pilgrimage back to Good Hope College, says, "I don't believe in looking at the past. I was born in Newark, New Jersey. Every time I go through on a train, I pull down the shade."

Actor-director Sam Wanamaker would serve in both capacities in this production, playing Miss Carroll's love interest Matt Cole while helming the show. Carroll, in her first and only Broadway show, received praise from most critics, and the show would run for more than a year, but Shirley's presence was credited for much of the show's appeal. In fact, some reports had it that Shirley had threatened to overshadow Miss Carroll in rehearsals, causing the producers to give some of Woody's lines to their leading lady. When it developed that they didn't earn the same quota of laughs in Carroll's hands, however, the jokes were returned to Shirley for safekeeping.

Even without a scriptwriter, Shirley was eminently capable of a quip. During rehearsals of one key scene, she watched with some annoyance as Wanamaker, playing Matt, began embellishing a bit of business involving a prop doll. Finally sensing that she was growing irritated with his fly-catching upstage, the actor asked, "Miss Booth, would you rather I did this at some other place?"

"Yes," Shirley replied. "Offstage!"[26] Columnist Leonard Lyons reported that director Wanamaker employed an unusual approach in rehearsing his cast. "At their first meeting he asked all of them ... to write a biographic sketch of the character each was portraying. These sketches were complete with details of early environment, education, business experience, intellectual background, romances, etc.— so that each actor would thoroughly understand the character he was portraying."[27]

Though most of the actors complied, Shirley balked at what she considered an unnecessarily academic approach, and said a copy of the script was all she needed to get down to work. After thirty years in the theater, she had her own ways of building a character, and critical response to her performance suggested that they worked just fine. *The Washington Post*'s reviewer said that women employed as secretaries would particularly appreciate Shirley's detailed portrayal of Woody, "a really wonderful creation. She's worked to death, smoothing the elegant passage of her chic employer through the busy ways of public life. Miss Booth makes Secretary Woods the epitome of bland exhaustion. She effects an ill-fitting business suit, can just about drag her feet across a room and yet manages to give you the impression she'll stick to her job."[28] Much of this, of course, was not specifically delineated in Kanin's script.

In early 1949, while still appearing in *Fancy,* Shirley made her debut in the new medium of television, appearing in a live benefit broadcast for the March of Dimes. The January 22 broadcast, aired on CBS-TV, was only a footnote in her career, giving little indication of how important television would become to her in years to come.

In April, Shirley received her first Tony Award for the role of Grace Woods in *Goodbye, My Fancy.* Honored at a dinner held at the Waldorf-Astoria Hotel with more than 1000 people in attendance, Shirley was deemed to have given the best female supporting performance of the 1948–49 season. Her male counterpart was *Death of a Salesman*'s Arthur Kennedy. The American Theatre Wing, headed by producer Brock Pemberton, awarded her a silver medallion engraved with the masks of comedy and tragedy, in what was only its third Tony ceremony.

5. Queen of Sheba

Radio was still the preeminent broadcast medium in 1949, and despite her experience with *Our Miss Brooks,* Shirley was still interested in a weekly series. That summer, while still appearing in *Fancy,* Shirley's comedy series *Hogan's Daughter* made its bow on NBC radio, under the sponsorship of Philip Morris. The new series, airing at 8 P.M. on Tuesdays, was the summer replacement for *This Is Your Life,* and, depending on the results of its summer tryout, could conceivably win a spot on the fall schedule.

An NBC press release explained the concept guiding Shirley's lead role of Phyllis Hogan: "*Hogan's Daughter* is a delicate flower, blooming among the tin cans and rattling trolleys of New York's tenement districts. A girl of great imagination, she has a picture of herself which nature and circumstances have hardly equipped her for. Working in a five-or-ten or a movie theater cage, she dreams of herself as a queen of the glamor [sic] world, model, actress, dancer, and so on ... depending on the pop tune she has on her 'hit' list at the moment."[1]

Aside from Shirley, the regular cast would include Howard Smith and Betty Garde as parents Tom and Kate Hogan. (Smith would later play bombastic Mr. Griffin on *Hazel*). Busy radio actor Everett Sloane was cast as Phyllis' boyfriend Marvin.

One of the only episodes of the series still in existence today, and available from collectors of Old Time Radio, is "The Television," scripted by John Whedon and Sam Moore, and originally broadcast on July 12, 1949. In that segment, Phyllis Hogan is jealous that her rival Marie Kaltenmeyer, whose family lives across the hall from the Hogans, has invited all their friends over to watch the Kaltenmeyers' new TV set. Phyllis fears that the lure of the small screen will help Marie win Marvin away from Phyllis. Though Phyllis' father Tom initially disdains television, he eventually warms to the idea of buying one, telling wife Kate it will "bring the whole world into our living room." Retorts Phyllis' pragmatic mother, "Do we want it there? I'm cleaning up all day anyway." In the show's climactic scene, Phyllis arrives home to learn that the Hogans are getting their own television, but she wants to go to the movies instead. Adding insult to injury, Mr. Hogan learns that the TV he bought to show up his neighbors is the same one Mr. Kaltenmeyer returned to the appliance store.

Other plots in the show's summer broadcasts mostly centered on Phyllis Hogan's ongoing efforts to get a good job, and improve her station in life. On the August 2 show, Phyllis landed a gig as a stenographer at an appliance company, but worried that her secretarial skills weren't up to snuff. Later shows concerned her efforts to help cure her father's supposedly bad leg (August 9), or persuade him to move the family to a new apartment (August

23). In "Personality Kid" (September 7), Phyllis has just benefited from a charm course, and decides to use her new talents to spruce up boyfriend Marvin.

Shirley's character basically called for her to play a likable, scatterbrained young lady with a short attention span, and no great intellect. The vocal impersonation of a flighty youngster was quite good, especially for an actress already in her early fifties. Phyllis Hogan sounded much like a sister to Dottie Mahoney, or Miss Duffy's niece. But the show itself, in the opinion of most critics, was nothing special.

Reviewing a slate of summer programs in his July 31, 1949, *New York Times* column, Val Adams thought the batting average overall was "indifferent." In the case of *Hogan's Daughter,* he reported that the show began well, "but then fell apart. It got off course when Hogan's daughter and her boy friend attended a giveaway radio program. This part of the script attempted to burlesque such activities, including commercials, but was too long drawn out and became more real irritating than the real thing. After that the show lost all elements of pleasant listening."[2]

John Crosby of the *Tribune* concurred, saying perplexedly, "I don't mean it isn't terribly funny. I mean it isn't funny at all. In fact, it's pretty grim." Nor did he understand the appeal of Shirley's character. "She's an authentic type all right," he conceded, "as authentic as the girl who waits on me at the delicatessen. Still, I see an awful lot of that girl at the delicatessen and I'm not especially anxious to run into her again on the air."[3]

Sounding a more positive note was *Variety,* whose reviewer thought *Hogan's Daughter* was "a summer series that should wear well around the calendar." He liked the show's down-to-earth quality, though he thought it needed more out-and-out punch lines. Shirley was praised, in typical *Variety* lingo, as "a thesper of considerable talents."[4]

For a while, it appeared that *Hogan's Daughter* might live beyond its initial summer run. In mid–August, *Variety* reported on the latest round of schedule-juggling, handicapping which shows would and wouldn't survive into the fall. At that point, Shirley's comedy series was still in the mix, but a few weeks later, enthusiasm for it had cooled, and it wasn't on the NBC schedule come September.

Hogan's Daughter wasn't the only project with which Shirley busied herself that summer. Also on the horizon was an offer from producer Brock Pemberton (who had staged Mary Coyle Chase's immensely successful comedy *Harvey* a few years earlier, and headed the organization that had awarded Shirley a Tony weeks earlier) to star in a new comedy by Doris Frankel. The show had gone

This NBC publicity photograph shows Shirley looking not much like the listeners of her radio series *Hogan's Daughter* would have pictured her.

through a plethora of titles, being known at various stages as *What's to Love?* and *Rondo in a Flat;* by August, it had been rechristened *The Time Is Yes.* Plans were for a brief road tour in early fall, to be followed by an October opening on Broadway. Shirley signed a contract that awarded her star billing in the production.

While busying herself with *Hogan's Daughter,* which would vanish after that initial summer run, and the Frankel play, Shirley quite nearly turned down the role of her career. That summer, she was sent the script for a play called *Come Back, Little Sheba,* written by a then-unknown playwright named William Inge. The Theatre Guild was mounting a try-out of the play, and asked Shirley to perform the lead role of Lola Delaney. Having been through some difficult times in recent months— Bill's health was still a concern — she praised the script, but declined the role, not interested in playing something so downbeat. Her friends at the Theatre Guild prevailed upon her, and Audrey Wood made a personal appeal to the actress. Finally, Shirley agreed to do a brief turn as Lola, while reminding them of her upcoming commitment to the Pemberton play. The Guild made plans to try *Sheba* for a week at the Westport Country Playhouse, at the close of the summer 1949 season.

In November, *Goodbye, My Fancy* posted its closing notice, having racked up more than 400 performances at four different theaters during its healthy run. Producers Michael Kanin, Richard Aldrich, and Richard Myers planned a touring production, to open shortly in Chicago, but admitted that the production would be largely recast. By then, actress Ann Harding was playing the lead, and the producers had engaged Jean Casto to replace Shirley as Grace Woods. In 1950, the show's enduring success resulted in the sale of film rights to Warner Brothers, where it would become a vehicle for Joan Crawford, and, in Shirley's role, Eve Arden.

Come Back, Little Sheba is the story of a lonely and disappointed middle-aged house-wife, Lola Delaney, whose husband is a recovering alcoholic. After years of marriage, both husband and wife are in a painful rut. "Doc" Delaney, whose addiction has damaged his practice as a chiropractor, is a saddened man whose early dreams were mostly frustrated by his shotgun marriage to Lola. Though he has achieved a full year of sobriety, he knows full well that his recovery is fragile.

As for Lola, she is bored and childlike, unhappily growing older with little satisfaction or interest left in her life. She has grown lazy and slovenly. Though her puppy, Sheba, disappeared months ago, she continues to call her name plaintively from time to time, hoping against hope that the lost dog will return.

The arrival of a boarder in the Delaney household, pretty college art student Marie Buckholder, sets into motion a chain of events that will uproot everything settled in the lives of the Delaneys. Although Marie has a developing relationship with a steady, responsible young man back home, she playfully encourages the attentions of muscle-bound college athlete Turk Fisher, whom she met when he posed for her life drawing class. For Lola, the flirtation between Marie and Turk is harmless, a pleasurable reminder of her own youth, when she too felt pretty and desirable. For Doc, however, it stirs up his latent resentment and frustration over having his future plans stymied by a youthful marriage to Lola. When he learns that Marie has allowed Turk to spend the night in her bedroom, he flies into a rage in which he falls off the wagon. The result is a climactic confrontation between husband and wife that would be electrifying in the hands of the right performers.

As the playwright's friend and mentor Tennessee Williams later wrote, "In each [Inge] play there would be one dark scene and it was always the most powerful scene in the play: but he loved his characters, he wrote of them with a perfect ear for their homely speech, he saw them through their difficulties with the tenderness of a parent for suffering children: and they usually came out well."[5]

As written by Inge, Lola Delaney is not very intelligent. She's a chatterbox, childish and tiresome at times. But by the time the curtain falls, the viewer comes to realize that she is also fiercely loyal, goodhearted, and unfailingly dedicated to her husband's well-being.

Onstage in her most highly acclaimed role: Shirley (pictured with John Randolph) in the moving drama *Come Back, Little Sheba.*

The many sides of the character made the role of Lola demanding for an actress. As Shirley herself later said, "All I had to do was prove to the audience that Lola was a colossal bore — without boring the audience."[6]

Shirley later contended that it was she who altered the concept of the role during *Sheba*'s early tryouts. "At first they made her a heavy, a villainous woman," she explained. "I felt that Lola turned out the way she did because life had been the villain, and I said so."[7] According to Inge's biographer Ralph Voss, the young playwright based Doc and Lola Delaney on his aunt and uncle, Dr. and Mrs. Earl Mooney of Wichita, Kansas, ultimately using them as prototypes for similar characters in several of his plays and novels. "Inge was fascinated with his eccentric aunt, who was the model for some of his most memorable female characters," Voss said.[8]

Voss concurs that the other Inge characters based on his aunt are often harsher than Lola Delaney, and considers it plausible that Shirley's take on the character may have been heeded. "It's a pretty good surmise," he says, "that if Shirley Booth had suggestions for Lola, both Danny Mann (directing his first big play) and Inge would have been quite willing to listen. The Theatre Guild had money invested and they, too, would have likely listened to what Booth had to suggest. Inge desperately wanted a hit, needed a hit, and would probably have gone into total eclipse if the play hadn't succeeded."[9] Also a factor was the fact that Inge's own struggles with the bottle had been sorely tested by the long wait to see his play staged, leaving him in less than tip-top shape to participate in the rehearsal process.

A bone of contention during the rehearsal period was Shirley's physical appearance. Inge had conceived the character as being overweight, a onetime glamour girl who's visibly let herself go. While Shirley didn't have a model's figure, she wasn't as frumpy as the director and playwright wanted. But she resisted their suggestion that she gain weight, or allow her costumes to be padded. Instead, refusing to bow to their pressure, she perversely put herself on a diet. "I'm supposed to be a professional actress," she reasoned, "and if I can't create the illusion of being overweight without fattening myself up like a hog for slaughter, I ought to turn in my union card."[10]

Instead of eating her way into the role, Shirley looked around her. Even as a little girl, she had been a people-watcher, and this would often be useful in fleshing out the characters she played. Walking down Sixth Avenue one evening, Shirley found her eyes following a grubby-looking woman meandering by with an equally dirty white poodle. From bits and pieces of this woman, and others she observed, Shirley began to envision how she would bring Lola Delaney to life.

Relegated to the dustbin was the stylized accent she'd employed so often, in *Hogan's Daughter* and elsewhere. "Now Lola was a common woman," Shirley explained, "like the Brooklyn character parts I've played — but she was mid-western, and she wasn't supposed to sound like a Flatbush floozy. I think I kept the accent out, but it was hard, real hard."[11]

The process of creating Lola Delaney took time, and her colleagues grew impatient when they couldn't yet see the finished product. Ironically, after wheedling Shirley into accepting the role, some at the Theatre Guild initially failed to be dazzled by her work. As *Time* magazine would later report, "After three days of rehearsals, Playwright Inge and Director Mann were desperate. They had concluded that Shirley simply could not handle the role. They were chiefly upset by her stock-company approach to rehearsals: she merely walked through the part, mumbling her lines."[12]

Nervous, Inge and Mann approached the Theatre Guild directors with a plea to bring in another actress, suggesting Joan Blondell as an ideal candidate. The Guild's Langner and Helburn balked, and within days Shirley opened up and played the role full throttle. For the first time, her director saw her true capabilities, and there was no more discussion of finding another star.

Appearing opposite Shirley was the veteran stage and film actor Sidney Blackmer, whose Broadway credits dated back more than thirty years. Newcomer Cloris Leachman assumed the role of ingénue Marie, while Lonny Chapman was cast as Turk.

The hastily assembled tryout at the Westport Playhouse, while affording the company

Shirley's leading man in the Broadway production of *Come Back, Little Sheba* was actor Sidney Blackmer. He would be passed over in favor of a bigger name star when the film was made.

the opportunity to fine-tune Inge's play outside the glare of New York critics, was nonetheless inauspicious. Coming at the tail end of the season, the play was missed by many of the Playhouse's subscribers. Not helping matters was the fact that the weather that fall was quick to turn chilly, and the theater was unheated.

A Sunday night dress rehearsal, played to an audience of mostly local people, provided the show with its ultimate test. As Inge's agent Audrey Wood explained: "There is one climactic scene in the second act of *Sheba* in which Doc, a usually quiet man, suddenly goes off the wagon, and in his demented drunken state threatens to kill his wife with a hatchet. Coming as it does after a long and quiet series of scenes between the two characters, it is highly melodramatic and something of a shock to an audience. I'd always felt, in reading the play, that this was the crucial scene. If it worked for the audience, if it held them, then I was certain Inge had written a viable piece of theater."[13] That shocking scene, which ran more than fifteen minutes in the show's second act, became unforgettable in the hands of Shirley, and Sidney Blackmer.

Over the next few days, word spread quickly in New York that the Theatre Guild's newest production was something special, and a number of theater notables made the trip to Westport to see Shirley and Sidney Blackmer in action. Other theatrical producers knew this show had real potential, and tried to pry the rights from the Guild's hands. Not surprisingly, the Guild directors weren't going to let go of the project now.

Variety's critic was among those who made the trek out to Westport that September, and he concurred that the show was Broadway-worthy. He found Shirley especially impressive: "Miss Booth neatly fuses the extrovert and the suffering woman, the gal whom a gentleman married because it was the decent thing to do. She is uniquely suited to the light monologue which runs through most of the first act and is profoundly affecting in the last act, when she discovers her man has again gone to pot."[14]

The widespread acclaim for *Sheba* left the denizens of the Theatre Guild — and, perhaps, Shirley herself — quite frustrated by her commitment to star in the Doris Frankel comedy that was now called *Love Me Long*. Stymied by Shirley's unavailability, Guild leaders even offered her producer Brock Pemberton a cut of *Sheba*'s profits if he would postpone his play and make Shirley available to take the Inge drama to Broadway. But Pemberton, confident that *Love Me Long* would do well, declined the offer.

Still, it was noted by the *New York Times*' Sam Zolotow that Shirley did not have a run-of-the-play contract with Pemberton. She had the contractual right to leave *Love Me Long* after giving two weeks' notice, and there was speculation that she would abandon the show after a brief run to reprise Lola Delaney on Broadway. In the meantime, she had voluntarily relinquished her sole star billing in the Frankel play, choosing to share featured billing with her co-stars who had roles of roughly equal weight.

November 7, 1949, would be the opening night for *Love Me Long*. Frankel's script cast her as a successful, larger-than-life actress Abby Quinn, twice divorced from the same man, who has recently remarried but still loves ex-husband Ike. Though Abby has married another man, and Ike is now engaged to a younger, more docile woman than Abby, both still covet the apartment they once shared. While Ike and fiancée Margaret have the better claim, it doesn't stop Abby from horning in to nab the apartment for herself and her current husband. The result is an uneasy weekend in which Abby, Ike, and their new loves all stubbornly hunker down in the much sought after apartment, and by Sunday it's no longer certain that the couples will still be mated in the same way they were on Friday.

The light, pseudo-sophisticated dialogue of *Love Me Long* was diametrically opposed to the downbeat drama of *Sheba,* and the chic and sophisticated character of Abby a far cry from Lola Delaney. Frankel's comedy probably seemed more commercially viable than the Inge play, and Shirley was human enough to appreciate being cast as an attractive and romantically viable woman after weeks of living Lola's downtrodden life. Still, by this point even Shirley must have been wondering if she made the right call in going forward with *Love Me Long.*

Variety's reviewer caught a mid–October tryout performance in Wilmington, and thought the show had definite possibilities. He found *Love Me Long* "bright and saucy," with "plenty of laughs sprinkled throughout," but found the plot garbled and the second act draggy. He liked Shirley's performance, noting, "Her deft handling of lines heightens the play's humor."[15]

Among the customary congratulatory telegrams Shirley received on opening night was a gracious one from her friends at the Theatre Guild, which read, "Wish you all the luck in the world. And we mean it."[16] Still, there was a pall that hung over the show. Producer Brock Pemberton suffered a heart attack in the final weeks of rehearsal. He survived, and returned to the theater shortly afterward, but the sight of Pemberton sitting in the wings, looking pale and weak but determined, didn't contribute to a happy feeling for the cast and company.

Though the Theatre Guild staff had prepared themselves to wait out Shirley's run in *Love Me Long,* they didn't have long to wait. As it turned out, New York reviewers had absolutely no love whatsoever for *Love Me Long.* Although the show had undergone some hasty rewrites during tryouts, the script still left much to be desired. The show was panned mercilessly, and would die a quick death.

Producer Pemberton defied the critical response for a few days, saying, "From now on it's got to be a word of mouth proposition. And I want to see what happens."[17] What happened, unfortunately, was a steady drop in business, and the show finally closed after only 16 performances. As Shirley would say years later, "Every time I tried to play a dressy part, one where I had some fancy clothes, the play was a flop."[18]

For Shirley, the failure was a blessing in disguise. It left her free to accept a Broadway run in *Come Back, Little Sheba,* and rehearsals were underway by early January. Most of the cast from the Westport production remained intact, though Joan Lorring replaced Cloris Leachman in the role of Marie. Over the next few weeks, the company took the show on tour to Wilmington, and then to Boston. In the latter city, when the critical reviews were less than expected, Shirley defied the prevailing mood by going out and buying herself an expensive new coat. Her show of faith in the play helped her colleagues get over the worries that had settled in since arriving in Boston.

Lorring, who'd been a Warner Brothers contract player in the 1940s, would be making her Broadway debut, and credited Shirley with giving her some solid advice on her portrayal at a time when she was floundering. Over dinner, Shirley explained, "You know, I keep calling Sheba all the time. And you know how I picture Sheba? She's little and she's white and she's fluffy and she's happy, and nothing ever gets her down. And when Marie comes to our house she's Sheba."[19] In an instant, Lorring understood her character's function in the play, and how to bring Marie to life.

After all the complications and delay, *Come Back, Little Sheba* made its Broadway bow on February 15, 1950. Though the critical response to the play itself was somewhat muted, all reviewers agreed that the performances were outstanding, especially that of Shirley. Also paying tribute to the show's quality were the many backstage visitors who would barely be able to congratulate Shirley and her co-stars, still choking back tears over her performance. On opening night, she walked into Sardi's, and received a standing ovation from her peers. Modest as ever, Shirley turned to see who had come in, before realizing that the applause was for her.

Even the First Lady of the American Theater, Helen Hayes, was an admirer. "She has perfect timing and perfect reading, and always has complete control of herself, her part and her audience," Hayes said of Shirley. "I have often gone back to watch her a second and a third time, trying to figure out how she does it, because the first time she has made it seem so effortless that I have forgotten I'm watching an actress."[20]

By this time, Shirley and husband Bill had, with some reluctance, sold their Pennsylvania farm. The daily commute from Bucks County had proven tiring, and they once again took up residence in their New York apartment. This also left Bill in closer proximity to medical attention, a necessity given his heart condition. He was now staying closer to home, pursuing more passive interests like painting, in which he also managed to enlist Shirley.

She admitted that, for a city girl and a devoted animal lover, there had been a downside to farm life. "We thought it would be wonderful to live in the country," she explained wistfully, "but I got much too emotional about killing chickens and selling calves for the market. I spent so much time painting the rooms in our house that I seldom got outside. I still love the feeling of the country. I guess this reflects a searching for peace I don't have in myself."[21]

On April 9, 1950, Shirley won her second Tony Award, with Blackmer similarly honored. That year's ceremony also included a tribute to her *Love Me Long* producer Brock Pemberton, who had died of a heart attack a few weeks earlier. The acting awards nabbed by Shirley and her co-star were among the few prizes that year *not* bestowed upon the hit musical *South Pacific.*

Despite the widespread acclaim, *Come Back, Little Sheba* enjoyed only a moderately successful run on Broadway. The downbeat drama was not a top-flight ticket seller, but did manage to last for almost 200 performances. Following the Broadway run, Shirley and Sidney Blackmer took the show on tour in the fall of 1950. The raves Shirley had received from New York critics were echoed in other cities like Washington, D.C., where *Sheba* played for two weeks in early 1951. By then, followers of *Sheba* had learned that another version of the show was in the works. The producers had sold the movie rights.

Through the fall, Broadway observers speculated on how Shirley would follow up her *Sheba* triumph. Always interested in demonstrating her versatility, Shirley nonetheless surprised her colleagues when she didn't accept another dramatic lead. Instead, she and Bill agreed that she should try something new. She signed to play a featured role in George Abbott's musical comedy adaptation of Betty Smith's *A Tree Grows in Brooklyn*. Shirley, top-billed despite her secondary role, would be cast as uninhibited Aunt Cissy, giving her the chance to display her musical prowess onstage for the first time since 1945's *Hollywood Pinafore,* with songs composed by Arthur Schwartz and Dorothy Fields. Happy to shed the mournful character of Lola Delaney, and the slumping posture that had given her backaches, Shirley threw herself wholeheartedly into the new role.

By early 1951, Shirley was spending long hours in rehearsals for her new show. On Sunday, March 4, with *Brooklyn* due to open in a few weeks, Shirley and Bill were relaxing at home in their apartment on West 54th Street. When the telephone rang in the bedroom, Shirley expected to hear Bill pick it up. When he didn't, she called out to him, but there was no reply. She walked into the bedroom and, within seconds, knew that her life had just taken a drastic turn. Bill had had another heart attack; Shirley had just become a widow.

Marcia Van Dyke (left), Johnny Johnston, and top-billed Shirley had lead roles in the musical *A Tree Grows in Brooklyn*. Shirley's look here is unexpectedly demure and classy, given the role she'd signed to play.

Only days after being widowed, Shirley returned to rehearsals for *A Tree Grows in Brooklyn*, which was scheduled to open in mid–April. Much as she had welcomed the opportunity to play a role so different from the drab and downtrodden Lola, it cannot have been easy, at the height of her grief, to go back to work. Deeply in pain over her loss, the actress nonetheless threw herself into preparations to play fun-loving, man-loving Aunt Cissy. Not long before, she and Bill had laughed together over the script, and Shirley had eagerly antic-ipated the lighthearted and showy role. Now he was gone, but Shirley kept her commit-ment to the show nonetheless.

A Tree Grows in Brooklyn, adapted from Betty Smith's 1943 novel, was typical of many Broadway musicals—singing and dancing extravaganzas based on serious and even down-beat works of literature. Though nowhere near as bizarre as later adaptations, such as the musical version of Stephen King's horror novel Carrie—notorious for creative challenges such as keeping the leading lady's microphone from shorting out in mid-song when a tub full of stage blood was dumped on her head—Brooklyn was primarily the story of a spir-ited 11-year-old girl growing up in a New York tenement neighborhood with a drunken and unreliable father, and an overstressed mother doing janitorial work to support her fam-ily.

As in the 1945 film classic adapted from the novel, the stage musical would get most of its lighter moments from the supporting character of Aunt Cissy. (Joan Blondell had played the role in the film, for which she received a Best Supporting Actress Oscar nomi-nation).

Young Francie Nolan (Nomi Mitty), just learning about boys and male-female rela-tionships, is intrigued by her carefree aunt, who has enjoyed relationships with a number of men, mostly without the encumbrance of marriage. Cissy, who calls all her men "Harry" rather than trying to learn a new name each time, was a showy role, complete with an atten-tion-getting song, "Love is the Reason," but Shirley was not playing the lead, despite her prominent billing. Cast as Francie's irresponsible father, and second-billed to Shirley, was nightclub singer and musical performer Johnny Johnston.

Not until the third scene of Act One would Shirley make her initial entrance, playing a character the author described thusly: "She's dressed for comfort in a flowered Japanese kimono which hangs open to reveal her combination, a thing of linen and ruffles and cherry-colored ribbons. She's proud of her sheer lisle stockings with their lace insets. Her red hair is beautifully coiffed. She makes herself comfortable and eats chocolate creams from a paper bag."[22]

Some observers had been surprised that Shirley had accepted the part, but she liked the idea of being seen in such a different light after Come Back, Little Sheba. Happy to play the freewheeling character, she nonetheless balked when the director wanted her current "Harry," (played by actor Nathaniel Frey), to make one of his entrances wearing only his long johns, which Shirley considered a cheap gag. Nor did she mind telling the esteemed George Abbott that it was a bad idea.

Abbott respected his star, and her professionalism. "In my 37 years in the theater," he said, "I've worked with more actresses than I can count, and to me Shirley is easily tops. How can there be any better, when she's perfect?"[23]

Betty Smith, author of the novel on which Tree was based, echoed his praise. "Shirley gives the character of Aunt Cissy dimensions that I never dreamed of, and I created the character. She knows more about Cissy than I do."[24]

Backstage, her co-workers also knew they were in the company of a trouper. When a scene called for an offstage voice to provide a baby's cry, Shirley volunteered. Never mind that she could otherwise have been comfortably ensconced in her dressing room during this scene, enjoying a well-earned respite from her demanding singing and dancing role. Or that most top-billed stars would have felt this task slightly beneath them. It was all in a night's work for Shirley.

Tree's uninhibited Aunt Cissy, as brought to life by Shirley.

While her personal life was in turmoil, professionally Shirley was on a roll, and critics lined up to applaud her when the musical opened a few weeks later. Reviews for the show itself were not uniformly positive — the contrast between Francie's serious story, and Aunt Cissy's comical interludes caused several reviewers to view it as two disparate shows awkwardly grafted together. Most of them, however, agreed that Shirley's performance was the chief asset of *A Tree Grows in Brooklyn,* and ticket sales for her first post–*Sheba* appearance on Broadway were brisk.

Offstage, Shirley's deportment was that of the trouper she was, but friends and coworkers saw through the façade. "I saw her right after her husband died," remembered a crew member, "and she was plenty busted up. But when they asked her how she felt, she said okay, fine, just fine. She knows how to hide her crying and nobody can tell. She's the kind of a gal who goes around laughing and cutting up, and wishing to hell she could drop dead."[25]

She admitted that it was difficult to go on living in the apartment she'd shared with Bill. "It's a two bedroom apartment that was fine for the two of us," she said, "but in which I do a good deal of rattling around."[26] The presence of her maid June Smith helped fill the void somewhat.

Always an animal lover, Shirley found that canine companionship helped her during this period. For a while, she had Candidate, a dog she and Bill had adopted together, but that soon changed. "Candy was a dog who preferred men to women," she explained. "Although I needed Candy, I knew it would be selfish to keep him under the circumstances, so he is now in the care of a male friend."[27]

Candy's successor, Gigi, proved a bit of a problem as well. Left at home to her own devices while her mistress went to the theater, Gigi was apt to disembowel a chair for recreation. Plan B, in which Gigi spent her evenings backstage in the star dressing room, worked a little better, though visitors wondered why Shirley didn't turn up the air conditioning, as the room was sweltering. She explained that Gigi didn't like the chilled air, and Shirley's friends shook their heads at the lengths to which she would go to keep her pets happy and healthy.

Though *Brooklyn* was a hit show for Shirley, there was another project near and dear to her heart that was still on the horizon — the film adaptation of *Come Back, Little Sheba.* Paramount Pictures owned the film rights, and producer Hal Wallis intended to make it one of the studio's prestige products for the year 1952. What was unclear in the spring of 1951, however, was whether Shirley would be asked to reprise her Tony-winning stage role.

A few months earlier, she had made the trek to California and performed in a test film for Wallis. But with movie studios suffering mightily from the new competition that television provided, there were serious reservations about moviegoers buying tickets to see a downbeat drama starring Shirley Booth and Sidney Blackmer. Shirley had never made a feature film, and although now considered a ticket-selling star on Broadway, did not enjoy that status with audiences outside New York. Blackmer was a highly regarded character actor who had dozens of film credits, but almost exclusively in supporting roles. Though he would have two films in release in 1951—*Saturday's Hero* and *People Will Talk*—the 55-year-old character actor was not considered star material.

Even if Wallis did decide to cast Shirley, she too had some reservations. She badly wanted to star in the movie, but she already had a highly successful stage career to protect. She was aware that most film companies liked to have their star names signed to long-term contracts; sometimes those contracts worked to the actor's advantage, sometimes not.

Producer Wallis, who would later title his memoirs *Starmaker,* was used to exerting control over the careers of his protégés. Though he had made stars of the young comedy team of Dean Martin and Jerry Lewis, they would ultimately wrest free of his control, as did a later discovery, actress Shirley MacLaine. This Shirley was not at all sure that she wanted to place her career solely in Wallis' hands, and give up the right to choose her own roles or to pursue a full-time film career in lieu of continuing to appear on Broadway.

Meanwhile, executives at Paramount, most of whom hadn't seen Shirley play Lola onstage, weren't necessarily wedded to the idea of casting her in the movie. There were plenty of experienced movie actresses in roughly the right age range to play the part, and whose names would bring audiences to the theater. Bette Davis, free-lancing in the early 1950s after terminating her long-term arrangement with Warner Brothers, was always a front runner for a prestige project, and was hot again after an Oscar nomination as Margo Channing in *All About Eve* (1950). Joan Crawford, too, was shopping for new scripts.

Unlikely as casting either Davis or Crawford as meek Lola might seem, there were other names being bandied about. Also considered was Judy Holliday, newly minted as a film star thanks to *Born Yesterday.* Holliday, who'd faced an uphill battle to reprise her stage role in the hit film, thought the idea of her playing Lola was ludicrous. "They spend two years trying to find out who should play my part in *Born Yesterday,*" Holliday said incredulously. "And then they spend two years trying to figure out who should play *Shirley's* part in *Sheba.* And then they decide I should play her part. Can you imagine?"[28] Bette Davis recognized that the part was a juicy one, but had seen Shirley play it in the theater, and felt that Booth had put her stamp on the role. Still, Davis would later say regretfully, "The character was a slattern, no clothes, no hairdo, but oh, those wonderful words."[29]

While the *Sheba* saga played out, another of Shirley's stage roles was recreated on film, with the May release of Warners' *Goodbye, My Fancy.* The show that starred Madeleine Carroll in New York, with Shirley featured, was transformed into a film vehicle for Joan Crawford, with some of the political material softened. Eve Arden, while still starring in the radio version of *Our Miss Brooks,* took Shirley's featured role as the congresswoman's sardonic secretary. In July 1951, Sheilah Graham's syndicated column reported that negotiations between Shirley's agent and Hal Wallis had run aground. Shirley, Graham reported, would continue in her *Brooklyn* role on Broadway, and let someone else play Lola Delaney on film. That, it seemed, was that.

But, as Shirley's agent Audrey Wood remembered, Paramount's plans slowly unraveled. "[T]hey gave the film script to practically every one of the available great Hollywood ladies who were then box-office names," Wood said. "In practically every instance, those film stars turned down the role. I understand that in one way or another, they all said the same thing: 'The only actress to play this character is Shirley Booth. Nobody else could do it.'"[30]

6. The World's Best Actress

In December, *A Tree Grows in Brooklyn* posted its closing notice, after more than 250 performances. While not the blockbuster producer George Abbott had wanted, overshadowed by the far more successful *The King and I* that season, the show had enjoyed a respectable run. By Christmas, Shirley was available for a new project, and Wallis' Paramount associates were coming to the conclusion that she might, indeed, be the right choice to star in the film version of *Come Back, Little Sheba*.

In early 1952, the deal was struck. Shirley signed a contract to star in *Sheba*, at a salary of $5,000 per week for a projected eight-week shoot. Though the contract gave Wallis the right to star her in subsequent productions, Shirley would share in the creative decisions. The deal hammered out with Audrey Wood allowed Shirley and Wallis to take turns selecting projects—when she'd starred in a role that she approved, he would then get to select the one to follow, and so on. "It's a good deal," Shirley said happily. "Each of us will have the chance to prove how right we are."[1]

Less fortunate than Shirley was her Broadway co-star Sidney Blackmer. Though Paramount executives had given in where Shirley was concerned, they insisted on having a box office name for the male lead. For a time, it looked as if the film might reunite Shirley with her long-ago stage co-star Humphrey Bogart. Bogart liked the role of Doc Delaney, and would have happily accepted the project, kidding Hedda Hopper that, though a teetotaler himself, he would do his level best to play a two-fisted drinker. Ultimately, however, Bogart's studio nixed the proposition, much to the actor's frustration. Hedda Hopper reported in March 1951 that Wallis was in discussions with Gregory Peck about the role. While the idea of casting Peck came to naught, the actor who ultimately emerged victorious was no less a surprising choice. Signed to play Doc Delaney in the film version of *Sheba* opposite Shirley was another of Hal Wallis' discoveries, actor Burt Lancaster.

Lancaster, in the early 1950s, was a brawny leading man who mostly played in adventure movies. A trained acrobat, Lancaster was at this point better known for his physical agility than his dramatic prowess. Roles in films like *The Crimson Pirate* made the 39-year-old actor popular with men who liked action films, and women who enjoyed the sight of his frequently bared chest. Fifteen years Shirley's junior, Lancaster loved the idea of playing Doc Delaney, but seemed at first glance ludicrously miscast as Blackmer's replacement.

"True, on the stage Sidney Blackmer gave you the feeling of an older man, one in his late 50s," Lancaster conceded. "But in the script he is actually indicated to be about 40 — which I'll be next year!"[2]

Burt Lancaster assumed the role of Doc Delaney in Paramount's film version of *Come Back, Little Sheba.*

By March, Shirley was in Hollywood. She was pleased that *Sheba*'s stage director Daniel Mann had also been brought out to California; like Shirley, he would be making his motion picture debut. Cast in key supporting roles were Terry Moore, as Marie, and Richard Jaeckel, as the arrogant, muscle-bound Turk.

Ketti Frings' script for the movie version of *Sheba* was a fairly faithful adaptation of Inge's play. Little would be done to "open up" the play, as was often done in movie adaptations. Doc could now be seen walking to work alongside Marie, but that was one of relatively few scenes that took the actors out of doors. Some of Lola's dialogue from the play would not survive the cut, either in the interests of time, or due to movie censorship codes. In the climatic confrontation between Doc and Lola in the second act, the axe used in the stage version was replaced onscreen by a knife. A slightly more hopeful ending was affixed to the script as well.

The motivation for Doc's final eruption was weakened slightly. In the stage version, he erupts upon realizing that the seemingly innocent Marie has bedded Turk. Frings' film script, having to pass more stringent censorship codes, modified the action. While Doc still believes that Marie has slept with Turk, it's made plain in the film that he is mistaken, that Marie ultimately refused the advances of her classmate when she realizes he wants only a sexual encounter.

After playing Lola so many times onstage, Shirley knew the character inside and out, and was undaunted by the notion of repeating the role in a new medium. Still, she admitted there were adjustments to be made. "There was hardly a hitch," she said, "except the first day when the technician with earphones started testing the mikes for sound. I took a good breath and spoke up real loud like I would on the stage, and suddenly all the dials on his machine went spinning around like mad and he clawed at his head as though I'd thrown a bomb at him. The poor man was half deaf the rest of the day, and I learned that you play parts a lot quieter in Hollywood."[3]

Shirley acknowledged that the scrutiny of the camera was occasionally unnerving. "I thought I had to underplay everything for the screen. Then I realized I could let myself go a little, like on the stage. Some of the things were wonderful. Others gave me the feeling that I was undressing emotionally. But as a whole it turned out beautifully. It was a labor of love."[4]

Burt Lancaster, nursing his own ambitions of being taken seriously as an actor, was impressed with Shirley, describing her to an interviewer as "a nugget, a diamond, a pot of gold. She's Babe Ruth. She's Mickey Mantle. It's a nice note for this town that a woman like Shirley can come in and by sheer personality bowl the place over."[5]

Terry Moore credited Shirley with aiding her own performance. Asked by columnist Hedda Hopper if she found it intimidating to work opposite such an accomplished performer, Moore said, "On the contrary, it's much easier to play scenes with good actors than bad ones. When you do a scene with an actress like Shirley Booth, you believe it. Believing it, you do it well."[6]

By summer's end, Shirley was back in New York, where she soon went into rehearsals for a new play. The acclaim Shirley received for the stage version, as well as the attention coming her way for the soon-to-be-released motion picture, raised her stock as an actress. Returning to Broadway to play the lead in Arthur Laurents' *The Time of the Cuckoo,* she was reportedly puzzled by the sign posted on the marquee as opening night approached in the fall of 1952. It consisted of four words—"Empire Theatre—Shirley Booth."

"When it went up that way at the end of rehearsals," said a co-worker, "Shirley kept waiting for them to finish the sign!"[7]

In fact, as Shirley herself must have realized, the wording on the marquee acknowledged that, after more than thirty years onstage, she was now a star whose mere presence in the show was expected to sell tickets. In fact, reviews of the show would confirm this, with critics often liking the star performance more than the script.

The show in which she was starring, *The Time of the Cuckoo,* cast her as Leona Samish, an American tourist

The nerve-wracking finale of *Sheba,* when Doc (Burt Lancaster) finally goes over the edge.

Voyeuristic Lola (Shirley, at left, with Burt Lancaster) is fascinated by the sexual chemistry that Turk (Richard Jaeckel) and Marie (Terry Moore) generate. Note that Jaeckel is more undressed in this Paramount publicity shot than he ever is in the actual film.

spending her summer vacation in Venice. While staying at a guest house, she becomes romantically involved with a local man who doesn't see his wife and five children as a barrier to enjoying Leona's company. Laurents based the play on his own experiences traveling in Europe, where he came to realize that the social mores concerning sex and relationships were quite different from 1950s America.

Although *The Time of the Cuckoo* was a success for Shirley, she would look back on the experience with ambivalence. She later confessed that she found the role of Leona uncomfortable to play. In Shirley's view, the character of Leona verged dangerously close to self–pity, a quality she felt certain audiences wouldn't embrace. She also found some elements of the play a bit risqué for her liking. Laurents' script deliberately left it to the audience to decide whether or not Leona is ever intimate with her Italian lover. While director Harold Clurman and others assured Shirley that it did not really matter whether or not Leona consummates the relationship, the star herself held a firm opinion on the subject.

"I've thought it out carefully," she later told an interviewer, "and I'm convinced she doesn't. Even Arthur Laurents, the author, argued about it with me, but I said, 'After all, Arthur, I should know — I was *there.*'"[8]

Though it made for an amusing anecdote, left unsaid was the genuine conflict that arose during production between Shirley, the playwright, and the director. With her increasing fame and experience, Shirley was no longer willing to give way to others when she felt strongly about characterization, line readings, or script changes.

Director Harold Clurman later said that the character of Leona hit a little too close to home to Shirley. "She was afraid that the woman she played, who was afraid of sex and

A lovely portrait of Shirley as wistful Leona Samish in Arthur Laurents' *The Time of the Cuckoo*.

afraid of taking a lover, was too close to what people would think she (Shirley Booth) was like," Clurman said. "That disturbed her, but she wouldn't ever admit it."[9]

In Laurents' opinion, the problem lay with Shirley's concern about losing audience sympathy. Given her background in comedy, Laurents said, Shirley tended to play it safe, balking at any line that might make her seem harsh. She was reluctant, he said, to play at full force a pivotal drunk scene, one in which Leona maliciously reveals a confidence that will endanger a marriage.

Nor did Shirley and Clurman find it easy to establish a rapport.

"He didn't know how to talk to her, nor she to him," Laurents said. "[E]ach spoke a different language — his was Stanislavsky as filtered through the Group Theatre, hers was George Abbott as filtered through inestimable experience."[10]

According to Shirley's friend Ralph Bellamy, she was eminently easygoing and agreeable in her personal life, but made of sterner stuff when it came to professional judgment. "She's balky," he said fondly. "In the theater she's steel. You do it her way or you don't do it."[11]

Despite the disagreements, Shirley grew friendly with her leading man, the inexperienced Dino DiLuca, who was playing a major acting role in English for the first time. Between rehearsals, she helped him with his language skills. She also kept herself busy by adopting two poodles, whom she named Prego and Grazi, both words that had figured in the *Cuckoo* script.

Lighter moments aside, however, Shirley's relationship with director Clurman remained difficult. Arthur Laurents claimed that the star fell into the habit of belittling Clurman to the other members of the company, challenging them to name a worse director they'd ever had, and then rejecting any nominees as less inept than he. Sometimes this was done outside of Clurman's presence, sometimes not.

When *Cuckoo* opened in October, it was an immediate success, and a personal triumph for Shirley. Whatever disagreements had taken place backstage were of no importance to viewers, who loved the show and, even more, its star. Playwright Laurents was praised for having written a lovely vehicle to showcase Shirley.

Despite his own difficult moments with the star, Laurents respected Shirley as the trouper she was. More than fifty years later, interviewed for a *Wall Street Journal* piece on the growing tendency of stage stars to call in sick, and let their understudies go on, Laurents made it plain that Shirley had not been of this ilk. He recounted an instance during the run of *Cuckoo* when she arrived at the theater in a miserable state, with a fever and sties in both eyes, "and she said to her understudy, 'I'll crawl on.'"[12]

For the star, it was a heady experience to be the top-billed star at the historic Empire Theatre. "Many's the time, when I first came to New York," Shirley said, "I used to sit in the top gallery and see the most unforgettable performances. It is a great pleasure to hear applause on that stage, as I look up to the top rim where I used to sit."[13]

As it happened, it was fortuitous that Shirley had the chance to do so. Not long after *Cuckoo* opened, members of the New York show business community learned that the theater's future would be short-lived. *The Los Angeles Times* noted that the historic Empire Theatre was scheduled to be razed upon the closing of *Cuckoo,* but noted, "The building wreckers, a group of cotton-textile manufacturers, cannot begin to tear down the theater until the end of the run of this last play to appear there. And, judging from the cheers of the first-night audience, there will be no knocking down of the historic brick walls of the Empire for more than several months."[14]

Her winning streak continued into December, when the film version of *Come Back, Little Sheba* opened, just in time to qualify it for Academy Award consideration the following spring. While filming was underway, word had already begun to spread that Shirley's performance was a tour-de-force, and once the film was in wide release the Oscar buzz began to grow.

Movie audiences getting their first glimpse of the noted stage star Shirley Booth saw a leading lady quite unlike the Hollywood norm. Shirley's first entrance in *Sheba* was the antithesis of Hollywood glamour, slumping down the stairs of the Delaney home in a terrycloth bathrobe, hair frizzled after a night's sleep. What followed over the next hour-and-a-half left most critics in awe.

Just two days after Christmas, *The Saturday Review*'s influential Arthur Knight weighed in as one of Shirley's biggest champions. Aware of her stage credentials, he nonetheless found himself taken aback by the skill and detail he saw in her film work. "The incredible thing," Knight wrote, "is how completely, how devastatingly she has recreated Lola in terms of the camera. From the first moment we see her, waddling sleepily down the stairs, pausing automatically to adjust the clock in passing, we know the essentials of Lola's life — a shabby, somnolent affair to be gotten through as easily and painlessly as possible. Then deftly, subtly, come the added touches — the endless platitudes, her simple good-heartedness, her pathetic dependence on her husband, her romantic visions of the past. And ever and again, the reminder of her slovenliness — the broken bedroom slippers, the formless housedress, the hairbrush on the kitchen table. Slowly, out of a myriad of incidents and tiny actions, Lola Delaney begins to take shape."[15]

On the night of February 9, 1953, the Academy of Motion Picture Arts and Sciences made it official. Among the nominees for Best Actress of 1952 were veteran movie stars Joan Crawford (for *Sudden Fear*), Bette Davis (*The Star*), and Susan Hayward (*With a Song in My Heart*), the epitome of Hollywood establishment. Alongside them, however, clearly indicating some of the changes that were imminent in the filmmaking community, were two experienced stage actresses and film novices repeating their Broadway triumphs — Julie Harris, for *A Member of the Wedding*, and Shirley Booth, for *Come Back, Little Sheba*.

Though the Academy Awards dated back to 1929, the ceremony to be held in the spring of 1953 marked the first time the awards would be broadcast on television. To many who worked in the movie industry, TV was still the enemy — the unexpected monster that caused people to stop going to the theater, and be entertained for free at home. The historic deal to broadcast the Academy Awards live on NBC-TV in March 1953 was made solely because the Academy badly needed the $100,000 paid by RCA Victor to obtain the TV rights.

Just because the show would air on TV, however, did not mean that movie actors would be willing to appear. Many were still expressly forbidden to make television appearances, and NBC executives had no assurance that studios would relax this rule for the historic Oscar telecast. Though the presentation of awards by the world's biggest stars would become a regular feature of future Oscar broadcasts, Shirley's fellow nominee Joan Crawford was only one of several big-name stars quoted as saying that they would step onstage during the May broadcast only should they should be called upon to receive an award themselves. Others, like Susan Hayward, were traveling and not expected to attend the ceremony at all.

Wanting to make sure that at least some star names ended up on camera, producers of the Oscar broadcast planned an unusually intricate bicoastal broadcast that was extremely ambitious technically for live TV in the early 1950s. While Bob Hope would host the majority of the Broadcast, emanating from the Pantages Theatre in Hollywood, the telecast would cut away occasionally to NBC's International Theatre in New York City, where former Academy president Conrad Nagel would oversee awards given to East Coast winners. Shirley, still starring in *Time of the Cuckoo*, would give her usual evening performance at the Empire Theatre, and then make a mad dash to the site of the Oscar broadcast.

In the weeks before the ceremony, the Oscar buzz for Shirley grew. In late February, she received the Best Actress laurels in *Look* magazine's 12th annual Motion Picture Achievement Awards. A few weeks later, *The New York Times* reported that the judges at the sixth International Film Festival at Cannes had declared Shirley no less than "the world's best actress," citing her performance in *Sheba* as "the best performance by any actress in films shown at the festival."[16]

By March, the trade newspaper *Variety* confidently predicted that Shirley had the Academy Award for Best Actress all sewn up. Having sponsored a straw poll that queried a substantial number of Academy members, *Variety* reported that the outcomes of some races were still open to question, but one in particular was not.

"Most amazing vote-getting ability," said the newspaper's write-up, "was racked up by Shirley Booth. Despite the usual undercurrent of comment about nominating an actress who was recreating a stage triumph, Miss Booth amassed enough of a lead to make victory certain."[17]

The nominations garnered by Shirley and by Julie Harris caused some predictable grousing. Was it fair to compare their work — recreating roles they'd long played onstage — to that of actresses who'd originated a movie role from scratch? Syndicated columnist Erskine Johnson reported that the controversy "about stage queens nominated for the Academy Awards" had led some Hollywood natives to campaign against Booth and Harris. However, he quoted actress Maggie McNamara (best known for Otto Preminger's *The Moon is Blue*) as taking exception: "It's ridiculous to say ... that Shirley Booth walked through *Come Back, Little Sheba* [the film] because she was so familiar with the character. Shirley Booth never walked through anything."[18] McNamara pointed out that the techniques required to play effectively in films were quite different from what stage acting entailed, and that in any event the script had changed.

On the night of March 13, 1953, Shirley began the eventful evening by turning on the TV set at home, strictly for Prego's benefit. She was to be escorted to the awards ceremony by producer Robert Fryer, but when he called for her at the theater following her evening performance, Shirley told him they'd have to skip it — she'd lost her tickets. Cooler heads prevailed, and according to columnist Leonard Lyons, "A phone call was made to NBC's Guest Relations Division."[19] Not surprisingly, the staff there reassured Shirley and her party that a place could be found in the auditorium for the Best Actress nominee.

At 10:30 p.m. (EST), while Shirley was still reciting lines onstage as Leona Samish, Bob Hope opened the historic Oscar telecast. Alluding to the live events more typical of the prime time TV schedule in 1953, Hope thanked "all the wrestlers who have relinquished their TV time"[20] to make the broadcast possible. He alerted home viewers accustomed to watching the outdated movies commonplace on early TV that they might actually see some movie stars more current than Theda Bara during the awards broadcast.

As in future Oscar telecasts, the biggest awards would not be handed out until later in the evening. Along the way, Gloria Grahame (*The Bad and the Beautiful*) beat out Shirley's *Sheba* co–star Terry Moore for Best Supporting Actress. Not until after a Supporting Actor win by Anthony Quinn (*Viva Zapata*), and the expected victory by Gary Cooper for Best Actor, was it time to hand out the Best Actress statuette.

To no one's great surprise, actor Ronald Colman opened the envelope and read Shirley's name. Immediately on her feet, Shirley, according to an Associated Press reporter, "ran up a short flight of stairs near the stage but tripped near the top. She didn't flub her big moment, though. She caught herself nicely and skipped out onto the stage."[21] She was welcomed onstage in New York by actor Fredric March, who kissed her cheek and described her to the audience as "a popular winner."[22]

Shirley in her best-known film role: Lola Delaney in *Come Back, Little Sheba.*

"I am a very happy and a very lucky girl," Shirley said emotionally as she held her newly won award. "My luck has many names on it — look at the screen credits. I could never have done it alone."[23]

Of the more than thirty-year career that had led to this moment, Shirley said, "I guess this is the peak. But the view has been wonderful all the way. I want to thank my old friends for their faith, my new ones for their hope, and everyone for their charity."[24]

As the *New York Times* reported the next day, "Instantly the viewers at home ... could

Fredric March congratulates Shirley on her Oscar win, as newsreel photographers capture the moment (Michael D. Strain collection).

see the actress 3,000 miles away in New York choke up with tears. Seldom has the immediacy and actuality of television been used so advantageously. The set owner's sense of being in three places at once — New York, Hollywood and at home — was thoroughly real."[25] Ratings surveys showed that more 70 percent of the television viewing audience was tuned in to the broadcast.

March 22, 1953: Shirley is surrounded by a barrage of reporters in the wake of her Oscar win.

Among those paying close attention to the broadcast was longtime Hartford resident Frances Williams Thatcher, almost thirty-five years after she'd shared the stage at the Palace Theater with young Thelma Booth. "Never has a woman in the past 25 years been more deserving of the Academy Award than Shirley Booth," said her former mentor proudly.[26]

As if the month had not already borne enough good news, Shirley won her third Tony Award on March 29. Chosen Best Dramatic Actress for *The Time of the Cuckoo,* she was once again caught by NBC television cameras in the act of being recognized by her peers. After almost thirty-five years as a working actress, 1953 was the year that Shirley truly became famous nationwide, enough so to grace the cover of *Time* magazine in August.

Meanwhile, if anyone had reason to be more delighted than Shirley by her Oscar win, it was executives and stockholders of Paramount Pictures. The publicity benefit of having not only Shirley, but Paramount's *The Greatest Show on Earth,* win Oscars resulted in additional bookings for the films that could put an estimated $1,000,000 into company coffers. On Friday, May 20, 1953, *Come Back, Little Sheba* began a fresh engagement in more than 250 theaters nationwide, and those who hadn't already seen Shirley's award-winning performance flocked to the box office.

After such a noteworthy film debut, Shirley's second feature film was, inevitably, a bit of an anticlimax. Little more than a footnote in her film career is the cameo appearance she shot in New York for *Main Street to Broadway,* which would be released by MGM in the fall of 1953. This oddball film, sponsored by the Council of the Living Theatre to promote interest in theatergoing, featured a once-in-a-lifetime cast of cameo players—aside from Shirley, the cast includes Tallulah Bankhead, Ethel and Lionel Barrymore, Rex Harrison and Lilli Palmer, Mary Martin, and even Rodgers and Hammerstein.

Shirley appears briefly as herself in the film's first few minutes, seen as she exits a theatrical office and is besieged by a group of mostly youthful fans clamoring for her autograph. The film also gave viewers a look at the historic Empire Theatre, home to *Cuckoo,* which was slated for demolition once the play closed. Helen Hayes, introducing the film, mentions that the theatre is soon to be demolished and replaced by an office building, reminisces about the great stars that have appeared there, and notes that the last of them will be "that exciting new star, our beloved Shirley Booth."

Time of the Cuckoo closed in May 1953, having run for more than 250 performances. Shirley marked the last performance in the Empire by leading the cast and audience members in a chorus of "Auld Lang Syne." *Cuckoo* subsequently became the basis for *Summertime,* directed by David Lean, which was released in 1955 with Katharine Hepburn assuming the role of Leona. That summer, after the Broadway run concluded, Shirley accepted a lucrative offer to bring *Time of the Cuckoo* to a theater in Colorado for three weeks, though she would not participate in the national tour that followed. Instead, in the fall of 1953, it was time for Shirley to make her next film with Hal Wallis.

Under the terms of her contract, it was Shirley's turn to choose a project. She happily embraced the lead role in *About Mrs. Leslie,* adapted by Ketti Frings from Viña Delmar's 1950 novel. Delmar had spent much of her career writing about women whose places in society found themselves outside the norm, penning titles like *Bad Girl, Kept Woman,* and *The Marriage Racket. About Mrs. Leslie* was Delmar's look into the life of the phenomenon of "the other woman."

Though Paramount publicity men would give the impression that the studio had purchased Delmar's novel expressly for Shirley's sake, this wasn't the case. In fact, Paramount had owned the rights for several years, but had been stymied by the difficulties of getting a script approved by the Production Code office. It was Wallis who ultimately figured out a way to tell the story of "Mrs. Leslie" and her lover in a way that censors found acceptable.

The woman who calls herself Mrs. Leslie lives quietly in a middle-class home outside Hollywood that she shares with several boarders, including aspiring performers Nadine and Lan, as well as elderly Mr. and Mrs. Poole, whose daughter is in a nearby hospital. Through flashbacks, the film reveals how Vivien Keeler, a toughened New Yorker, met and befriended a well-to-do industrialist, whom she knows as George Leslie.

In 1940s New York, Vivien was eking out an existence as a nightclub singer. One night, she meets George, a well-to-do but lonely businessman who's been dragged to the club by some friends. When the lonely man impulsively invites her to spend a few weeks with him at a secluded beach house as his paid companion, Vivien accepts. Brassy Vivien and low-key, scholarly Mr. Leslie are surprisingly happy together, and their vacation becomes an annual event.

Grateful for her companionship, George gives Vivien the money to become a partner in a dress shop. She is hurt and dismayed to learn, unexpectedly, that her beau is in fact prominent executive George Hendersall, who's just been tapped for an important wartime assignment, and who has a wife and two sons. After thinking it over, she allows the relationship to continue.

In the summer of 1945, as World War II is coming to a close, she receives the news

The brassy singer (Shirley) and the harried businessman (Robert Ryan) make a surprisingly compatible couple in *About Mrs. Leslie*.

that Hendersall has died of a heart attack. Back in the present, Vivien is pleased to learn that Lan and Nadine, whose real name is Alice, are planning to be married. Giving them the benefit of her own bittersweet experience, she advises them not to do things halfway, but to hold out for the full life they should have together. Lan and Alice leave to begin their new life together, and the Pooles also move out, after the death of their daughter. As the film comes to a close, Vivien is, once again, alone.

Frings' screenplay was, by Hollywood standards, a faithful adaptation of Delmar's novel, following largely the same structure and using the same characters. Like the book, the film of *About Mrs. Leslie* alternated between Vivien's story and those of her roomers. Among the changes from novel to film were the locale of the beach house — Florida in the book, California in the film — and the point in the relationship at which Vivien realizes she is a married man's mistress, which happens earlier in the book's narrative. (In the interests of appeasing film censors, it's deliberately left unclear that Vivien and George do in fact have a sexual relationship, though adult moviegoers could presumably read between the lines. The scene in which Vivien first arrives at the beach house, and is shown to her own guest room by George, was probably the compromise that helped the script get the OK under the Production Code).

Another revision for the purposes of the film found the unusual couple's first meeting in a nightclub, where Vivien is employed as a singer. This would allow Shirley the only opportunity of her film career to showcase her singing voice, which was by then familiar to Broadway audiences.

Various actors were considered for Shirley's leading man before filming got underway in the fall of 1953. Among them was Ray Milland, who loved the role, but was too busy between *Dial M for Murder* and his new TV sitcom *Meet Mr. McNutley,* which premiered on CBS in the fall of 1953, to join the company. Since Shirley was already committed to go into another Broadway show in early 1954, it wasn't feasible to wait on Milland. Instead, paired with Shirley for the film was actor Robert Ryan (1909–1973), an up-and-coming leading man better known for action films and tough guy characters. His casting as the bookish Mr. Leslie was considered out of the norm for the actor. Ryan, who had worries about being typecast, saw the role as an opportunity to do what Burt Lancaster had done co-starring with Shirley in *Come Back, Little Sheba* — demonstrate that he could play a broader range of role than he'd previously been assigned.

About Mrs. Leslie afforded Shirley the most glamorous role she would ever play on film, cast as a faded but still desirable nightclub singer of questionable virtue. Shedding the droopy posture and drab clothes she'd used to play Lola Delaney, Shirley slipped into a bathing suit for a romantic seaside scene with Ryan, surprising some of Wallis' staff who thought the star would balk at the skimpy costume.

She admitted that the glamorous treatment was quite a change from her first film assignment. "I used to come on the set, do my own hair, and wrap a kimono around myself," Shirley commented of her *Sheba* days. "Now I have to come in early, put on these fancy clothes, and have a big makeup and hair session. People are always fixing my curls so they're just right. I'm not so sure I didn't like it the other way."[27] The famed Edith Head designed her extensive wardrobe for *About Mrs. Leslie,* which cost many times what had been invested in her cheap *Sheba* attire.

Some of Shirley's best moments in the film are silent ones. Twice in the film, she learns shocking bits of news about her lover George Leslie, both of them while she is alone amidst a crowd of strangers. In one instance, she is watching a newsreel in a crowded movie theater; the other takes place in Times Square on V-J Day. Both times, Shirley's facial expressions and eyes beautifully convey the depth of emotion that Vivien Keeler feels.

Said Shirley's young co–star Marjie Millar, "She's utterly fascinating to work with. I've never seen anyone use their hands to help express emotion the way Shirley does. She studies everything she does. She reads all the off-stage cues. She offers to help you with your lines, and then she thanks you."[28]

On the beach with Mr. Leslie (Robert Ryan) in *About Mrs. Leslie.* Producer Hal Wallis' staff had wondered if Shirley would balk at doing swimsuit scenes.

A rare photograph from Shirley's costume fittings for *About Mrs. Leslie*. Edith Head designed her wardrobe (Michael D. Strain collection).

Though she was perfectly capable of playing a middle-aged woman falling in love, Shirley made it plain that there were few such episodes in her own life. The widowed actress predicted (correctly) that she would not remarry, and explained that she didn't see it as a priority.

"You see," she said, "I just am not a woman who needs companionship. If it comes along, and it is just right, that is wonderful. But when you don't need a husband, you don't drive yourself in that direction." She admitted that any signs of interest from a man tended to put her off these days. "I really don't know what it is," she commented. "But the minute a man starts giving me the straight gaze I back off. Scared. It's the old inferiority complex again, I guess."[29]

Contemporary critics were lukewarm to *About Mrs. Leslie,* most of them regarding it as inoffensive but unremarkable. *Variety*'s reviewer thought it had some box office potential, but clearly regarded it as soap opera, saying snidely, "Matinees in particular should be above average."[30]

About Mrs. Leslie was a box office disappointment. Although Shirley liked the film, and received some good critical notices for her work, producer Wallis seemed to take its box office returns as an indication that she lacked wide audience appeal as a leading lady.

It's not likely that theater owners screening the film boosted their box office take by following the inane promotional suggestions made in Paramount's "Showmanship Manual" for the film. Among other flights of idiocy, theater owners were urged to mark up local

Shirley plays a scene with her friend Philip Ober in *About Mrs. Leslie* (Michael D. Strain collection).

streets with graffiti reading, "Learn the truth 'About Mrs. Leslie.'" (Paramount's publicity boys reminded them they should "obtain official civic permission beforehand, of course.") Another "sure–fire" idea: "Have 'Mrs. Leslie' paged in all the local hotel lobbies, airports, bus terminals and railroad stations for several days in advance and throughout your entire run. This should be done at frequent intervals throughout the day and evening."[31]

By the time it opened, Shirley had once again retreated to Broadway, where she was starring in her second musical production for Herbert and Dorothy Fields, *By the Beautiful Sea*, which premiered in April 1954. More of a star vehicle than *A Tree Grows in Brooklyn* had been, Shirley's second Fields show cast as Lottie Gibson, proprietress of a Coney

Pressbook ad for *About Mrs. Leslie.*

Island boarding house circa 1900. Her leading man was actor Wilbur Evans, playing a Shakespearean performer who moves into Lottie's boardinghouse and catches her romantic eye. Other cast members included jazz singer Mae Barnes. The show was budgeted at $300,000.

In its early stages, *By the Beautiful Sea* also spotlighted a young Joanne Woodward, in what would have been her first notable Broadway role (though she'd already served as an understudy in *Picnic*). Woodward said that she was hired for the ingénue role in *By the Beautiful Sea,* but lost the job during the early days of rehearsal. It was Shirley, said Woodward, who insisted on the casting change. Apparently Woodward, trained in the methods of the Group Theatre, spent too much time in rehearsal questioning her motivation for every step she took, and not enough time learning her lines. "Shirley Booth put up with this for about four days and then said, 'She's gotta go' and I was fired," Woodward explained some fifty years later, seemingly holding no rancor.[32]

The lead role in a musical comedy was a boatload of work, more than some performers in their mid–fifties might have relished, but Shirley was undaunted. "I feel exactly the same as I always have," she said. "You don't get older, just more tired ... As a matter of fact, the company thinks I'm indefatigable. If I enjoy my work, I can go on forever."[33]

Reviews were lukewarm for the show, but as always journalists loved Shirley. Critic Walter Kerr was amazed by the ease and self–assurance the star displayed onstage, even in a flawed show. "You feel that a thousand things could go wrong — the lights could go out, the scenery fall, the other actors collapse in despair — and she would go right on puttering about the stage, humming to herself, tidying things up. Miss Booth is so happy to be in the house that her happiness affects even the ushers. She is so radiantly confident that the marquee outside glows brighter for having her in the neighborhood. I think the term 'professional' must have been coined to describe Shirley Booth."[34]

Variety took note of the wide range of opportunities that Shirley's role afforded her in the course of two-and-a-half hours. "She handles such straight tunes as 'The Sea Song,' picks up the audience and stops the show in a hoofing turn with a grinning colored urchin named Robert Jennings, has a couple of romantic duets with Wilbur Evans ... makes a balloon ascent and parachute jump, plays a laughable-touching scene with the petulant soubrette and finally brings down the house with her little girl impersonation vaude act."[35]

The latter song, "Lottie Gibson Specialty," found Shirley assuming the role of a noxious, Baby Snooks-ish child who violently rejects the notion of sharing her parents' affection with a baby brother. Another standout number was the witty "I'd Rather Sleep Alone," in which Shirley's character bemoans the motley crew of men who've come along in her life.

Much as Shirley did indeed love performing, *By the Beautiful Sea* began to sap her energy as its run continued. By summertime, Shirley was looking ahead to spending some down time out of the public eye, relaxing at the house she'd bought on Cape Cod. "They told me it's 200 years old," she said of the retreat she'd nicknamed "The Nest," "but they say all houses there are 200 years old. I'm just going to putter. I'm a frustrated interior decorator — no talent, but lots of ambition — and I'll get a can of paint and be quite content."[36]

Left unsaid was the fact that, for the time being, Shirley's Paramount movie career was in limbo. Though Hal Wallis hadn't yet given up on her, despite the disappointment of *About Mrs. Leslie,* it would in fact be three more years before she faced the film cameras again.

7. Hot and Cold Spells

Throughout 1955 and 1956, Hal Wallis was working to find the right movie script for Shirley, but there were obstacles at every turn. He'd thought her perfectly suited to the lead role in *The Solid Gold Cadillac,* but his bid for the film rights was unsuccessful. In March 1955, Louella Parsons reported that Wallis had decided on *Route 66,* a romantic comedy by Erna Lazarus, "about a shopworn show girl and a lazy, lovable, tinhorn sport who are thrown together on a cross country trip."[1] However, this too fell through (Wallis eventually recycled the script as the Martin and Lewis vehicle *Hollywood or Bust,* though he presumably didn't inform either of them that he was playing the Shirley Booth role).

Even before filming *About Mrs. Leslie,* Shirley had claimed that she never counted on a lengthy movie career. "In the first place," she said, "I never pined away for a screen job because I was sure they didn't have room for a person like me — a character actress who had no resemblance to a movie queen. I'm still surprised."[2] Now, with plans for her next movie up in the air, Shirley began looking toward a new Broadway engagement instead.

This was simplified by the fact that Wallis' attention had been caught by another actress. Always on the prowl for new talent, he was intrigued by *The Rose Tattoo,* which would introduce actress Anna Magnani to American audiences. Moving full steam ahead on that project left Shirley feeling as if she was no longer his top priority. "You see, last year's rose," she said wryly of herself.[3]

In the summer of 1955, Shirley kept busy with an engagement at the famed Cape Playhouse in Dennis, Massachusetts. The Playhouse, only twenty miles from home, booked her for a four-week run, with a different show each week. Her repertoire consisted of three of her best-known Broadway shows—*Sheba, Time of the Cuckoo,* and *My Sister Eileen* — plus a production of *The Vinegar Tree.* It was a pleasant summer, commuting daily by convertible with Prego in tow.

Meanwhile, bigger things were about to happen. She signed a contract to return to Broadway in the fall of 1955, starring in a light comedy called *The Desk Set.* William Marchant's play would cast her as Bunny Watson, head of the research department at a large New York television company (reportedly based on CBS' operation). The script detailed the conflicts that arose when Bunny opposed plans to automate her department. Actor Byron Sanders was her leading man in *The Desk Set,* with future television star Doris Roberts *(Everybody Loves Raymond)* and actor Louis Gossett, Jr. *(An Officer and a Gentleman)* among her supporting players. Also in the cast was a now grown-up Joyce Van Patten, former child star of 1943's *Tomorrow the World,* though the actress does not believe that her previous history with Shirley was the reason she was cast.

Though *The Desk Set* would ultimately emerge as another hit for Shirley, the road to opening night was unexpectedly bumpy. According to Joyce Van Patten, the lengthy road tour, which encompassed New Haven, Wilmington, Boston, and Philadelphia, was a chaotic one, in which cast and script changes abounded. Film actress Glenda Farrell, originally cast in the featured role of Peg Costello, left the show during its road tour, a casting change attributed publicly to the usual "creative differences" during rewrites. Original director John Cromwell (perhaps best known for directing Bette Davis' performance in the 1934 RKO film *Of Human Bondage*) also fell by the wayside.

When the script was deemed in need of an overhaul, Shirley's colleagues from *My Sister Eileen,* Joseph Fields and Jerome Chodorov were brought in. Marchant's original script was punched up in the interests of a zanier feel to the show. Fields ultimately assumed the role of director as well.

Joyce Van Patten, who said the cast of *The Desk Set* found the heads-are-rolling atmosphere of the road tour unnerving, says of the changes, "I think most of this came from Shirley, frankly."[4] She said Shirley had trouble communicating with director Cromwell, and wanted an actress older than Glenda Farrell (who'd recently turned 50, but looked younger) in the key role of Bunny's best friend. Dorothy Blackburn stepped in as Peg before the New York opening, which was delayed a couple of weeks beyond the initially announced mid–October premiere.

According to syndicated columnist Dorothy Kilgallen, among the late amendments to the script was a scene that turned out to be one of *The Desk Set*'s show-stopping moments. In mid–October, with opening night imminent, Kilgallen reported that "a vignette of the classic office Christmas party complete with white collar workers and a wine-filled water cooler" had been inserted to "boost the comedy content."[5] This would become one of Shirley's strongest and most memorable scenes in *The Desk Set.*

Upon its opening, *The Desk Set* earned what were becoming typical reviews for Shirley during this period — praising the star for enlivening a so-so script. Said critic Walter Kerr, "All those people who swore they'd go to see Shirley Booth read the telephone book now have their opportunity."[6] *The Daily Mirror* thought the show "lightweight, but Miss Booth's performance will make it a hit."[7] It was, as Joyce Van Patten points out, a "star vehicle"[8] of the type that no longer exists on Broadway.

Shirley agreed that the play held no deep messages, but she was content to play a role that simply gave the audience an enjoyable evening at the theater. "In New York observers reported that people leaving the theater after seeing our little comedy were invariably smiling at one another," Shirley later said. "It's wonderful to be able to put audiences into a good humor."[9] Theatergoers returned the favor by keeping the box office humming, and Shirley settled back into the routine of a successful Broadway star.

Actress Elizabeth Wilson, another of Shirley's co-stars, grew friendly with her during the run of *The Desk Set.* She remembers a group of players from the show that socialized often — Wilson and her current boyfriend, Doris Roberts and her then-husband, Michael Cannata, and Shirley. Acting as Shirley's frequent escort was another of their co-stars, actor Frank Milan. "I always felt very comfortable with Shirley," Wilson says.[10] She remembers one night when she was abruptly taken ill. Lying down backstage, Wilson looked up to see the star approaching her, who'd brought a flower to cheer her up.

By the summer of 1956, Shirley had announced plans to leave the Broadway company of *The Desk Set,* agreeing to play a Los Angeles engagement. The producers opted to keep the New York show open, recasting the lead with actress Audrey Christie, but the play was not a hit without Shirley, and closed a few weeks after Christie's debut in the role.

The Los Angeles production, however, was a smash success with Shirley at the helm. The *Los Angeles Times* reviewer raved about her performance: "The skill, charm, and humanness of this exceedingly clever actress were disclosed to marked advantage in the comedy of the business world, which requires just the neat interpreting that only a knowing performer as Miss Booth herself can supply."[11] He admired the seeming spontaneity of her masterful drunk scene, noting that even her co-stars seemed to be struggling to avoid bursting into giggles at her playing. Joyce Van Patten, who watched that scene played countless times during the New York run, concurs: "It was always just spontaneous and brilliant."[12] She clarified that the spontaneity arose not through ad-libbing, but from Shirley's ability to keep each performance individual and fresh.

Ticket sales were a producer's dream, and the show was held over at the Carthay Circle Theater after setting "a record of having practically doubled the gross business of any previous stage attraction."[13] The production finally closed just before Labor Day 1956, so as to accommodate the plans Shirley had made for a European vacation. (The young producers of *The Desk Set* would have an even bigger hit with their next show, *Auntie Mame,* for which they briefly considered offering Shirley the lead).

In 1957, *The Desk Set* became a 20th Century–Fox film vehicle for Katharine Hepburn and Spencer Tracy, the second Hepburn film role taken from one of

An ad for Shirley's 1955 Broadway hit *The Desk Set,* emphasizing the many glowing reviews the star received.

Shirley's plays. Shirley later explained that she had accepted the lead in the Broadway production knowing that the film rights had already been sold, and without giving her first crack at the movie version. "Such a provision could have held up the sale," she later said, "and I do not think that would have been quite right."[14] She continued, however, to have a fondness for the show, and it would be one of her favorites to revive during her later stints in summer stock theater.

While both Joyce Van Patten and Elizabeth Wilson came away from *The Desk Set* with nothing but admiration for Shirley's work, both found her in some ways difficult to know, and perhaps not a terribly happy person. Although Van Patten had felt quite close to Shirley during *Tomorrow the World*, she says the atmosphere was different when they met again as adults. By the time of *The Desk Set,* says Van Patten, Shirley "was surrounded by people who protected her,"[15] and didn't reach out as readily as she had to a little girl in 1943.

Wilson, despite the general camaraderie that the female cast members had enjoyed during the show's run, vividly remembers what may have been her last encounter with Shirley. It was at a party given by Doris Roberts and her husband. Knowing that *The Desk Set* was due to close soon, Wilson asked Shirley to sign a photo of herself as a memento of the experience. She was startled by the star's response.

"Are you a friend, or a fan?" Shirley asked her fellow actress, with whom she had spent so much time over the past several months. Wilson says she didn't get the photo, and did not stay in contact with Shirley in later years.[16]

Bluntly saying that most of the biggest stars with whom she worked during her long career were "incredibly insecure," Elizabeth Wilson believes that description can be fairly applied to Shirley as well, and aptly describes the mixture of qualities that made her performances so memorable. "She was a wounded lady who could make other people laugh."[17]

Also that year, Shirley accepted the lead role in a *Playhouse 90* segment called "The Hostess with the Mostes,'" which cast her as famed Washington, D.C. hostess, and U.S. ambassador, Perle Mesta. Mesta's life story had already been the basis of Ethel Merman's hit musical comedy *Call Me Madam.* The 90-minute live broadcast, in March 1957, was a demanding one for Shirley, who was off-camera only briefly for costume changes between scenes. Among the scenes was one that cut close to home for Shirley, in which Mrs. Mesta is suddenly and startlingly widowed when her husband collapses at home. It had been only six years since she'd lost Bill in almost exactly the same way.

She boned up for the role by carrying around a recording of Mesta speaking, playing it repeatedly during the rehearsal period as she learned to match the ambassador's vocal quality. A good supporting cast, including Louise Beavers and Robert Lowery, helped. There was even a cameo from ex-actress and Hollywood columnist Hedda Hopper, and a role for Shirley's friend and frequent escort Frank Milan. But the lion's share of the airtime was devoted to Shirley.

Variety had nothing good to say about the broadcast. "The cloyingly slow-moving unveiling of the life of Mrs. Mesta, her childhood frustrations, love life, and the Washington segment made for a tedious story that was both trite and unmoving.... Having the script hew to the biographical sketch of Perle Mesta sadly handicapped Miss Booth. None of her warmth, individuality or abundant talents were given a break."[18]

In retrospect, even producer Martin Manulis didn't view "The Hostess with the Mostes'" as one of *Playhouse 90*'s finer moments. "The Mesta story was disastrous," he admitted, "and I felt bad because it was Shirley Booth's first TV drama. It sounded good to me at first, and I agreed to do it, but it turned out not to be a story. There wasn't enough conflict, for one thing."[19]

By the time she had completed her commitment to *The Desk Set,* Shirley was once again talking with Hal Wallis about her film career. This time it was Wallis' turn to choose a project, and he gave Shirley the script for *Hot Spell,* a melodrama set in New Orleans about a dysfunctional Southern family. It was based on a moderately successful play variously called *Mrs. Gibbons' Boys,* or *Next of Kin,* written by the young Lonnie Coleman (later best known for his *Beulah Land* series of potboiler historical novels).

Once again, the choice of script demonstrated the limited range of roles Shirley's movie producer thought suitable for her. *Hot Spell* cast Shirley as yet another downtrodden wife, this time the naively trusting spouse of middle-aged playboy Anthony Quinn. Featured were Shirley MacLaine and Earl Holliman as Shirley's children, and Oscar winner Eileen Heckart as a friend and neighbor who, in a memorable scene, tries to teach Shirley's character to smoke, drink, and talk tough.

Publicly, Shirley tried to downplay the similarities to her earlier film work. "In *Hot Spell* the character I portray may have a nodding acquaintance with the one in *Come Back, Little Sheba,*" she conceded, "but the environment is utterly different. The setting is Louisiana, where the Cajun influence prevails. Anthony Quinn is my husband and Shirley MacLaine [another Wallis protégé] my daughter, which gives us two pictures together."[20]

Cast once again as a cast-off wife, she told reporters that she was comfortable with

Hot Spell: Fen (Eileen Heckart) gives her friend (Shirley) some sage advice on how to keep a man in line.

herself in middle age, content to be recognized more for her acting skills than her beauty. "I know a lot of beautiful people but I don't care to be with them more than five minutes ... they are so dull," she explained. "People worry too much about appearances. When beauty becomes self-conscious and artificial it loses its appeal."[21]

Nineteen fifty-eight would see the release of Shirley's final two theatrical films. More interesting to Shirley than the role in *Hot Spell* was the chance to play Dolly Levi in *The Matchmaker,* adapted from Thornton Wilder's successful play which had starred Ruth Gordon as a turn-of-the-century widow who arranges everyone's love life, including her own. When Paramount agreed to release *The Matchmaker* prior to *Hot Spell,* though the latter was the first to be filmed, Shirley felt assured that audiences would see her abilities to play varying roles.

Despite her numerous successes playing comedy on Broadway, film audiences had seen Shirley only in downbeat dramas. Don Hartman, who produced *The Matchmaker,* said, "She is exceptionally suited to the starring part, and she is giving an exceedingly sincere, simple, and sympathetic performance, besides evidencing her unique comedy abilities."[22] The finished film tried to retain some of the feel of the stage production, with Shirley speaking "asides" to the camera occasionally, as the character had addressed the audience onstage.

Her co-stars included stage and TV veteran Paul Ford, as the object of her pursuit, as well as the new young star Anthony Perkins, cast as a shy store clerk who falls for MacLaine's

Rising star Anthony Perkins (right), co-starred with Shirley in *The Matchmaker* (Paramount, 1958), and quickly grew to admire her. At left is actor Robert Morse.

character. Perkins, who had worked in New York theater and was the son of a prominent stage actor, was quite taken with Shirley, telling reporters she was his "favorite actress."[23] They socialized occasionally during the shoot, with Perkins visiting his co-star at the Chateau Marmont.

Shirley worked well with producer Hartman, despite a difficult moment when he considered cutting one of her favorite scenes—the soliloquy, in which Shirley's character reflected on her life before being widowed, and the personal philosophy that she had evolved. "To me it was the heart of all that the picture meant," Shirley explained. "I went to Hartman and he said, 'Well, if you want it, it stays.'"[24]

By the time of *Hot Spell*'s release, it was clear that movie producers' faith in Shirley was fading. While she received her contractually stipulated star billing in *Hot Spell,* publicity for the film centered largely on the rising star Shirley MacLaine, with poster art of Miss MacLaine in her slip far more prominent than Shirley Booth's face was in advertisements.

Hot Spell did little to excite audiences, but critics noticed Shirley's work nonetheless. *The New York Times'* Bosley Crowther, who was frequently disdainful of more established movie stars like Joan Crawford, was intrigued

A sample ad for *The Matchmaker,* from Paramount's pressbook.

by Shirley's performance. "Miss Booth," Crowther said, "whose character portrayals seem to ripen more in each film she plays, does here a blistering exposure of that sacred American idol, 'Mom' ... she turns what would seem to be a wistful and respectable character into a pathetically stupid wife and mother whose own weak posturings have brought her home to ruin."[25]

Films and Filming critic John Cutts called Shirley's performance in *Hot Spell* "one of the most exciting, exacting things I have ever seen ... Shirley Booth uses the words provided her only as a starting point for characterization; words, in her delivery of them, are not so much spoken as *born* within her ... to say that she plays with depth is not enough—she goes further than that, indeed, she brings to her part a third dimensional quality of personality that takes us completely off-guard."[26]

By the fall of 1957, with both films in the can and awaiting release, Shirley once again

Onscreen, the relationship between the characters played by Shirley and Anthony Quinn was tense. When the cameras weren't rolling, however, the actors indulged in an ongoing chess game.

went home to New York. After spending so much time in front of movie cameras, she was ready for a return to the stage, and had already chosen the vehicle for her comeback. While on tour with *The Desk Set*, she'd received the script for a drama called *Miss Isobel*, written by two neophyte playwrights, Michael Plant and Denis Webb. Producer Leonard Sillman, best known for his *New Faces* talent revues, had optioned the play after discovering it during a trip to England in 1955. He thought Shirley perfect for the lead in *Miss Isobel*, and wasn't daunted by her agent's warning that she would have to complete her film commitment to Paramount before taking on a new play.

Another obstacle, said Sillman, was his awareness that "Shirley Booth hated to read scripts," and received more than she could absorb. He enlisted the help of *New York World-Telegram and Sun* drama critic Bill Hawkins, a mutual friend, to persuade Shirley that this script was worth her attention. A few days after air-mailing the script to her in San Francisco, Sillman reached her by telephone, and was delighted by her response, "I want to do it!"[27] Now, almost a year after accepting the part, Shirley went into rehearsals that fall for Sillman's show, under the direction of actor Sir Cedric Hardwicke.

Shirley's title character in *Miss Isobel* was a widow living in San Francisco with her unmarried daughter, who's being courted by a fortune hunter. As the *Washington Post* reported, "The daughter's frustrations have made her grab for a sleazy fortune-hunter whom her mother refuses to finance in a catering business. The daughter's rasping character and her frantic discovery that there is cash in her mother's room unhinges Miss Isobel's mind. She thinks that once again she is a bride from Australia and slowly she drifts back into childhood."[28]The show's theme struck a chord with Shirley. "Regression is one of the overlooked problems of the aged," she said. "I've discussed the psychological angles of most of my recent roles with a psychiatrist friend. I think that no matter what you may feel is wrong with this play, audiences are intrigued by Miss Isobel's retreat to her childhood."[29]

Unfortunately, *Miss Isobel* would be Shirley's first real flop since being elevated to full-fledged stardom in the early 1950s. Reviewers, almost to a man, hated the script, called it unplayable, and wondered why the star had taken such a role. One of the few more tempered reactions came from the *Washington Post*'s Richard L. Coe. Coe admired Shirley's performance, and credited the play with "a title role of unusual appeal and the story has the ingredients of heartbreak."[30] In his opinion, the script of *Miss Isobel* represented a good first draft that could have been greatly improved, and turned into a viable Broadway property, had it been molded and shaped patiently in community theater tryouts before being produced professionally.

Former co-star Joyce Van Patten attended a performance of *Miss Isobel* with a group of friends from *The Desk Set,* who sided with the show's harsher critics. "We all went to see it.... We all thought it was terrible." She considers it just a flawed attempt to build a show around Shirley's large audience following in the wake of her earlier hits. "They were looking for vehicles for her," Van Patten says of this period.[31]

Shirley herself had no such misgivings, and was quite surprised by the show's failure. Years later, she would look back on the *Miss Isobel* experience, still mystified as to why audiences and critics had not liked the play as well as she did.

"There were never so many letters from audiences, saying they were delighted and charmed," Shirley said. "Sometimes you can console yourself with such letters. They take out some of the sting."[32] She also acknowledged that she had been the beneficiary of much critical praise throughout her career, and figured it was only logical that she couldn't expect to be that lucky every time at bat. Though Shirley had racked up her share of unsuccessful shows early in her Broadway career, the parts she chose in the late 1950s would bring her an even worse run of misfortune. A year or so earlier, she'd been approached by the producers of a musical comedy then being called *Daarlin' Man,* which would eventually be retitled *Juno.* This part Shirley thought herself unsuited to, and she passed — initially. In the wake of *Miss Isobel*'s demise, however, there was renewed interest in signing Shirley for the lead in Marc Blitzstein's musical version of Sean O'Casey's *Juno and the Paycock.* Despite her initial misgivings, she allowed herself to be persuaded to sign for the lead role, at an starting salary of $3,000 per week. Co-starring with Shirley, for $2,500 per week, would be 57-year-old film star Melvyn Douglas, making his Broadway musical debut.

Douglas, who frankly appraised his own his singing and dancing abilities as minimal, was dubious about performing in a musical. Nor was he impressed by Shirley's talents in these areas. "Miss Booth couldn't sing or dance any better than I could," Douglas later said. "We were like a carnival of blind acrobats."[33]

From the show's early performances out of town, it was evident to all concerned that things were not coming together. Director Vincent Donehue, acclaimed for his previous hit *Sunrise at Campobello,* was viewed by the producers as lacking decisiveness, allowing Shirley to infuse her role with more vulnerability and softness than the character needed.

Shirley with her leading man Melvyn Douglas in the ill-fated *Juno*.

Perhaps it was the fear of yet another flop that caused Shirley to act in a way that some of her *Juno* colleagues characterized as difficult. The esteemed Agnes de Mille, signed to choreograph *Juno,* took a dislike to Shirley, with whom she had a power struggle during rehearsals.

"Shirley was sassy, raw, and mean," de Mille later her told her biographer. "One day she said something like, 'You have changed your mind three times. Make up your mind what you want me to do!' Very bitchily."[34] Was Shirley being difficult, or was she just a sixty-year-old woman whose feet and back hurt after a long and unproductive rehearsal? Whatever the cast, the show was in disarray. Original director Vincent Donehue was abruptly replaced by José Ferrer, who made changes amidst a general feeling that the show was sinking fast.

According to Douglas, it was co-star Jack MacGowran, making his Broadway debut in the troubled show, who best summed up the unhappy experience that was *Juno*. Mac-Gowran, unlike most of his colleagues, was an Abbey Theater veteran who actually knew from experience the character and tenor of life in Dublin. Growing increasingly frustrated by *Juno*'s deviance from the original source material, MacGowran one day erupted into a alcohol-induced tirade that no one present would soon forget. Berating the assembled company of cast and crew at the top of his lungs, MacGowran bellowed, "No one here knows a f——thing about O'Casey or this f—— play and you don't have the slightest notion of what the f—— playwright is saying, or what the f—— actors are saying or what any of you f—— people are trying to do."[35]

Though some of the men paid to serve as theatrical critics liked *Juno* at least a little better than MacGowran did, most considered it at best a mixed bag. *Juno* opened in March 1959 to dismissive reviews, and fell apart in less than two weeks, closing after only 16 performances. A cast album featuring Shirley and Melvyn Douglas would be one of the few tangible reminders of the failed show.

Though *Juno* failed, some critics in later years would regard it as a missed opportunity. Broadway historian Ethan Mordden credited it with "a truly memorable score," but acknowledged that the subject matter might have been too grim for ready commercial acceptance. He speculated that a stronger direction, along the lines of Joshua Logan, or Jerome Robbins, might have pulled the show together successfully.[36]

Continuing her dismal run of luck onstage in 1959, Shirley accepted an invitation to be reunited with playwright William Inge and director Daniel Mann, who'd been so important to her career, in a new drama, *A Loss of Roses*. Since Inge had given her the most prestigious role of her career in *Come Back, Little Sheba*, Shirley signed for the role of Helen Baird despite some misgivings about the script. By this time, she had begun to have doubts in her own judgment, and surely remembered that she hadn't initially been that enthusiastic about *Sheba*, either.

The new play, set in a suburb of Kansas City during the Depression, cast Shirley as Helen Baird, a nurse and mother of a 21-year-old son, Ricky. Helen worries that her adult son seems to lack ambition, and to be content to live at home with her indefinitely. She's appalled when her son impetuously proposes marriage to an older woman, an unemployed actress who is an old friend of the family.

Underlying the conflict that develops between the two women is the implication that the close relationship between mother and son borders on the inappropriate. When Ricky tries to give his mother a kiss, Helen draws away, saying, "You're too old to still be making love to me like you did when you were a baby." Affronted, Ricky retorts, "Forget it. I'm just trying to be nice to you and tell you I can look after you, and you act like it was something unholy."

Cast as Shirley's son in *Roses* was a young Warren Beatty, whose credentials up to that point were minimal. His presence in such a prestigious production was attributed largely to his mentor Inge, who was widely believed to have a crush on the young actor, and who interceded on his behalf when director Mann suggested Beatty be replaced with a more seasoned performer.

Expectations were running high for *A Loss of Roses,* and in July Louella Parsons reported that Hollywood producer Buddy Adler had secured the movie rights for a whopping $400,000. "Yes, we paid a big price," he told Parsons, "but Inge writes only hits.... There were a number of producers trying to buy *Loss of Roses,* so we were lucky to get it."[37] Some would later classify that statement under the heading of "Famous Last Words..."

Throughout rehearsals and a tryout in Washington, D.C., Shirley began to find her role in *A Loss of Roses* unsatisfactory. She complained that the younger actress Carol Haney, then a rising star because of her role in *The Pajama Game,* was being showcased at her expense. Other members of the company remembered that Shirley grew frustrated with the amount of attention director Mann was giving to the untrained Warren Beatty, leaving her feeling a lack of direction.

Shirley's agent, Audrey Wood, found herself in a difficult spot, since she represented all three of the show's principals—Shirley, Inge, and Mann. "It became much worse," Miss Wood recalled, "when she announced, during our out-of-town tryout, that unless certain changes were made by Bill for her in the script, and unless Mann would concentrate on her performance rather than spending so much time with Beatty's, she would not come into New York with the play."[38]

In late November, only days before the show's scheduled opening at the Eugene O'Neill Theater, Shirley abruptly resigned from the production, telling a reporter, "It's a third-rate part.

"I didn't want to do it in the first place," Shirley explained, "but I had faith in Inge and in Daniel Mann's directing. I thought maybe they'd develop the problem of the mother and the son a little more, but they're not going to and there's nothing else for me to do. It's not that I'm telling them what to do, but rather what I'm not going to do."[39] She claimed to bear her colleagues no ill will, and to believe that the show would be a hit without her.

Unable to keep the peace, Wood had finally realized that Shirley's departure was the only viable solution to the contretemps. She later recalled that she advised the playwright to postpone the opening upon Shirley's departure. Inge, who had invested a considerable amount of his own money in the production, thought it over and decided to disregard her advice. At least, that was Wood's account—Inge remembered it differently.

"[In] the last few days of our out-of-town engagement," he later said, "suddenly I realized that the play I thought I had written was not happening on the stage. By that time, it was too late to make all the changes that would have been necessary. I tried to prevent its coming into New York but this would have brought me a greater personal financial loss than I could have handled. I have never felt so trapped."[40]

Interestingly, Inge himself basically agreed that the role of Helen Baird was not the star role Shirley had expected. When Random House published the play in 1960, using a text edited and approved by the playwright, the final scene no longer focused on Helen and Ricky, but on Lila. As Inge ultimately admitted, "It is really Lila's play."[41] That would become even more obvious a couple of years later, when the film adaptation *A Loss of Roses* was named *The Stripper,* clearly acknowledging the prominence of the younger female character.

The Washington Post's Richard L. Coe, always in Shirley's corner, called her departure from Inge's play "simply an inexorable fact of the star system [which] led audiences to expect that as Miss Booth was the only player listed above the title, this would be her story.... The result was the imbalance that baffled first-nighters."[42] Coe claimed that the original plan had been to sign Marilyn Monroe for the Carol Haney role, and that only after she proved to be unavailable did Audrey Wood conceive the ill-fated notion of reuniting the team of Inge, Mann, and Booth for *A Loss of Roses.*

Now that the play had no star name to be billed above the title, Carol Haney would share featured billing with Shirley's replacement. Inge, who had a personal acquaintance with actress Betty Field, persuaded her to join the production in the other female role. Shirley would continue to appear in the Washington company at night, while Field was rehearsed during the daytime in preparation for the New York opening, by then only a few weeks away.

Field gave up a film role to step into Inge's play, but arrived with very little time to rehearse before opening night. *A Loss of Roses* opened in late November, and died a quick death, with at least one prominent critic calling Shirley wise to have resigned from such a flawed show. Acerbic Dorothy Kilgallen, in her syndicated column, opined, "It is now clear why Shirley Booth exited from the play during the tryout period; the mystery is how she ever considered doing it at the beginning."[43]

Gossip, charges, and counter-charges were laid out in a *New York Times* article. Inge, while declining to say that his complaints referred specifically to Shirley, told journalist Maurice Zolotow he was tired of being rewritten by performers during the rehearsal process. "Don't you think actors ought to have more respect for writers? Why don't they trust the dialogue, the characters, give themselves time to grow into it? No, instead they try to bring the author's prose down to the level of everyday speech. Oh, you'll get demands for changes even at the first reading!"[44] He continued to believe that *A Loss of Roses* ranked with his finest work as a playwright, though few critics or scholars agreed.

Free of her commitment to the Inge play, Shirley didn't remain idle long. By Thanksgiving 1959, newspapers reported that she had signed to play the lead in *The Other One,* adapted from a novel by Colette. Once again, Leonard Sillman, who had cast her in *Miss Isobel,* would be her producer, with actor Jean-Pierre Aumont signed to play the male lead. Shirley would portray a married woman who learns that her husband's secretary, played by Nina Foch, is also his mistress. The unexpected relationship that develops between the wife and the mistress formed the crux of the play.

Aumont respected Shirley as "a great American actress," but was less enthusiastic about Foch, whom he claimed "couldn't say a line without the advice of her psychiatrist,"[45] or about the Actor's Studio graduate who played his son. Thirteen years Shirley's junior, Aumont considered himself oddly cast as her husband, and would remember being regularly entreated by producer Leonard Sillman to age his appearance with a fake mustache and artificially colored white streaks at his temples.

By the time the play opened in April 1960, it had undergone a title change, and was being called *A Second String.* By any title, it failed to make an impression on theatergoers, and once again Shirley's name was attached to a Broadway failure.

In the summer of 1960, Shirley was onstage in Westport, Connecticut, starring as Abby in *The Late Christopher Bean.* Adapted by Sidney Howard from René Fauchois' *Prenez Garde à La Peinture,* the play cast Shirley as a loyal maid whose longtime employers try to swindle her out of the valuable paintings left behind by a destitute painter who was a boarder in the Haggett household. *The Late Christopher Bean* had been a Broadway hit in 1932 with Pauline Lord in the role of Abby, and proved a favorite vehicle for Shirley in summer stock.

Still, she was anticipating making her own Broadway comeback that fall. She'd signed with producer-director Richard Myers for a show called *Come Away with Me,* to co-star Kenneth MacKenna. A September opening was anticipated. During the summer, however, problems developed with the show, and there was an unexpected shortage of available theaters. By August, Myers announced that the show would not open on schedule, and that he was releasing his stars from their obligation.

By that time, Shirley's confidence had taken a few blows. In 1955, she had been regarded as the star so beloved that she could sell tickets to a mediocre play, and make the audience enjoy the journey. By 1960, she had endured four upsetting misfires in a row, and had little reason to be more optimistic about her film career. The sum total of her experiences in *Miss Isobel, Juno, A Loss of Roses,* and *A Second String,* along with the disappointment of *Come Away with Me,* left her frustrated, and at loose ends.

The combination of those factors, coupled with an unexpected job offer, would soon lead Shirley to the most famous role of her career.

8. Here Comes Hazel

Shirley's fame with modern audiences rests largely on the five years she spent in the early 1960s playing the starring role in TV's *Hazel*. But in 1960, when word got out that the Oscar winner and possessor of multiple Tony Awards was considering such a venture, her colleagues in the theatre and motion picture world were taken aback.

Despite the fact that her last three Broadway shows had flopped, and her contract with Paramount Pictures had come to an end after 1958's *Hot Spell*, it wasn't really that Shirley *had* to do television. Although she was by no means the type of leading lady usually show-cased in Hollywood films, she was still in demand as an actress. Around the time she entered negotiations to star in *Hazel*, she was approached by director Frank Capra to play the lead in his *Pocketful of Miracles*, a remake of his earlier success *Lady for a Day* (Columbia, 1933).

Miracles, like its predecessor, was based on the Damon Runyon stories of Apple Annie, a New York bag lady who's dressed up by her friends as a society woman so as to help Annie's daughter impress the young man she wants to marry. The story seemed an ideal fit for Shirley, who'd long demonstrated her ability to mix tears and laughter. During negoti-ations, however, Capra made the tactical error of arranging a screening of the original film, intending to show his potential star what a juicy role she'd be getting. Instead, Shirley, always a fan of other actors, was greatly impressed by actress May Robson's performance as Apple Annie in *Lady for a Day*, and reached the conclusion that she couldn't better it. Capra ultimately cast Bette Davis in *Pocketful of Miracles*, released in 1961 to mixed reviews, while Shirley looked elsewhere for her next gig.

As Shirley's friend Alice Bellamy had observed years earlier, and as the star herself read-ily admitted, Miss Booth was pretty straitlaced. Some of the roles she was offered in the early 1960s offended her sensibilities. She'd been uncomfortable with the oedipal aspects of her role as Warren Beatty's mother in *A Loss of Roses*, but that kind of candor was becom-ing increasingly common on Broadway and in films. Tennessee Williams offered to write a play for her, but told her he envisioned her playing the madam of a bordello. She later told Hedda Hopper that she had no interest in such a role, whether for Williams or in the film *Walk on the Wild Side* (Columbia, 1962): "I'm not interested in parts of that sort. My erstwhile agent offered it, and that's why he's erstwhile. I think no one should accept such parts, no matter how desperate he may be to get a job."[1] (Barbara Stanwyck ultimately accepted the role, for which she was duly chided by Hopper).

At this point in her career, Shirley wasn't a complete stranger to television, though her experiences with it were limited, since she'd spent most of the 1950s acting onstage and in films. Still, she'd made a TV guest appearance as far back as 1949, participating in a New York-based variety special, and occasionally turned up on panel shows like *This is Show Business* (CBS, 1949–56). In February 1960, she was a guest on CBS' popular *The Garry Moore Show,* clowning with series regular Carol Burnett. But in the wake of her Oscar win and subsequent film roles, many critics now regarded Shirley as a dramatic actress, forgetting that she had long gone back and forth between serious theater works and lighter fare like her radio comedy shows.

In early 1961, before *Hazel* got underway, Shirley accepted an offer from her old colleagues at the Theatre Guild to appear in their critically acclaimed TV series, *The U.S. Steel Hour.* This dramatic anthology, seen regularly from 1953 to 1963, was an offshoot of radio's *Theatre Guild on the Air.* Shirley was signed to play the lead in a drama by N. Richard Nash called "Welcome Home," which aired in March 1961. Foreshadowing the much more famous TV role that was just around the bend, Shirley played Jenny, described by a reviewer as "an individualistic and unselfish domestic who for twenty-five years has dominated the household in which she was employed."[2]

Shirley saw her character a little differently. "This is a gentle, lost creature. She's been with one family for years and now with their children grown they don't know what to do with her. They can't just discharge her after all these years..."[3]

The *New York Times* commented favorably on Shirley's performance, saying, "It was Miss Booth's first TV dramatic role since 1956 and there were a few moments when she did not seem entirely sure of herself before the cameras. But during most of the telecast she provided a convincing and touching portrayal of the tender-hearted Jenny. She should be given another opportunity soon to display her artistry on television."[4]

That opportunity wasn't long in coming. By the time "Welcome Home" aired, Shirley had already been signed by the Guild's producers to make a return engagement to *The U.S. Steel Hour.* She would be paid $5,000 for her starring role in "The Haven," by Tad Mosel, which had originally been produced on *Philco TV Playhouse* with Shirley's *Hot Spell* co-star Eileen Heckart cast in the lead. "The Haven," taped in the spring of 1961, cast Shirley as a wife who must deal with the infidelity of her husband, played by Gene Raymond. That, too, was well-received, with critic Bill Fiset calling Shirley's performance Emmy-worthy, and saying "Miss Booth and Raymond, as husband and wife, performed with such utter simplicity and skill that even the playwright could hardly have asked a fragment of improvement."[5]

Meanwhile, in California, Screen Gems executive William Dozier was looking for the right actress to star in the company's new project, a TV adaptation of Ted Key's cartoon character Hazel. Cartoonist Key had been drawing Hazel cartoons for *The Saturday Evening Post* since 1942. His single-frame cartoons depicted a comfortably plump, hook-nosed maid in a suburban household, unflappably able to handle any situation that arose with a quick wit and a dose of common sense. His work for the *Post* was popular enough to be reprinted in anthologies like *Here's Hazel* and *All Hazel.*

The Curtis Publishing Company, owners of the *Post,* refused for a number of years any options to adapt Key's character to other media. In the late 1950s, however, the company finally consented to market the TV rights to Hazel, and several production companies were interested in launching a *Hazel* television program.

As Key later recounted in a *TV Guide* article, George Gobel's Gomalco Productions (best known for *Leave it to Beaver*) proposed to cast Ann B. Davis (of *Love that Bob* and, later, *The Brady Bunch*) as Hazel. David Susskind's Talent Associates thought it a perfect

STANDARD AFTRA ENGAGEMENT CONTRACT
FOR A SINGLE TELEVISION BROADCAST

Dated: **February 14th,** 19 **61**

Between___**SHIRLEY BOOTH**_____
c/o **Wm. McCaffrey Agency** Name
501 Madison Ave.
New York City _____ hereinafter called "Performer,"
                    Address

and

THE THEATRE GUILD, of 27 West 53rd Street, New York 19, New York, hereinafter called "Producer."

Performer shall render artistic services in connection with the rehearsal and broadcast of the program designated below and preparation in connection with the parts or part to be played:

TITLE OF PROGRAM: THE UNITED STATES STEEL HOUR

TYPE OF PROGRAM: Dramatic—Network and Commercial

SPONSOR: The United States Steel Corporation

DATE AND TIME OF PERFORMANCE:* Wednesday **within one year from the date of pre-recording** 10:00-11:00 P.M.
PRE-RECORDING
PLACE OF PE**RFORMANCE**: Studio #61 CBS, New York City

AFTRA CLASSIFICATION: Actor

PART TO BE PLAYED:___**Eunice in THE HAVEN**_____

COMPENSATION: $ **5,000.00** by check, payable to and in the name of: **WILLIAM McCAFFREY AGENCY, said payment to constitute full payment to above performer.**

REHEARSALS* **and PRE-RECORDING to take place between**
Date **March 13, 1961 and**   Date
March 22, 1961.
Date   Date

Date   Date

Date   Date

Execution of this agreement signifies acceptance by Producer and Performer of all of the above terms and conditions and those on the reverse hereof and attached hereto, if any.

THE THEATRE GUILD (Producer)

___*Shirley Booth Baker*___
   Performer
C16465   By ___*Sara Greenspan*___
Telephone Number

111-07-7619
Social Security Number

*Subject to change in accordance with AFTRA Code

Attached hereto as "ADDITIONS NOT PART OF STANDARD FORM" is an agreement between Producer and Performer. In the event that any of the terms and provisions of the said attached agreement are less favorable to the Performer than, or inconsistent with the expressed provisions of this Standard Form contract, such provisions of the said attached agreement shall be deemed to have no force and effect whatsoever.

Shirley's contract, signed "Shirley Booth Baker," for the television drama *The Haven*.

post–*Honeymooners* vehicle for Audrey Meadows. But it was Screen Gems that won the TV rights to Key's character, and set out to turn the popular cartoons into a workable sitcom.

Not only was Screen Gems a studio with a track record for launching successful sitcoms (such as ABC's *The Donna Reed Show*, which also gave a TV berth to an Oscar winner), but they had already scored a hit with a series based on a cartoon character. *Dennis the Menace,* based on Hank Ketcham's long-running newspaper strip, had premiered on CBS in 1959, and would enjoy a four-year run. Clearly the studio had demonstrated its ability to use this type of source material in developing a viable series. However, the character of Hazel posed some challenges of her own.

"For many years I had drawn a maid who never lost a battle," Key wrote. "She was designed that way; that was the 'joke.' I tried to make her real and believable. But the one line always had to be hers. This placed a special burden on the producers and writers [of the proposed series]. No human being could continually top others, line by line, for almost 30 minutes and be made to appear sympathetic or credible. Invincibility had to be maintained and yet it had to be tempered."[6]

Armed with 20 pages of Key's notes on characterization, Screen Gems executive Harry Ackerman and producer James Fonda appointed writers William Cowley and Peggy Chantler, who had worked on *Dennis,* to develop *Hazel,* the series. Their pilot script, titled "Dorothy's Birthday," centered on the conflict that arose when an overworked Hazel is pressed into service at the last minute to put together a luncheon for Mrs. Baxter and her friends, and then left at home that evening to relax while the Baxters take Dorothy out to dinner. The episode's conclusion reinforces the idea that Hazel is one of the family, when George realizes his mistake at leaving her out of the birthday dinner.

The idea of casting Shirley Booth to play the lead was not an immediate one. In fact, there was little reason to believe that she would want to do a sitcom. The name actresses who came to television during this period more often chose to do an anthology series along the lines of Loretta Young's 1953–61 show. June Allyson did a similar show in the late 1950s, and Barbara Stanwyck had signed to topline a dramatic anthology on NBC in the 1960–61 season.

Screen Gems considered character actress Thelma Ritter, memorable as a supporting player in *All about Eve* (Fox, 1950) and other critically acclaimed films. Also in the mix at one point was Agnes Moorehead, who would gain her own TV immortality a few years later as Endora on ABC's *Bewitched* (1964–72).

When Screen Gems executive William Dozier sent the *Hazel* pilot script to Booth's agent, naysayers thought he was wasting his time and postage. Still, unable to cast the role to his satisfaction, Dozier decided to give it a shot, despite Shirley's well-known stance on regular TV work.

"Why are we looking for somebody like Shirley Booth to play this part?" he purportedly told his staff. "I don't care what she's said in the past ... if I'm not going to get her I want her to tell me why."[7] He submitted the pilot script to Shirley's agent, William McCaffrey.

"I got a call from my agent," Shirley later explained to *TV Guide.* "I told him, you know how I feel about TV. But when he said Hazel I agreed to read it. He was so surprised he almost dropped the phone. Well, I did read it. And I agreed immediately to do it."[8]

In fact, Shirley had considered playing Hazel a few years earlier, when Key had collaborated with writer Robert Cenedella on a stage adaptation. She'd read the play, but thought that it didn't sustain itself well over the length of an evening in the theater, and declined the role. Though the play never came to fruition, she had liked the character of Hazel, and considered it a much more suitable concept for a TV series, especially as Cowley and Chantler had adapted it in the pilot script. The financial incentive was also strong — Shirley, in her early sixties, was thinking about the kind of monetary security that a lifetime of stage work, despite its prestige, hadn't given her.

In February 1961, syndicated columnist Hedda Hopper reported that Shirley had arrived in Hollywood to shoot a pilot episode of *Hazel.* Shirley's theater colleagues were horrified. As Burt Lancaster, her co-star from *Come Back, Little Sheba,* later admitted, he was among the many who thought his friend was lowering herself by accepting a TV sitcom, and told her so.

"I'm ashamed of you, Shirley," she later quoted Lancaster as saying, "lowering yourself with a thing like this *Hazel* series. I wish you'd get out of it."[9] Much later, Lancaster credited Judy Garland with setting him straight, telling him, "If Shirley Booth can be cheapened in any way, they haven't invented the medium to do it yet."[10]

The lady herself expressed no such doubts. "Actors love good parts," Shirley explained. "Hazel is a good part. She is a good human soul, honest and likable."[11]

That the interfering, know-it-all, busybody Hazel would emerge as likable could, in fact, largely be attributed to Shirley. This aspect of the character, in accord with Shirley's wishes, would be more apparent on TV than it had been in Key's cartoons. *The Saturday Evening Post*'s Marione R. Nickles, in an introduction to one of Key's published cartoon collections, described the Hazel of the printed page as a "big-hearted tyrant," and added, "Not that Hazel doesn't know her place. She does indeed. It is in her opinion several cuts above the other members of the family."[12]

Shirley, whose reluctance to play unsympathetic characters was well-known in Broadway and movie circles, freely admitted that her conception of Hazel was in some ways a departure from what Ted Key had created. "I took the astringency from the character as Ted had conceived her, and gave her a maternal feeling toward the household. I feel that comedy has to touch depth to avoid getting very boring. In the theater and in movies I always look for the tear, just as in drama I always look for the light things because I believe this is life."[13] Luckily, Key, who considered Shirley ideally cast as Hazel, recognized the need to adapt to a different medium, and didn't take offense at the changes made to his original characterization.

Having succeeded in attracting the attention of a bona fide star, Screen Gems was open to Shirley's input, and rolled out the red carpet to sign her for the role. She would be given billing above the title in *Hazel,* as well as a generous salary and profit participation in the series. Well-known Broadway and film composers Sammy Cahn and James Van Heusen contributed the theme music and song for the new series, giving the new enterprise an added touch of class.

Still, TV's *Hazel* encountered a few bumps along the way to prime time success. Cast as George Baxter in the original, never-to-be-aired pilot was veteran character actor Edward Andrews. An avuncular actor, usually seen silver-haired and with his trademark glasses, Andrews was a familiar face throughout the 1960s and beyond, playing McMann and Tate clients on *Bewitched,* and featured in Doris Day movie comedies like *The Thrill of It All* (1963). His casting suggested that the original intent was for George, as well as Hazel, to be a comedic character. Completing the main cast were Whitney Blake as Dorothy Baxter, and ten-year-old Bobby Buntrock as the Baxters' young son Harold. Blake, a beautiful blonde in her mid-thirties and the mother of a later generation TV star, *Family Ties'*

Meredith Baxter Birney, had a solid list of credits that included playing the murder victim in the premiere episode of TV's *Perry Mason* (CBS, 1957–66).

After the pilot had been shot, though, executives realized that the show's chemistry was wrong. Andrews and Blake made an oddly matched couple, not just because they were eleven years apart in age (and looked farther apart than that). One scene in Chantler and Cowley's pilot episode features George and Harold joking about Dorothy receiving her birthday whacks. When the fatherly George, as played by Andrews, grinningly confides that Dorothy has already been spanked by him, the scene doesn't play as cute, as was doubtless intended, just creepy.

More importantly, producers realized that Shirley needed a strong adversary in the series. If the comedy was to center on Hazel running roughshod over the family that employed her, no matter how amiably, she needed a viable opponent who could stand in her way. Just as the heroine of a later Screen Gems comedy, ABC's *Bewitched* (1964–72), needed a mortal husband who would put his foot down when the magical doings got out of hand, Hazel needed a boss who could say no. Andrews was dropped from the cast of *Hazel,* and instead movie and TV actor Don DeFore was approached about assuming the role of George Baxter.

DeFore, a Warner Brothers contract player in the 1940s, had made a smooth transition to television work in the 1950s, spending several years playing "Thornie" Thornberry, neighbor and sidekick to Ozzie Nelson in ABC's *The Adventures of Ozzie and Harriet* (1952–66).

"I was television's first neighbor character," he told a reporter in 1964. "After that, Burns and Allen developed the Mortons. Thornie — my part — finally was dropped because Ozzie and Harriet just had too many characters to establish — five, counting me — and there just wasn't time to follow through with so many after the children became more important in the show."[14]

After leaving that show in 1958, DeFore's career momentum had slowed. A pilot for his own TV sitcom, "Daddy-O," produced by *Dobie Gillis* veteran Max Shulman, had been optioned by CBS but ultimately rejected. In recent years, DeFore, a family man with five children, had supplemented his erratic acting income by going into the restaurant business, along with other sidelines like a textile company. Still, he didn't immediately jump at the chance to join the cast of *Hazel.* Not only would his character likely be upstaged by the boisterous Hazel, but Hollywood rumor had it that there wouldn't be much money left for any other cast members once Miss Booth's paycheck had been cut.

Nonetheless, DeFore met with Screen Gems executives, and signed a contract calling for co-star billing on *Hazel.* Whitney Blake and Bobby Buntrock would be carried over from the original pilot cast to play opposite him and Shirley. (Portions of that pilot segment, interspersed with new footage of DeFore replacing Edward Andrews, would air as *Hazel's* 23rd episode). Chosen instead to introduce the series to viewers was a script called "Hazel and the Playground."

Initially unsure how his character fit into the show, and knowing he was expected to bring in something different from the talented actor who'd been dismissed, DeFore analyzed the situation and realized, "I saw a man fighting a giant. I knew then that the constant struggle to be master in his own house works only if Mr. B constitutes formidable opposition. If he's a midget, she's no longer a giant. Also, it's not funny." During the course of filming his first episodes, DeFore "learned how far down to push the anger button, the frustration button, the righteous-indignation button — and the valve of affection that George, despite his best efforts, holds for this infuriating woman."[15]

The casting change, and DeFore's fine-tuning of the characterization of George, made for a more cohesive show, though it also called for adjustments in Shirley's performance.

Shirley in her best-remembered role, as the irrepressible maid *Hazel*. Playing her employers during the show's 1961–65 run on NBC-TV were Don DeFore (as George Baxter) and Whitney Blake (Dorothy).

She didn't mind: "I come into a part with no preconceived ideas—ever! Except that the character interests me. After we're into rehearsal and I see the people who are going to do it with me, then I decide what I'll do. You have to adjust to other people."[16]

Screen Gems didn't have much trouble lining up a sponsor and a time slot for its new show, signing a deal with Ford to place *Hazel* on NBC's 1961–62 schedule. Ironically, were it not for Shirley's father's edict years earlier not to use the family name onstage, Ford could have had a great publicity gimmick, sponsoring a show starring an actress named Ford. Instead, they took out full-page ads in popular magazines like *The Saturday Evening Post* (*Hazel's* original home) to promote "a great new comedy series starring Shirley Booth."

Once the series was sold, Shirley set up residence in California, initially taking a suite at the Chateau Marmont hotel. Treating the role in *Hazel* as seriously as she would a theatrical performance, she dug into the character she'd be playing, and spent long hours rehearsing and studying her scripts.

Despite her years of experience, Shirley had to do some adjusting to the way television worked. "Serial work is unlike anything I've ever done before, and can be tricky," she told a reporter that first year. "For instance, scenes are often filmed for TV at the same time for different sequences. If there's a scene in front of a fireplace in as many as a dozen or so scripts, we film those scenes at the same time while the lights are up before the given set. That means we skip around in episodes of several weeks at a time, parts of as many as six half-hour shows being done in one hectic day.

"All that, I don't need to tell you, requires a concentration tougher even than stage or screen. The result is I spend every night boning up on the next day's shooting schedule, trying to find the continuity that just isn't there on the set."[17]

Though she missed the presence of a live audience, which had always been so important to her, Shirley said there were compensations. "I'm working under the most favorable conditions," she said. "When I'm playing an emotional scene, our director, Bill Russell, sits there intently, and when I'm finished tears are streaming down his face. I don't miss having an audience, because Bill is it. And the cast is grand."[18]

Hazel premiered on NBC's Thursday night schedule on September 28, 1961. With the original series pilot scrapped, the first episode dealt with Hazel's efforts to have half of a nearby botanical garden turned into a neighborhood playground for Harold and his friends "Hazel and the Playground" gave America its first look at Shirley's new TV character in a brief prologue as she walks down the sidewalk with a bag of groceries in her arms. She speaks her first lines to a little girl, Laurie, when Hazel stops to admire the chalked lines some children have drawn for a hopscotch game. When Laurie disdainfully says that she's too old to play such a game, Hazel grins and says, "Oh, are you? I ain't!" She skips happily down the sidewalk.

The premiere episode also introduced two other recurring characters, the wealthy and clueless neighbors Herbert and Harriet Johnson, played by veteran actors Donald Foster and Norma Varden. Foster, who'd played Shirley's father in the Broadway hit *My Sister Eileen* twenty years earlier, was one of a number of her former stage and film co-stars who would be given a showcase on *Hazel*.

Early reviewers of the show weren't impressed. Snapped *Variety's* critic, "If *Hazel* makes it on NBC-TV this season, there will be tangible support for the theory that the mass television audience has the mentality of a 12-year-old."[19] He considered the show "grossly unworthy of its star, Shirley Booth." Back in New York, her hometown newspaper, which had so often covered her many stage triumphs, described her as "the latest member of the Sardi aristocracy to go West in pursuit of those satisfying film residuals," saying with some

The role of Hazel occasionally required Shirley to master a few new skills. Here she tackles lawn maintenance.

condescension of her TV work that "there'll be nothing but understanding for a grand trouper."[20]

If not the most artistically challenging role of Shirley's career, playing Hazel did come with its own set of difficulties. A running joke in the series was Hazel's blithe competence at almost everything she undertook, especially in matters athletic. Not only was the sassy maid a championship bowler, she was also seen to place-kick a football in the pilot segment, supposedly with such vigor that it landed smack in the chimney of a neighbor's house. For Shirley, whose own leisure time pursuits were more passive, the athletic prowess didn't come naturally.

"You have to do things for your art," she said laughingly of the sporting feats assigned to her, for which she was given coaching by various experts. "This is the physical art, you know. But I have discouraged them about any ideas of making me catch a baseball. I could never learn to catch a ball without wincing and closing my eyes."[21]

Though some actresses might have balked at playing the deglamorized role of Hazel, Shirley saw it as a plus. Her younger co-star Whitney Blake would spend long hours being fitted for the glamorous wardrobe she wore as Dorothy. In contrast, Shirley was perfectly content to climb into Hazel's drab uniform and sensible shoes, not to mention the red wig that spared her the bother of a long daily session with the studio hairdresser.

That same lack of pretentiousness, despite Shirley's impeccable credentials, made an impression on a journalist who visited the *Hazel* set during filming of an early episode, and came away newly impressed by Shirley. "As I watched," he later wrote, "I realized that greatness in an actress ... is more than talent and more than professional training."[22]

Noting that Shirley had her lines memorized from the earliest rehearsal, rather than carrying around the script as many actors did, he watched her interact with director Bill Russell. When Russell gave Shirley some direction, correcting the way she was playing a scene, Resnik fully expected the star to resist. "I have seen lesser stars blow their tops at this type of proceeding," he commented. "I have seen lesser stars directing the director and the director taking the directions. Not Miss Booth."[23]

Not only did Shirley change her approach in the scene in accord with Russell's instructions, she later told the reporter that she welcomed being corrected. "It is a good idea to stop people before they get grooved in a bad habit," she explained. "Our director was right in what he told me. He is consistently right — an excellent director."[24]

Shirley minus her *Hazel* wig, though recognizable to her fans just the same (Michael D. Strain collection).

Journalist Cynthia Lowry, who'd written often about Shirley in the days prior to *Hazel*, was also impressed by the star's ability to inhabit this character. "Miss Booth," Lowry wrote after a set visit in 1962, "is an intelligent, poised, and attractive woman, who dressed conservatively and well, reads widely, and has cosmopolitan tastes." But when it was time to face the NBC cameras, "her facial expression changed. Her body slumped and she looked pounds heavier. Her speech became more casual. Her walk was different. She had changed into Hazel."[25]

Those early episodes provided a bit of background for the character of Hazel. She had dropped out of high school when her mother died, called upon to take care of her younger siblings. Going into domestic service, she had worked for Dorothy's family since the future Mrs. Baxter was a little girl, and came along when she married George, now a prominent attorney. Hazel's most serious boyfriend had been a man named Gus, whose picture she still kept by her bedside, even though he had long ago left her to enter military service and never came back.

Although some observers questioned whether viewers would be able to relate to the great stage actress playing a maid, Shirley had no such concerns, and saw significance in the character. "There used to be a lot of Hazels," she told a journalist. "Today women seem to think they're lowering themselves to work in another woman's home. But domestic service can really be a noble way of life. There are so many lonely women who, if they could come into a home and take care of a family, would acquire a sense of being needed — which is what Hazel gets from the Baxter family."[26]

Some viewers saw a resemblance between Hazel and Shirley's long-ago radio character of Miss Duffy, but the star begged to differ. "Actually, Hazel and Miss Duffy are more unlike than alike," she said. "Hazel is more intelligent, has a softer heart."[27]

In fact, Shirley would be so loved in the role that some viewers took exception to the function that Don DeFore played as her TV adversary. DeFore, a genial sort in real life, explained, "I've had mail from fans threatening to punch me in the nose if I don't stop being so mean to Hazel. Even my own mother says she thinks I'm too mean."[28] Conversely, other *Hazel* fans took him to task for letting a domestic servant run roughshod over him. In fact, DeFore was the epitome of an effective supporting player, and Shirley, with her innate show business wisdom, was the first to acknowledge this.

"Don's contribution is incalculable," she said at the time. "The show couldn't be without him. He gives off the complete aura of frustration without rancor. He is a wonderful man — you read it in his face and you are comfortable with him."[29]

Though Whitney Blake's role as Dorothy Baxter was less prominent than DeFore's, and widely considered somewhat thankless, she too contributed to the show's success, giving her thinly developed character charm and warmth. Other performers who made their mark on the show included the veteran radio and television actress Cathy Lewis, who would make several guest appearances each season as George's snobbish older sister Deirdre. Shirley excelled at playing the side of Hazel that effortlessly stuck a pin in the side of characters full of hot air, and Lewis' Deirdre, who abhorred Hazel's down-home mannerisms and overly familiar attitude, would make one of Shirley's best onscreen combatants. Also introduced that first season was the gifted character actress Maudie Prickett, as Hazel's fellow maid and "Sunshine Girl" Rosie Hamecker.

Having taken the plunge into series television, Shirley was rewarded with affection from viewers that translated into high ratings. That fall, *Hazel* was part of a block of new programs on NBC's Thursday night schedule that included another immediate hit, Richard Chamberlain's *Dr. Kildare* (1961–66). *Hazel* would finish its inaugural season on NBC with ratings that placed it among television's top five shows, easily beating out another sitcom, ABC's short-lived *Margie* (1961–62), which went head-to-head with it.

Although critical response to the series was never more than lukewarm, Emmy voters quickly took notice of Booth's performances. On May 22, 1962, with *Hazel* completing its first season, Booth was named Outstanding Lead Actress in a Series, defeating contenders like Donna Reed and *Pete and Gladys* star Cara Williams. Shirley accepted her award with a one-liner familiar to *Hazel* audiences, saying, "Boy, this is a doozy!"[30]

Critics like *The Washington Post*'s Lawrence Laurent contended that Shirley deserved the award even though he had no affection for her show. "Miss Booth is one of the fine actresses of our time," he wrote, "and this has been proved weekly by her ability to overcome a collection of stereotyped characters, soggy scripts, and completely undistinguished production. Shirley Booth gets fire out of ancient chestnuts to keep *Hazel* going."[31]

Once the first year's episodes were in the can, Shirley was free to leave her temporary berth at the Chateau Marmont to spend the summer at her home in Cape Cod.

When the show returned for its second season in the fall of 1962, *Hazel* became one of television's first situation comedies regularly broadcast in color. One first-season episode, called "What'll We Watch Tonight?" had been colorcast as an experiment before NBC and Screen Gems agreed to making the change permanently. Other major shows that premiered that fall, like CBS' *The Lucy Show* (1962–68) and *The Beverly Hillbillies* (1962–71), would air in black-and-white for their first few years, but NBC, which had a corporate affiliation with RCA, used *Hazel* and a select few other shows to intrigue home viewers into buying the relatively uncommon — and expensive — color TV sets that were then still a novelty.

Also acknowledging *Hazel*'s success were the inevitable imitations that sprang up in those years. Screen Gems itself sold ABC *Our Man Higgins,* a sitcom casting *My Fair Lady*'s Stanley Holloway as an English butler working for a suburban American family. That show failed to catch on, as did *Grindl* (NBC, 1963–64), in which Imogene Coca played a domestic worker sent out on short-term assignments by an employment agency.

If critics considered *Hazel* relentlessly commonplace, Shirley saw it differently. "Good situation comedy," she said in a *Saturday Evening Post* magazine profile, "makes the audience feel that the things that happen in their daily lives are important. By dramatizing these things— actions as commonplace, perhaps, as cleaning out a closet or washing the dishes— a show can make their lives more interesting. There's no violence on *Hazel,* there's plenty of emphasis on the home, and it shows people how members of a healthy family behave toward one another."[32]

Midway through the show's run, a piece of Shirley's history came to a close when her ex-husband Ed Gardner died. He'd been out of the spotlight for several years, never topping his 1940s success with *Duffy's Tavern.* A TV version in the early 1950s had not been a success, and his most recent exposure had been in reviving his Archie character for brief bits on NBC's radio series *Monitor.* Though he and Shirley no longer kept in regular contact, she told Hedda Hopper in 1962 that her ex-husband had phoned her after seeing an early episode of *Hazel* and complimented her, saying, "It's a delight to have a show that's not pretentious. You can go along on the strength of the story and the laughs come naturally."[33]

Gardner's death on August 17, 1963, at the age of 62, left behind the wife he'd married in 1942, the former Simone Hegemann, and two teenage sons. Gardner was reported by United Press International to have died of "a diseased liver," suggesting that his years of carousing had taken their toll. (An unidentified friend quoted in the same obituary also

Shirley relaxes between takes with her beloved dog Prego in this 1964 publicity shot.

noted that Gardner "kept terrible hours and smoked like Pittsburgh."[34]) Several celebrities who'd worked with Gardner were among the mourners at the memorial service held at All Saints' Episcopal Church in Beverly Hills, including film stars Edward G. Robinson and Randolph Scott. Shirley, understandably, wasn't among them.

Wary of overexposure, Shirley would do little outside television work during the run

Dancing cheek-to-cheek with the star of *The Andy Williams Show* during her November 1964 guest appearance. She would make only a handful of such appearances during her run on *Hazel* (Michael D. Strain collection).

of *Hazel*. Unlike many performers, who considered appearances on talk, variety, or game shows to be good promotion for their series, Shirley didn't believe in spreading herself too thin. She thought that TV viewers who wanted to see Shirley Booth should tune into *Hazel,* and also believed that actors who constantly sought publicity were destroying some of the mystique she saw as vital to her profession. This, of course, didn't apply to appearing on the annual Emmy Awards broadcast, where she accepted her second Best Actress Emmy for *Hazel* in the spring of 1963.

With the series a success, Shirley put down roots in California for the first time in her life. In 1964, she bought a house in Beverly Hills, purchasing a second one in nearby West-wood for her sister Jean. Being a homeowner, with old friends like the Ralph Bellamys living in the same area, gave structure to her life for the months that *Hazel* was in production each year. She didn't, however, intend to become a year-round resident of the West Coast. She maintained her Manhattan apartment — "so I will always have a foot in New York's door," she explained, "and of course I still go to the Cape [Cod] every summer."[35]

By this time, *Hazel* had become an enduring part of her life. "The series is confining," she admitted to a reporter as the fourth year got underway. "It limits my time and what I can do but it has never been a drag. I'm not the least surprised it has lasted. I had complete faith in it from the beginning, even before it went on the air."[36]

She began the new season a few pounds lighter. "Went on a salt-free diet," she explained to a reporter. "I got too fat last winter. That's all I had time to do, eat and work. And that uniform isn't all that inspiring. Some actresses have to stay thin to stay in their Mainbocher wardrobe. I can always cover up with an apron."[37]

In early 1965, as *Hazel* played out its fourth year on NBC, network programmers were skeptical about the show's future. Still ensconced in its usual Thursday night slot, the series took a hit in the ratings that year, largely because of an unexpected one-two punch from the usually beleaguered ABC. That network's 1964–65 schedule had introduced two massive hits — the prime time soap opera *Peyton Place* (1964–69), and a new situation comedy from Screen Gems, *Bewitched* (1964–72). Both *Hazel* and *Kildare* took a hammering from the new competition. While NBC would renew *Kildare* for a fifth year, trying to revitalize it with a change in format that would make it more like the unexpectedly popular *Peyton Place, Hazel* was shown the door. Though the show would continue to play on NBC through its summer 1965 rerun cycle, by January Screen Gems had been notified that a fifth-season renewal would not be forthcoming.

9. Hanging Up the Uniform

Though NBC had canceled *Hazel* after four seasons, Screen Gems executives weren't yet ready to give up on the show that had been in television's Top Ten a few years earlier. Concluding that the show had grown stale, they decided that a new format was needed to extend *Hazel*'s life.

"They told me we could jazz it up by moving Hazel to Hollywood and using some guest stars," Shirley said that spring. "But I thought they meant move Mr. B and the whole family to Hollywood." Instead, she found out that bigger changes were imminent. With a shrug, Shirley said, "I said I'll wait till I see a script. So far, they haven't shown me one."[1] She was sanguine about the possibility that the show might simply be retired instead, or so she said, though she would certainly honor her contract if a deal could be made.

Since NBC executives considered Shirley's series played out, Screen Gems negotiated throughout the spring and early summer to place the show elsewhere for a fifth year. In February, *Variety* reported that ABC wanted *Hazel* for its Saturday night schedule. When the dust finally settled, however, Booth's show would land on CBS instead. The deal called for CBS to air a fifth season of original episodes, and also obtain rerun rights to the series for its CBS Films division.

Although the future of her TV series had been up in the air for several months, Shirley claimed she lost no sleep over the negotiations. "Sure, we were cancelled last January," she told a journalist, "and we weren't bought to return to television until April. But I had more optimism than anyone else at Screen Gems. I just knew it would happen."[2]

Disappointed with some of their sitcom pilots that spring, CBS programmers thought Shirley's four-year-old show a better bet than the newbies—something NBC perhaps should have considered. The network that let Booth slip away filled its fall schedule with the likes of *Mona McCluskey* (which was awarded the time slot vacated by *Hazel)*, *Camp Runamuck, The John Forsythe Show,* and, most notoriously, *My Mother, the Car.* None of them would see a second season.

While Screen Gems personnel worried about the future of *Hazel*, Shirley spent her summer 1965 hiatus reprising one of her best-known pre-television roles. She accepted an offer from a 3,000-seat theatre outside Hollywood to revive *Come Back, Little Sheba.* Coming into the homestretch of her five-year TV contract with Screen Gems, she had begun to think of what would come next for her after *Hazel,* and was curious to see how people would respond when she revisited her roots as a dramatic actress. The production would re-team Shirley with her original Broadway co-star, Sidney Blackmer, as Doc.

The result impressed attendees like *Los Angeles Times* critic Cecil Smith. "There is such warmth and such humor in Miss Booth's portrayal," said Smith's rave review. "Lola is a terrible woman who spies on young lovers for a vicarious thrill, who opens other people's mail, who eats chocolates and listens to radio rhumbas rather than clean house—a shapeless, flabby horror of a housewife. That the actress draws sympathy and understanding for her is the work of a consummate artist."[3] Shirley's performance routinely drew standing ovations from audiences during the two-week run at the Valley Music Theatre.

Not only were reviews laudatory, but she was intrigued by the reaction her stage turn produced on the set of *Hazel*. "All the production people had been to see the play," she explained to King Features' Harvey Pack. "And when I came back to work it was, 'Welcome back, Miss Booth,' instead of 'Hi, Shirley.' I considered that quite a tribute, but after a few days they went back to calling me Shirley. However, if I was able to sell people who had worked with me for years on *Hazel* on the idea of appearing as another character, I know I'll have no trouble with the public."[4]

Though Shirley was prepared to do a fifth year of *Hazel*, which would finish her five-year contract with Screen Gems, the starring role in *Sheba*, plus the weekly series, represented an ambitious schedule for a performer in her late sixties. She had experienced some health problems in 1965, among them a bout with exhaustion that earned her a week's stay in the hospital. When planning got underway for *Hazel*'s fifth season, the producers were notified that Miss Booth's doctor wanted her working hours reduced.

The need to reduce Shirley's screen time, as well as give the show a new energy going into its run on CBS, led to some changes. Rather than beefing up the roles of the familiar characters played by Don DeFore and Whitney Blake, the producers opted for a cast shakeup in preparation for the move to CBS. Child actor Bobby Buntrock would remain a cast member, but DeFore and Blake were rather unceremoniously jettisoned that spring in favor of fresher faces.

One journalist reported in February that the new format would be what he described as "Hazel in Hollywood," and would feature Shirley as "the maid in a household of a Hollywood talent agent and his wife."[5] The revamped show that emerged, however, represented a less radical change. In the storyline, Mr. and Mrs. Baxter were called out of the country for an extended period on business. (TV historians Harry Castleman and Walter J. Podrazic joked, "Perhaps George and Dorothy Baxter were not really transferred to Saudi Arabia. Perhaps they just made up the whole story to get out of town and get rid of Hazel. Hopefully they found a nice quiet town somewhere and began living a more independent life, free of domination from their domestic."[6])

The departure of George and Dorothy left son Harold, and Hazel, to move in with George's younger brother Steve and his wife Barbara. Another new character would be Harold's young cousin Susie, played by child actress Julia Benjamin. Producer Fonda said that the changes were needed in order to open up new story avenues for the show after more than 100 episodes. It's likely that Screen Gems also achieved some cost savings, as the younger actors (described in a *Variety* column blurb that April as "Ray Fulmer, stage actor, and Lynn Borden, one-time 'Miss Arizona'")[7], presumably drew smaller salaries than the original series co-stars.

Both newcomers recognized the importance of the opportunity they were being given to work with Shirley. Midway through the season, Lynn Borden told a *Los Angeles Times* writer, "I've learned a lot from her and that's why I hope we can go another year. I keep telling her, 'please help me!' If I don't feel right about something, I ask her—and I write

Hazel underwent major cast changes upon its move to CBS-TV in 1965. Here Shirley appears with Bobby Buntrock and Julia Benjamin as Harold and Susie Baxter.

down what she tells me in case I should forget some time. I learn everything I possibly can from her, because I may never again have the opportunity of working with someone like her."[8]

Concurred Ray Fulmer, who had previously appeared in theater productions opposite actresses like Rosalind Russell, Eve Arden, and Gloria Swanson, "These are the ones you learn from. Working with Shirley, I feel I've arrived at the apex of my career. I was one of about a dozen that they auditioned, and I've got to be the luckiest guy in television."[9]

Hazel's new employers were younger than the original Baxters, and Steve would not be as stern an opponent for her as stuffy George had been. Although the season opener "Who's in Charge Here?" found Steve vowing to lay down the law to Hazel as his older brother never had, he soon figured out the futility of butting heads with her. The character changes brought out a more maternal side of Hazel in the series' last year. "Hazel's relationship to them is changed," she told a reporter. "She is more protective and motherly — less a manager."[10] The new format also allowed Hazel to interfere with Steve's work as a real estate agent, taking upon herself to show houses and help her boss close sales that were in jeopardy.

Aside from Fulmer, Borden, and Benjamin, other actors created new recurring roles for the show's fifth season. Mala Powers was cast as Barbara's friend Mona Williams (with Charles Bateman seen occasionally as husband Fred), while young Ann Jillian (then billed as "Jilliann"), would play Millie Ballard, a giddy teenager who worked part-time after school as the secretary in Steve's office. With the move to a new location, some of the show's original recurring characters, like mailman Barney (played by Robert B. Williams), would be dropped, though Cathy Lewis (as snobbish Deirdre Thompson) and Maudie Prickett (Rosie) would continue to appear from time to time.

The show's new time slot, at 9:30 P.M. (EST) on Mondays, placed it opposite the popular *Andy Williams Show* on NBC, and the third year of another popular sitcom, *The Farmer's Daughter,* on ABC. *The Andy Griffith Show,* airing at 9 P.M. on CBS, would give a strong lead-in to *Hazel. Variety,* reviewing the fifth-season opener that laid out the new premise, saw "no reason to doubt the continued success of this situation comedy series" despite the change in cast and network, adding that Shirley "carried off the role with usual aplomb."[11]

A few weeks into the season, ratings indicated that *Hazel* was still popular with viewers, though there was some drop-off in ratings from *Griffith,* a Top Ten show. During its first month, *Hazel* ranked at #26 in the ratings, solid enough to please CBS and the sponsor. As filming continued that year, however, Shirley was aware that her original five-year contract with Screen Gems would soon be at an end.

Pat Cardamone, a child actor under the stage name Pat Cardi, made several appearances on *Hazel* during the show's last season, playing the recurring role of Jeff Williams, Harold's friend and classmate. Though he shared relatively few scenes with Shirley, he maintains a strong impression of her behavior during his debut episode, "My Son the Sheepdog."

The plot concerned an effort by Harold and his friends to form a musical group, and get a booking on a television variety show called *Pandemonium.* Cardi found it an unpleasant experience working with *Hazel*'s director, whom he remembers as "a large (not fat) imposing older man who resembled LBJ and was just as demonstrative. He seemed to be very quick to yell at actors, no matter how old! He was hard of hearing, and made us shout our lines in a ridiculous fashion. If we didn't yell loud enough he would intimidate us and tell us we were terrible actors and would be fired and replaced."

Into the maelstrom stepped Shirley, who finally told the director, "Stop yelling at the children!" He promptly did so, leaving Cardi grateful for the star's intervention. Appearing periodically throughout the remainder of the 1965–66 season, Cardi remembers today that Shirley "was very nice to me, very quiet on the set, and seemed to know her lines quite well so that there were few retakes."[12]

By the spring of 1966, Shirley was ready to let go of *Hazel,* and discouraged any discussions about continuing the series into a sixth season. Had she wanted to continue, she might well have done so—the show's ratings on CBS, while not as strong as they might have been with the popular *Andy Griffith Show* as lead-in, were still quite acceptable. According to Pat Cardi, there were inquiries from producer James Fonda about signing on for another season of *Hazel,* with the idea that the role of the Williams family would be expanded. By that point, however, Cardi was committed elsewhere (to the new CBS sitcom *It's About Time*), as were the actors who played his parents on *Hazel.* As for Shirley, she was tired, experiencing some health problems, and ready for a change. By letting *Hazel* come to an end, she would clear the way for the show's successful second life in syndication. The money she would make from its multiple reruns would keep her very comfortably for the rest of her life.

When shooting concluded on *Hazel,* it was Shirley's intention to take things easy for a while. She liked the idea of spending a year or more relaxing at her home in Cape Cod, where she'd never before been able to witness all four seasons.

"Of course, I've been offered lots of guest star roles," she noted, "and some series. I really don't want to get into another series but I'm very reluctant to say 'never' about anything because something might come up and I'll change my mind."[13]

A visitor described the serene atmosphere at Shirley's Cape Code hideout, a "grayshingled, low-ceilinged old house ... on a country road which ends at the beach, a few yards from her house. From her windows, you can see the bay.... The front door and the side door are painted bright yellow and brick walks go to both doors. There is a sheath of corn on the side door and a wreath of pine cones on the front. She bought the wreath at the sale at the Congregational Church. Along the road, close to the house, is a privet hedge, six feet tall, a protection against prying eyes."[14]

Shirley could happily have stayed there quietly for the next several months. Her preferred pastimes were passive, relaxing ones—knitting while watching television, reading, collecting and furnishing the house with antiques. Instead, however, her best-laid plans were quickly undone, though it was by her own choice. Within weeks of her departure from the Screen Gems studios, Shirley was at work again. In August, syndicated columnist Sheilah Graham interviewed her as she prepared to begin filming her first TV-movie, based on a book called *Package Deal.* Once that assignment was complete, she would depart for England, where she had signed a deal to star in a television production of *The Glass Menagerie* for producer David Susskind.

"I'm delighted as I love England," she told Graham. "If you want to know why I'm doing *Package Deal,* by the way, it's because so few pleasant parts are offered you these days. There are so many sick parts. I have to take the good ones when they are offered."[15]

Package Deal was itself part of a package deal, one of ten early TV-movies made by Universal Studios under the umbrella title "World Premiere." Others included Rod Serling's airplane drama *The Doomsday Flight,* and *How I Spent My Summer Vacation,* starring Robert Wagner. NBC hoped that the two-hour color films, heavily populated with familiar faces, would lessen its reliance on theatrical films in its prime time schedule, but

Smooth-talking Harry Miller (Charles Drake) ropes an unwitting Mrs. Hudson (Shirley) into crime in the NBC TV-movie *The Smugglers.* The "World Premiere" was filmed in 1966, but didn't air until late 1968.

something went awry where Shirley's movie was concerned. Although Shirley finished filming by early September 1966, the TV-movie would stay on the shelf for the next two years. It finally surfaced for broadcast on NBC in late 1968, under the title *The Smugglers*.

Meanwhile, *The Glass Menagerie*, which aired on CBS in December 1966, was a prestigious undertaking, but not a satisfying one for its star. She would receive yet another Emmy nomination for her performance, but Shirley was dissatisfied with the production. She had disagreed with the director on her interpretation of Amanda Wingfield. Having greatly admired the performance given by Laurette Taylor—"she really contributed something to theater with it"[16]—Shirley wasn't content to settle for doing a pale imitation of the original.

"I never give a complete characterization," she explained during shooting. "I try to leave a little for the yeast of the audience's imagination and interest to work. I was never pretty, you know. I always had to catch an audience other ways. When they aren't interested in your beauty, you've got a better opportunity to make them interested in the person you are supposed to be."[17]

Not having seen the finished film until it aired, Shirley was unhappy with the finished product. She felt that director Michael Elliot had taken his revenge over their creative differences by cutting the film to her disadvantage, focusing mostly on her younger co-star Barbara Loden instead. "I could have phoned it in," she said of her role.[18]

Still, reviewers noticed her work. Noting that her performance was far removed from viewers' memories of Hazel Burke, the *Washington Post*'s critic said, "This Shirley Booth was tough and pitiful, brave and silly, strong and defeated repeatedly by life and times. Miss Booth has the range to handle all the dimensions of a complex and indomitable character."[19]

Shirley, late 1960s (Michael D. Strain collection).

Though Shirley received an Emmy nomination for the role, she shrugged it off. "That's one acceptance speech I'll never have to make," she cracked, and her prediction proved correct.[20]

In the spring of 1967, on short notice, Shirley joined the cast of "Do Not Go Gentle into That Good Night," a drama being produced as an episode of *CBS Playhouse*. Loring Mandel's script had originally been cast with actor Fredric March playing the lead, an elderly man who rebels against his confinement to a nursing home. March's actress wife, Florence Eldredge, had a supporting role as a fellow resident who is a love interest for the star. When March fell ill, he and his wife withdrew, and producers asked Shirley's *Juno* co-star Melvyn Douglas to step in. Shirley agreed to play Eldredge's featured role in the 90-minute drama, which was videotaped for a fall broadcast.

"It's a very small role; I only have four scenes," Shirley remarked. "But I had to do it for the producer, George [Schaefer]. He has had such a terrible time. First the TV strike. Then Freddy March got sick, and naturally his wife Florence wanted to be with him. Freddy is an old friend, and I wanted to help out."[21]

The show was produced much like a stage play, with three weeks of rehearsal preceding five days of taping at CBS' Television City complex in May. Aside from Shirley and Melvyn Douglas, Schaefer assembled a fine cast that included Claudia McNeil (of *Raisin in the Sun* fame), Warren Stevens, and Karl Swenson.

Shirley's character, Helene Michaud, makes her first entrance midway through the show's second act. Helene, a retired department store buyer, is content with her life at the Holly Valley Home for the Aged. The never-married Helene, who's alone in the world except for a brother who lives far away, offers friendship to the angry Peter Schermann (Douglas). She tries to help him find enjoyment in his new circumstances, as she has:

"You haven't gone to the village?" she asks him. "A movie house, there's a park, there's a botanical garden.... I walk, I enjoy seeing the children, the windows ..."[22] Her placid acceptance of her world fails to convince her new friend, who rails against the Holly Valley Home, and others of its ilk, as "a sealed box for old people who die."[23]

Producer-director Schaefer pointed out that Mandel's play did not argue wholeheartedly for the rightness of any one position concerning nursing homes, and the treatment of the elderly. "In Loring's drama, many different attitudes toward geriatrics are dramatized, yet no character in the play is either absolutely right or completely wrong. The viewer is expected to participate; to reject or approve what he is watching in the light of his own knowledge."[24]

In March 1968, the *New York Times* reported that Shirley was headed back to Broadway, to star in a revival of her 1955 hit *The Desk Set*. According to the *Times,* the project would be produced by Robert Fryer, Lawrence Carr, and Joseph Harris, with John Bowab as associate producer. Gus Schirmer was said to be Shirley's choice to direct her in the new production. For reasons unknown, however, this project died aborning, although Shirley did do a summer stock revival of *The Desk Set* that summer.

Despite being downed by a virus, Shirley appeared for a luncheon held in her honor during the July run of *The Desk Set* at the Famous Artists Summer Playhouse in Syracuse. "My doctor has been giving me some of those mysterious little capsules that you swallow with faith and hope, but little charity," she cheerfully told attendees. Explaining why she had chosen to revive the Marchant play rather than appear in a new show, Shirley said she "would rather walk down the street with an old friend she could be proud of, than with one that embarrassed her."[25]

By 1968, *Hazel* was in daily syndication, and the reruns were soon playing to substantial ratings on stations all over the country. Though this did not result in the financial windfall many assumed, as she claimed to have collected little of her profit participation during these years, it did keep her visibility high among younger viewers. It also freed her to turn down roles not to her liking, and hold out for projects that would allow her to maintain her standards.

On Christmas Eve 1968, her TV-movie, *The Smugglers,* filmed in 1966, was finally scheduled for broadcast on NBC. When it was finally broadcast, however, the film suffered yet another indignity. Midway through the telecast, the network interrupted *The Smugglers* for live coverage of the Apollo 8 space mission, and the astronauts' entry into lunar orbit.

A complicated caper plot with numerous twists and turns in just less than 90 minutes, *The Smugglers* has an odd feel to it, as if the makers couldn't quite decide whether or not it was intended to be funny. The plot, adapted from Elizabeth Hely's 1965 novel, centers on naïve American tourist Mrs. Hudson (Shirley), who's vacationing in Austria with her stepdaughter Jo (played by Carol Lynley). Crooked Harry Miller, who's been foiled in his attempt to smuggle some contraband across the Italian border, befriends Mrs. Hudson and persuades her to deliver the package, which she believes contains a religious statue.

Mrs. Hudson delivers the package to Harry's friend, who lives in a secluded castle, with a meek, half-witted servant, Piero, and wangles an invitation for herself and Jo to stay overnight. In the nearby village, Jo meets a handsome Frenchman, M. Cirret, and confides the story to him, not knowing that he's a policeman on vacation from the Surete on vacation. Cirret alerts the local police inspector to the possible transport of contraband just in time to bail out the unsuspecting Mrs. Hudson, who's once again been persuaded to deliver someone else's belongings—this time the corpses of Frank Miller and his mistress Anna.

Producer-director Norman Lloyd enjoyed a long association with *Alfred Hitchcock Presents* (CBS, 1955–65), and at its best this TV-movie has something of a similar feel. Silver-haired Shirley, though top-billed, isn't given a lot of interest to do, but gives her character a charmingly vague quality. Among her co-stars are several other TV stars, then-current and future, among them Broadway veteran Kurt Kasznar, then a regular on Irwin Allen's *Land of the Giants* (ABC, 1968–70), and a dark-haired Donnelly Rhodes, who later played genial ex-con Dutch on *Soap* (ABC, 1977–81). Michael J. Pollard, who plays the castle servant Pietro, was fresh from his Oscar nomination as Best Supporting Actor in *Bonnie and Clyde* (1967).

Aside from *Hazel* reruns, Shirley was little seen onscreen in 1969, but did turn up as a guest star on ABC's *The Ghost and Mrs. Muir,* in the episode "Medium Well Done" (November 6, 1969). She played Madame Tibaldi, a spiritualist hired by sneaky realtor Claymore Gregg to exorcise the ghost of Captain Gregg from Gull Cottage. Madame Tibaldi, who tells Mrs. Muir she discovered her special psychic gifts "about six reincarnations ago," was a splashy and fun role for Shirley. It also allowed her to play opposite an old friend, series regular Charles Nelson Reilly. A few months later, Shirley was a guest on *The Dean Martin Show,* appearing in a fun sketch as a pet inspector who checked out prospective dog owners before allowing them to adopt.

Probably the biggest role that got away during this period was the part of elderly stowaway Ada Quonsett in producer Ross Hunter's *Airport* (1970). By this time, Shirley's physical ailments, notably her bursitis, occasionally interfered with her ability to work, and the role ultimately went to Helen Hayes. Hayes was excellent in the role, nabbing a Best Supporting Actress Oscar, but it's a pity that Shirley didn't have the opportunity to be seen in such an enormous hit film.

In 1970, Shirley signed to make a return to Broadway, set to play the lead in a musical called *Look to the Lilies.* Adapted from the novel *Lilies of the Field,* and the acclaimed 1963 movie adaptation, Shirley's new project would feature Al Freeman, Jr. in the role made famous by Sidney Poitier. She would play the Mother Superior, a role created in the film by Lilia Skala. As in previous versions, the plot centered on a group of nuns who enlist the help of a young African-American convict to build a church.

Shirley was pleased with the project. "I'll be playing a mother superior and you can't get any nobler than that. Nowadays it is not easy to find something you are proud of doing; this show has great appeal and I just adored the picture." She added that Leonard Spigelgass's book for the show "opens new vistas for the stage version and elaborates on the screen characters."[26]

Shirley was cast as a medium in her guest appearance on ABC's *The Ghost and Mrs. Muir.* Also pictured is series star Edward Mulhare.

Back on Broadway for the first time since 1960's *A Second String,* she acknowledged before opening night that it had been a long time since her last appearance. "My last three plays were flops. I suppose I'm being very brave, but I'm not worried about it."[27] The talent behind the scenes was impressive. *Look to the Lilies* boasted music and lyrics by Jule Styne and Sammy Cahn, while Joshua Logan had been recruited as director.

As she had often done in the past, Shirley showed her faith in the new undertaking by getting out her wallet. When others had doubted the viability of *Come Back, Little Sheba,* she had bought a mink as a symbol of the success she believed the show would be. This time, her purchase was a little bigger; Shirley celebrated signing for *Look to the Lilies* by adding to her property holdings at her winter home in La Quinta, California. "I'm a great believer in positive thinking," she said, in explaining the logic behind her spending. The California desert was a long way from her New York apartment — in more ways than one — but Shirley had learned to love the arid environment. "There are a lot more lizards than humans out there," she noted. "Also roadrunners and sidewinders."[28]

Unfortunately, her return to the stage proved a highly touted flop. Though reviews of *Look to the Lilies* were mixed-to-positive, with several writers delighted to see the multiple Tony winner resuming her stage career, the show closed after only 25 performances. Shirley's co-star, actress Taina Elg, later voiced a familiar complaint concerning the star's performance, saying that she had undercut some of the dramatic tension the show needed by balking at playing the character as written. "The show didn't work because Shirley Booth had her own ideas," Elg said, noting that the role needed someone "very determined and very tough," to balance the heroic character of the ex-convict. "The contrast worked very well. But Shirley Booth wanted to be a nice Mother Superior — and you couldn't have two goody-goodies. There was no conflict."[29]

Styne, who'd lobbied for Ethel Merman to play the Mother Superior, concurred. "Shirley's a buttercup," he later said, "bad picking for that part." Equally displeased with the choice of Al Freeman, Jr., whom he thought lacked the gentle and noble qualities that character needed, Styne said, "I knew we were dead from the first week of rehearsal."[30]

With *Look to the Lilies* a goner, Shirley took her usual turn in summer stock. In July, she was onstage at the Westport Country Playhouse, starring in a new comedy by James Elward, *Best of Friends*. Shirley played the wife of a well-known author, who comes back into her life several years after he was supposedly killed in a plane crash. Complications ensue when her husband, played by Donald Woods, asks her for a divorce so that he can marry his current mistress. Also in the cast were Patrick McVey, Jo Henderson, and Jennifer Warren. In August, the show moved on to the Pocono Playhouse. *Best of Friends* was being eyed for a Broadway run, but this did not materialize.

Later that year, however, Shirley toplined a Broadway revival of Noël Coward's 1925 comedy *Hay Fever*, achieving an even shorter run. Her character, Judith Bliss, was an actress whose flair for drama was as apparent in her private life as it was onstage. The plot revolves around the complications that ensue when Judith, her son and daughter all invite house guests to the family estate for the weekend.

Though the production boasted some impressive talent, including a then little-known Sam Waterston, the play didn't seem to catch the interest of Broadway audiences in 1970. Looking back on that production, she would later say, "It was a lead balloon, dear, to put the very best face on it. We had a strange assortment of dialects in that play, and Noel Coward takes a very light touch, which the director didn't have."[31] Most New York critics also considered her miscast in the production, feeling that, despite her own undeniable star status, she was ill-suited to play the elegant and dreamy actress character that Coward had based on his friend Laurette Taylor.

"Shirley Booth is a natural comedian and often a touching character actress," said her *Time of the Cuckoo* director Harold Clurman in analyzing the problem, "but she is not a *poseuse*, an actressy actress. Her forte is the middle class, and she is out of her element in this play."[32]

Shirley would later refer to this period as her "Gobi desert" years. She was having a

Shirley played the Mother Superior in *Look to the Lilies,* her next-to-last Broadway outing. She is pictured with co-star Al Freeman, Jr.

difficult time keeping busy as an actress. Many of the roles available for actresses in the late 1960s and early 1970s offended her sensibilities. She saw Jane Fonda's critically acclaimed 1971 film *Klute*, in which Fonda played a hard-edged prostitute, and pronounced it "pornographic."[33] On Broadway, shows like *Grin and Bare It*, in which the entire cast performed key scenes in the nude, existed on a planet completely removed from the theater she had once known.

Shirley could still remember playing Sadie Thompson in *Rain* as a young leading lady in stock, and the audience shock that produced audible gasps when she addressed Reverend Davidson as "you psalmsing son of a...," though prevailing censorship dictated that another actor cut in before she finished speaking the phrase.

In 1971, she was angered to hear a television commercial for Colgate-Palmolive's Burst laundry detergent, one that featured an endorsement from none other than "Hazel." Shirley, who had nothing to do with the promotion, and said she had "refused enormous sums" to do TV commercials, filed a $4 million lawsuit against Colgate and the Ted Bates advertising agency. "I think it's hard enough to keep the mystique of the theater going without commercials," she said.[34] Court testimony elicited an admission from the actress who'd voiced Hazel for the commercials that she'd based her performance on Shirley's, but Booth lost her case nonetheless when it was demonstrated that the ad agency producing the commercials had properly licensed Ted Key's copyrighted character.

Though TV audiences around the country continued to see Shirley in syndicated reruns of *Hazel*, summer stock would be her chief professional activity in the early 1970s. While her Broadway revival of *Hay Fever* had not been a success, there was still an audience in other American cities happy to see stars appear on local stages in familiar roles. The fall of 1971 found Shirley touring in a revival of *Harvey*, opposite actor Gig Young. Publicly she had only praise for Young.

"Gig is wonderful in the part," she told reporter Bob MacKenzie. "Better than Jimmy Stewart, in my opinion. Jimmy always seemed competent to cope with whatever might happen, but Elwood is really beyond coping. He has a mystical quality about him, that dreaminess. Gig has that wonderful sense of whimsy, that faraway quality."[35] Offstage, according to Young's biographer, the actor's growing problem with alcohol made the entire production a difficult one.

Still, for Shirley, there were compensations. She particularly enjoyed the show's run in San Francisco, where she had previously played in productions of *Come Back, Little Sheba*, *The Desk Set*, and *The Philadelphia Story*. The management of the Raphael Hotel allowed her to keep her poodle in her hotel room, much to Shirley's delight. "My dog is beautifully trained and it's better than traveling with a gigolo," she joked.[36]

The following summer, Shirley agreed to play the lead in a new show at the Ogunquit Playhouse, *Mourning in a Funny Hat*. Actress-comedienne Dody Goodman, known to audiences for her many guest appearances on Jack Parr's *Tonight Show*, and later for a featured role in *Mary Hartman, Mary Hartman*, was the author of the play, which she had based on her mother's experiences adjusting to life after being widowed. Shirley would play the lead, Rachel Gibson, a woman who resists the efforts of friends and family to plan her life for her. She liked the role, with one small exception—a line of dialogue that called for her to say the word "crap."

As an actress, and frequent talk show guest, Goodman's specialty was dithery confusion. As a playwright, having her first show produced, she was apparently made of sterner stuff. Hearing that Shirley balked at saying "crap," Goodman mounted the stage, looked

her star in the eye, and said firmly, "Honey, I'm not asking you to hold it in your hand—
I'm just asking you to *say* it!"[37]

Reviews for the show itself were mixed, but those for Shirley were not. "There is no
question at all about Miss Booth's ability as an actress for she is superb," said the reviewer
for the *Kennebec Journal*.[38]

As it turned out, playing a recent widow in *Mourning in a Funny Hat* was a harbin-
ger of things to come. Just when she was adjusting to the idea of occupying herself with
summer stock theater, then spending winters in solitude at her home near Palm Springs,
Shirley received an unexpected offer to do a second weekly TV series.

10. Living with Grace

In the early 1970s, producer Norman Lear's successes with *All in the Family* (CBS, 1971–79) and *Sanford and Son* (NBC, 1972–77) had started a trend toward adapting sitcoms from popular British shows. ABC took a liking to the idea of turning *For the Love of Ada,* an English comedy about the adventures of a lively, fun-loving widow, into an American sitcom to be called *A Touch of Grace.*

Co-executive producer Herman Rush had previously worked as a packaging agent, and had played a key role in turning England's *Till Death Do Us Part* into America's *All in the Family.* Now, venturing out on his own, he acquired the American rights to *Ada,* which he thought had the potential to become as big a hit with stateside audiences. "This is basically a love story of two elderly people who think young," Rush explained. "It uses the generation gap, but in reverse. Her daughter and son-in-law are young, but they think old. Grace is 63, but she thinks and acts young."[1]

He'd devised that synopsis for the purpose of attracting Shirley Booth to the star role. As it turned out, the sales job wasn't necessary. Rush's partner, Ted Bergmann, flew to Cape Cod for a meeting with Shirley, and was happily surprised. Shirley liked the pilot script, and though she had previously called it unlikely that she would ever do a second television series, accepted the lead role of Grace Simpson. She viewed Grace as similar to Hazel Burke with her lack of pretension and essential honesty. Co-starring in the show were character actor J. Pat O'Malley, as Grace's love interest Herbert Morrison, Marian Mercer (who'd appeared with Shirley in *Hay Fever*), as Grace's stodgy daughter Myra, and Warren Berlinger as her son-in-law Walter. Carl Reiner, who'd helmed the highly acclaimed *Dick Van Dyke Show* (CBS, 1961–66), signed on to direct the pilot episode.

A reporter visiting the *Grace* set in February watched in fascination as Shirley rehearsed a monologue in which Grace visits the cemetery and tells her late husband Henry of her new romance. When she was finished, series producer Saul Turteltaub had tears in his eyes, and said to partner Bernie Orenstein, "By God, that woman can act."[2]

She was equally at ease with the script's comedic aspects. It's at the cemetery that Grace meets Herbert, who is employed there. "But Mother," says daughter Myra, "he's a gravedigger!" Replies Grace with a shrug, "Well, it's a good steady job!"

In another bit, she bemoans her subsistence on a monthly stipend of $120.00 from Social Security, cracking, "What kind of security is that?" Later, discussing a friend who's endured multiple surgeries, having various organs removed, transplanted, or repaired, Grace comments, "She must be almost completely hollow by now."

Artist's rendering of the cast of Shirley's 1973 ABC sitcom *A Touch of Grace*.

Despite the networks' usual fears about older stars, the show appealed to a wide range of viewers. "There are a lot of kids in the audience when we tape the show," said Orenstein, "and they really react when Shirley and Pat do a scene together."[3]

Shirley's only quibble with the series was the more permissive dialogue she found creeping into the scripts, which she viewed as the producers' misguided need to compete with shows like *All in the Family.* In her own way, the star set about to tackle the problem. "I am the censor," she told an interviewer. "I'm trying very hard to moderate that risqué element in the scripts. It takes a while to change things and a woman is supposed to do things gently. I think I'll be able to do it."[4]

In the meantime, Grace's eagerness to become a grandmother was a running joke in the show's early scripts, leading to some dialogue that never would have passed NBC's censors during the *Hazel* days. Bemoaning daughter Myra's failure to conceive, Shirley's character says, "I don't know what you and Walter do in bed. He's doing everything right, isn't he? ... I blame those electric blankets. In my day it was either sex or shiver." Though she enjoyed playing the *au courant* Grace, Shirley admitted that her own values were pretty much what they had always been. "I know I'll be accused of being old-fashioned and square," she said, "but I don't approve of couples living together and having children without marriage. I don't approve of four-letter words and explicit sex in films, or nudity in films or on stage." Calling the Broadway hit *Oh, Calcutta!* "disgusting," she added, "Sometimes I fear mankind is losing its sense of dignity."[5]

TV production methods had changed since Shirley starred in *Hazel.* While that show was filmed like a motion picture, on a soundstage, *Grace* was videotaped. Using the technique then in vogue, Shirley and her co-stars performed the show before a live studio audience. Tapings were on Tuesdays, with performances at 5:30 P.M. and again at 8 P.M., the final air show cut together from the best moments of the two performances.

Writer-producer Saul Turteltaub, whose other sitcom credits include *That Girl* (ABC, 1966–71) and *Sanford and Son* (NBC, 1972–77), has only fond memories of working with Shirley on *A Touch of Grace.* "We all fell in love with her," he says today. "She was a nice person, a good person, and perfect for the part." The cast and crew recognized that she had high standards, and strove to emulate them. "You wanted her to respect you," Turteltaub says.[6]

Shirley liked her co-workers, and often accepted a standing invitation to go out with them for a celebration once the show was in the can. After a long day, though, she felt the strain. "On Tuesday nights," she sighed, "I sometimes feel as though I've been beaten with sticks."[7]

If the 74-year-old star found the workload challenging, it wasn't readily apparent to her colleagues. "I don't remember her once, ever, missing a line," says Turteltaub.[8]

Like her *Hazel* co-stars, the actors on *Grace* were respectful of Shirley and her well of experience. Of playing opposite her, Marian Mercer said, "If Shirley thinks you're saying it wrong, she tells you. If you're smart, you listen."[9]

Her leading man J. Pat O'Malley had been in semi-retirement, living near San Juan Capistrano, when the series role came along. "This thing came out of the blue," he said, "and when they mentioned Shirley Booth, I said, 'Oh, boy, this is really something.' She's wonderful, we have two of the best writers in the business. They make the show folksy, but believable."[10]

O'Malley liked the fact that *A Touch of Grace* was lighter in tone than shows like *All in the Family.* "These shows are getting a little preachy and political," the actor opined.

A Touch of Grace: Grace (Shirley Booth) agrees to take an overnight trip with beau Herbert (J. Pat O'Malley, at left), in "The Weekend." Also pictured are co-stars Marian Mercer (Myra) and Warren Berlinger (Walter).

"People want to sit down and be entertained. People need to laugh; they don't need all the problems of the world."[11]

A Touch of Grace was paired with another new entry, *Here We Go Again,* which starred Larry Hagman and Diane Baker as newlyweds faced with constant intrusions and problems caused by their ex-spouses. ABC unveiled both shows on January 20, 1973, filling the Saturday night hour just vacated by *Alias Smith and Jones* (1971–73). According to the network's copywriters, in a *TV Guide* ad announcing the show's debut: "You'll love Shirley Booth as the lively widow whose modern ideas shock her 'young fogey' family."

That magazine's longtime critic, Cleveland Amory, did in fact love Shirley, though not her show. While he liked Booth's performances, he found the supporting characters of Wally and Myra "so square they are less funny than pathetic." As for the show's scripts, said Amory, noting the frequent gags about gravedigging, "It's too bad they couldn't inter, along with the jokes here, most of the plots. If it's possible to base a whole episode on what is a tasteless idea to begin with, these writers will do it."[12]

The *Chicago Tribune*'s Clarence Petersen thought the show flawed, particularly in the development of the younger characters, but said, "Still, Miss Booth and O'Malley dominate the show, and they are just marvelous, totally believable, funny when they should be funny, touching when they should be touching. They are charming, interesting, human; they are never abrasive ... They exhibit the serenity one hopes for in his own old age."[13]

One dissenting voice who liked neither the show nor its star's performance was *The Los Angeles Times*' Burt Prelutsky, who earned the small distinction of giving *A Touch of Grace* perhaps its meanest review. Calling the show even "hokier and dumber" than its time slot competitor, *Bridget Loves Bernie,* Prelutsky complained, "You sit there trying to remember how great an actress Shirley Booth used to be — but watching her simultaneously fumble her lines and trying to keep her dentures from falling out makes it difficult."[14]

Still, the show did have its followers, and not all of them were in Grace and Herbert's age range. Said a *TV Guide* reader, "I am 22 years old and I absolutely love the show. Every time I watch it I see my grandmother who is 70 and a swinger, in the sense that she enjoys life now as she did when she was 50. My grandmother lives in Florida and I live in New York so I don't get to see her very often. But when I watch *Grace* it's like she is right here with me."[15]

Unfortunately, the powerhouse *All in the Family* gave CBS a virtual stranglehold on the Saturday night audience. Younger viewers, or those who wanted more action than Lear's sitcom offered, changed the channel to NBC, for Jack Webb's *Emergency!* (1972–77), leaving few to sample Shirley's new comedy and its companion show.

Ratings from the show's premiere were discouraging. According to the *Los Angeles Times,* Shirley's new show placed at #54 its first week out. The shows flanking it on the ABC schedule, however, did even worse, with *Here We Go Again,* going head-to-head with *All in the Family,* only one step short of the bottom of the ratings chart at #64, with only an audience share of only 17. Julie Andrews' ABC variety hour, which followed *A Touch of Grace,* was also in the cellar, at #60. Subsequent weeks showed similarly dismal results for the new ABC Saturday lineup.

By late February, ABC and its competitors were still tinkering with their fall schedules, but the low ratings of Shirley's show made it a long shot to be renewed for the 1973–74 season. Still, as syndicated TV columnist Bettelou Peterson reported, *Grace* "has been outpointed by the competition but the general feeling is that the show 'works' and Shirley Booth is an audience pleaser. She may get another chance."[16]

However, Ms. Peterson's prediction failed to come true, and ABC did not place *A Touch of Grace* on its fall schedule. By the time a splashy profile of Shirley appeared in a May issue of *TV Guide,* trumpeting her return to television, the fate of *A Touch of Grace* was already sealed. The final of the series' 13 installments showed Grace accepting Herbert's marriage proposal, but not enough viewers were there to witness it. Both of ABC's new sitcoms were off the air by early summer, probably before many viewers knew they existed. There was brief talk of a letter-writing campaign to convince the network to reinstate *A Touch of Grace,* but nothing came of it.

Ironically, *TV Guide*'s Arnold Hano had asked Shirley during their interview whether she could see herself doing *A Touch of Grace* for five years, as she had done with *Hazel.* "Think? I know I could," Shirley said. "And I'd be privileged."[17]

That summer, as Shirley's TV comeback was winding down, *Come Back, Little Sheba* playwright William Inge committed suicide in Los Angeles. He was said to have been plunged into depression by critical reaction to his novels, and had recently been hospitalized with a drug overdose. The 60-year-old playwright killed himself with fumes from his car in the garage of his Sunset Strip apartment. A few months later, Shirley's original *Sheba* co-star Sidney Blackmer was also gone, dying of cancer in October 1973.

After enjoying a comfortable five-year run with *Hazel,* Shirley was hurt to have *A Touch of Grace* end so abruptly. Nevertheless, another project did come along in the wake of her series' cancellation. She accepted an offer to voice Mrs. Claus in the Rankin-Bass special *The Year without a Santa Claus,* which made its debut on ABC-TV during the 1974 holiday season. The one-hour program tells the story of what happened when Santa Claus comes down with a cold at Christmastime, decides his work is no longer meaningful to people, and takes to his bed for a sabbatical. Mrs. Claus enlists the aid of two elves and Vixen, the reindeer, to help restore the holiday spirit.

The program, which was created with stop-motion animation, was adapted from a 1956 book by Phyllis McGinley, and offered six original songs, as well as some holiday favorites. Aside from Shirley, who narrated and sang, the cast included Mickey Rooney as Santa, as well as Dick Shawn and George S. Irving as the memorable "Snow Miser" and "Heat Miser," still fondly remembered today by a generation of baby boomer kids.

According to an ABC press release, it was Shirley's admiration for author Phyllis McGinley, a Pulitzer Prize winner, which led her to accept the role of Mrs. Claus. "I was very impressed with much of her writing," Shirley said, "and was carried away with her when I read 'Saint-Watching.' I wanted to be associated with her work and was anxious to do the show."[18]

She was intrigued by the techniques used to assemble the musical performances, which were combined from multiple recording sessions. "Do you know that I have not ever met [Mickey] Rooney, but yet in the show I end up singing a song with him? He was in Chicago somewhere and I was in New York, but we do a duet in the show."[19]

The Year without a Santa Claus became a holiday perennial that played every holiday season for years to come, and was subsequently released on video and DVD. It was also Shirley Booth's television swan song. By the mid–1970s, Shirley's career was essentially over. In her late seventies, her health was beginning to falter, and she would spend the remainder of her life quietly at her home in Cape Cod.

In 1974, she suffered a stroke that left her paralyzed for a time. She rallied somewhat, and publicly she put a good face on her situation. "Oh, once in a while I have to slow down," she told a syndicated columnist in 1975, "but other than that I'm fine. I won't be able to do another TV series like *Hazel*—it's just too grueling. But I'm looking forward to guest appearances and maybe even to a movie."[20] Sadly, this was not to be.

Shirley's liking for solitude frequently caused her to be labeled as "lonely," a tag she disputed. "That's wrong," she said. "I'm alone a lot, but I'm never lonely. I find hundreds and millions of things to do. I'm very sorry for people who can't be happy alone. Up here [on the Cape] there are lots of widows, and many of them had never in their lives prepared to be alone. They're going to pieces, and it's just too bad. They start to drink, and they go up and lock themselves in their rooms for weeks at a time."[21]

Though out of the public eye, Shirley was still held in high esteem, as demonstrated by her 1979 induction into the Theater Hall of Fame. The organization, founded in 1972, had taken a hiatus in recent years from announcing new members, due to lack of funding. Shirley, who was chosen back in 1974, was part of an illustrious group of 51 inductees including Leonard Bernstein, Tennessee Williams, David Merrick, and Jessica Tandy. Also on the honor roll were Booth friends and colleagues like 82-year-old Morris Carnovsky (her co-star from *My Sister Eileen*), Abe Burrows (who'd written for her on *Duffy's Tavern*), and her Cape Cod neighbor Julie Harris. Shirley did not attend the award ceremony at the Uris Theater, leaving Celeste Holm to accept in her absence.

In the 1980s, her health began to give way, and for the last several years of her life she seldom left her home on Cape Cod. For as long as she was able, however, she continued to putter happily around her house. In 1984, having just turned 86, she told a *New York Times* reporter that she "looked like a leper," having tangled with a patch of poison ivy in her garden, but that "her spotty appearance had not affected her spirits or her future digging and weeding plans."[22]

She spoke regularly by telephone with old friends like Charles Nelson Reilly and *Hazel*'s Don DeFore. A neighbor with whom Shirley became friendly was Frances Hammons, a founder and columnist for the community newspaper, the *Cape Cod Chronicle*. Hammons described Shirley as "a delightful person to meet," saying that she and the actress enjoyed exchanging books, and talking about antiques.[23] Shirley also enjoyed regular visits with a longtime friend, actress Julie Harris, who owned a home nearby on the Cape.

By the mid–1980s, Shirley's eyesight had begun to fade, forcing her to give up some favorite activities, like needlework and painting, but she plowed ahead. Animals continued to be a great source of contentment to her, and during this period she was mistress to two Siamese cats, Cash and Carry. A 1988 article in a supermarket tabloid told readers that TV's *Hazel* was now blind, and suffering from the results of a stroke, but proclaimed that she hadn't given up.

"Shirley has a terrific attitude, even though she can hardly walk since her stroke last year and has lost her sight," said neighbor and friend Rose Caliri. "Shirley has absolutely no self-pity ... She says she's had a very full life and has no regrets."[24] The *Globe* article made Shirley seem plucky indeed for an 81-year-old woman. Little did the reporter or her readers know that the actress was in fact 90 years old.

Shirley died of natural causes at her home in North Chatham on October 16, 1992. Her sister, Jean Coe, told reporters that she had suffered a broken hip a year or so earlier, further restricting her activities. Most obituaries noted that her age, according to the 1907 date listed in reference books, would have been 85. However, a spokesman for the Nickerson Funeral Home told reporters she was 94 years old, confirming her August 30, 1898 birth date. After a private memorial service, she was buried in the Baker family plot at Mount Hebron Cemetery in Upper Montclair, New Jersey. The family asked that any donations in Shirley's memory be made to the American Heart Association.

Shirley and friend at home in Cape Cod. Her inscription apologizes for her "terrible" scrawl, explaining, "I am legally blind" (Michael D. Strain collection).

According to her hometown newspaper, the *Cape Cod Chronicle,* "In recent years Ms. Booth had been reclusive and was seen around town infrequently ... Chatham friends remember Ms. Booth as a quiet and unassuming woman who pretty much kept to herself."[25]

Though Shirley's passing was covered by all the major wire services, as well as urban newspapers around the U.S., the amount and type of coverage varied. Surprisingly, her *New York Times* obituary was a relatively brief one, running less than 1000 words. Had Sam Zolotow, the *Times* reporter who'd so ably covered Shirley's Broadway career for many years, still been on the staff, it seems likely that a fuller and more thoughtful appreciation of her work would have appeared. Unlike most other media outlets, however, the *Times* did not lay the emphasis primarily on Shirley's television work, not even mentioning *Hazel* until the fifth paragraph of her obituary.

That Shirley Booth will not soon be forgotten is evident from the comments that have surfaced in the years since her retirement whenever her classic stage roles are assumed by other performers. In the spring of 1993, *Three Men on a Horse* was revived by Tony Randall's National Actors Theatre, with Ellen Greene stepping into the featured role of Mabel that brought Shirley her first major success in 1935. *The Philadelphia Story* was revived on Broadway in 1980, featuring Mary Louise Wilson as Liz Imbrie, but lasted only a few weeks. Perhaps most frequently reprised, however, is *Come Back, Little Sheba*.

When *Sheba* has resurfaced, the actress playing Shirley's Tony and Oscar-winning role has often been unfavorably compared to the original. A TV-movie version in December 1977 was mostly well-received, with critics praising the performances of Joanne Woodward as Lola, opposite Sir Laurence Olivier as Doc Delaney, and Carrie Fisher, at the height of her *Star Wars* fame, as Marie. However, *Time* magazine damned actress Shirley Knight with faint praise for her turn as Lola in a 1984 production at New York's Roundabout Theater, crediting her with "attain[ing] a lumpish sweetness,"[26] if not much else. Reviewing a 1987 Los Angeles production, with *Cagney and Lacey* star Tyne Daly in the role, the *Los Angeles Times'* Dan Sullivan thought the performances lacked strength and vigor, robbing the play of its full import, and concluded that Shirley was still "the definitive Lola."[27] Perhaps the oddest rethinking of Inge's play was the 1974 musical *Sheba,* starring actress-comedienne Kaye Ballard, which died a quick death in Chicago amidst poor reviews. In the fall of 2007, yet another (non-musical) revival of *Come Back, Little Sheba* was Broadway bound, after a successful run at Los Angeles' Kirk Douglas Theatre. Ironically, the role of vulnerable Lola had once again been cast with an actress best known to audiences for playing a tough female cop on television. This time, actress S. Epatha Merkerson (*Law and Order*) was set to play Shirley's role.

Shirley Booth does have a star on the Hollywood Walk of Fame, though surprisingly it is not for her television stardom, nor for her Broadway career, but for her work in motion pictures. However, her 1992 obituary in the *Los Angeles Times,* while duly noting her many roles and awards, concluded that "the diminutive tragicomic will probably go down in show business annals as the lovably cantankerous Hazel."[28] *People* and *Entertainment Weekly* took a similar stance. Both titled their memorial articles "Maid to Order," devoting almost the entire text to a discussion of Shirley's television work.

In the years since Shirley's death, most of her castmates from *Hazel,* as well as many of her theatrical colleagues, have passed away as well. *Hazel* co-star Don DeFore died of cardiac arrest in December 1993, at the age of 80. Several months later, Burt Lancaster, her leading man from the film version of *Come Back, Little Sheba,* passed away as well. The last major survivor of the original *Hazel* cast, Whitney Blake (Dorothy) died in 2002, at the age of 76; aside from her work in *Hazel,* she was acknowledged as co-creator of the hit sitcom *One Day at a Time* (CBS, 1975–84). Amazingly, Shirley's 1930s colleague from *Three Men on a Horse,* writer-producer George Abbott, survived her, passing away on January 31, 1995, at the age of 107.

Shirley in her iconic role as TV's *Hazel*

However, there are still a number of friends and colleagues who remember Shirley with fondness, and express admiration for her work. Actor Dick Van Patten, with whom Shirley worked in radio's *Duffy's Tavern,* lost touch with her in later years. Nonetheless, he vividly remembers a turning point in his career that he attributes to Shirley's influence. In the early 1970s, when Van Patten was appearing in a West Coast production of Elaine May's *Adaptations,* Shirley attended a performance and encouraged a studio casting director to do likewise. From that encounter came an offer for Van Patten to play a role in the CBS sitcom *Arnie* (1970–72). Though that series was short-lived, it represented the actor's first major exposure in Hollywood after a career spent doing mostly live theater and television in New York. Today, Van Patten feels that the successful television career he ultimately enjoyed, including his starring role in ABC's *Eight Is Enough* (1977–81), began with that favor done for him by Shirley.

"I really owe everything to Shirley Booth," he says today.[29]

Julie Harris, still living near Shirley's former home at Cape Cod, is another admirer. Though the two stage stars never performed together, they greatly admired each other's work, and their paths had crossed numerous times over the years. Fellow nominees for the Best Actress Academy Award in 1953, they were also both Emmy nominees in 1962. In that instance, both ladies won a Best Actress trophy — Shirley, in the Continuing Performance category for *Hazel,* and Harris, for her one-time role in a television version of *Victoria Regina.* In 1973, both starred in ABC sitcoms — Shirley's *A Touch of Grace* ran from January to June, while Julie Harris starred in *Thicker Than Water* that summer. Today, Miss Harris says of her one-time neighbor, "Shirley Booth was a consummate actress. Her role in *Come Back, Little Sheba* will be in my memory always."[30]

And, of course, there is still *Hazel.* If not the most substantial achievement of her much-honored career, it still represents a welcome opportunity for new generations to experience an unforgettable actress. As for Shirley herself, if ultimately she is to be best remembered for her famous television character, it's unlikely that she would have any strong objections to that. "I'd rather have affection than admiration," she said in 1971. "Affection is warmer, and it lasts longer."[31]

Most of the viewers, critics, and colleagues who watched at her work over the course of a fifty-five year career would probably say that she had — and deserved — plenty of both.

Appendix A: Broadway Performances

Hell's Bells (1925)

CREDITS: A comedy in three acts by Barry Conners. Produced by Herman Gantvoort; staged by John Hayden.

CAST: Eddie Garvie (D.O. O'Donnell), Tom H. Walsh ("Jap" Stillson), Humphrey Bogart (Jimmy Todhunter), Shirley Booth (Nan Winchester), Violet Dunn (Gladys Todhunter), Camilla Crume (Mrs. Amos Todhunter), Virginia Howell (Abigail Stillson), Ernest Pollock (Police Chief Pitkins), Joseph Greene (Horace E. Pitkins), Olive May (Mrs. Buck), Fletcher Harvey (Dr. Bushnell), James Cherry (Halligan), Clinton Self (Swartz), Converse Tyler (Riordon)

HISTORY: Opened January 26, 1925, at Wallack's Theatre. 120 performances.

SUMMARY: Elderly "Jap" Stillson and his friend pay a visit to his hometown, where they lead people to believe they have struck it rich with mining investments. Stillson's relatives plot to confine him to an institution so that they can assume control of his wealth.

NOTES: *Hell's Bells* originally toured under the title *Fool's Gold*.... In Shirley's Broadway debut, she plays an ingénue opposite young leading man Humphrey Bogart.

REVIEWS: "*Hell's Bells* is a clean, funny play, but Barry Conners has overwritten it and its direction hasn't improved matters a great deal ... several charming love scenes between the juveniles."—*Variety*, 1/28/25 / "*Hell's Bells* chimed with a doubtful harmony.... The playing ... was uneventful."—*Time*, 2/9/25

Laff That Off (1925)

CREDITS: A comedy in three acts by Don Mullally. Produced by Earl Carroll; staged by Roy Walling.

CAST: Alan Bunce (Leo Mitchell), Shirley Booth (Peggy Bryant), Thomas W. Ross (Rob't Elton Morse), Wyrley Birch (Mike Connelly), Hattie Foley (Mrs. Connelly), Norval Keedwell (Lindau), Pauline Drake (Emmy)

HISTORY: Opened November 2, 1925, at Wallack's Theatre. Produced by Earl Carroll; staged by Roy Walling. 263 performances.

SUMMARY: Three bachelors who share quarters in a boardinghouse offer shelter to pretty, down-and-out Peggy Bryant. While two of the men promptly fall for Peggy's charms, it is Leo, who rescued her, whom she prefers. After leaving to seek her fortune in Hollywood, Peggy returns two years later on Christmas Eve. Now a successful actress, Peggy nonetheless wants to resolve the unfinished business with the young man she left behind.

REVIEWS: "...a well-made comedy. It runs the gamut of the comic emotions; tears and smiles are neatly alternated and mingled."—*New York Times*, 11/3/25 / "The company is only mildly talented."—*Time*, 11/16/25 / "Shirley Booth plays the girl attractively."—*Charleston Daily Mail*, 11/15/25

Buy, Buy, Baby (1926)

CREDITS: A comedy in three acts by Russell Medcraft and Norma Mitchell, based on a play by Francis R. Bellamy and Lawton Mackall. Produced by Bertram Harrison.

CAST: Laura Hope Crews (Janice Marvin), Alison Skipworth (Esmeralda Pottle), Malcolm Duncan (Carteret Flotten), Thurston Hall (Henry Marvin), Edwin Nicander (Ronald Bradford), Shirley Booth (Betty Hamilton), Verree Teasdale (Pauline Lunt), Mabel Colcord (Norah), Maurice Burke (Harold Boland), Charles Mather (Burglar)

HISTORY: Opened October 7, 1926, at the Princess Theatre. 12 performances.

SUMMARY: Three young couples compete for a prize to be awarded by their wealthy aunt to the first of them to produce an heir. Nephew Harold has kept his marriage to Betty, a secretary, secret, but their baby wins them the million-dollar reward.

NOTE: The show's original title was *Pay to Bearer*.

REVIEWS: "The authors of *Cradle Snatchers* have again turned their hands to a farce of innuendo, and the resulting play was revealed ... before an audience which seemed to find a good deal of it funny.... A cast of generally excellent players has been encouraged to shout from the rostrum the sturdy nuances of the comedy, and situations already obvious are thus additionally pointed." *New York Times*, 10/8/26 / "...before the evening is over *Buy, Buy, Baby* becomes a deadly bore."—*The New Yorker*, 10/16/26

High Gear (1927)

CREDITS: A comedy in three acts by Larry E. Johnson. Staged by Roy Walling.

CAST: Shirley Booth (Mary Marshall), William Shelley (Harvey P. Marshall), Erman Seavey (Uncle Elmer), Edith Gordon (Stella), Olga Krolow (Sylvia Allen), Royal C. Stout (Limpy Lanigan), Peggy Shannon (Florence Ainslee), Cecil W. Secrest (Dr. Gerald Niles), Martin Malloy (Officer Shea)

HISTORY: Opened October 6, 1927, at Wallack's Theatre. 20 performances.

NOTE: A flop on Broadway, this play later toured under the more provocative title *Mary's Other Husband*.

SUMMARY: A young lady with an overactive imagination has written letters to her uncle boasting of the privileged life she and her wealthy husband lead, then must keep up the charade when the uncle arrives for a visit.

REVIEW: "As the fluttery and wide-eyed young wife, Shirley Booth contributes an acceptable performance in a role that easily might be made to seem more silly than it is."—*New York Times*, 10/7/27

The War Song (1928)

CREDITS: A play in three acts by the Spewacks and George Jessel. Staged by Albert Lewis.

CAST: George Jessel (Eddie Rosen), Clara Langsner (Mrs. Rosen), Shirley Booth (Emily Rosen), Lola Lane (Sally Moss), Raymond Guion (Sid Swanson), William Gargan (Pvt. James Perkins), Joseph Latham (Pvt. Harris Winters), Edward Leiter (Bob Elkins), Paul Ker (Herman Wagner), T.F. Benson (Pvt. Chickopopolis), Patricia Kenny (Mrs. James Perkins), Ted Athey (Dr. Hayman), Eda Heinemann (Social Worker), Paul O'Brien (Cpl. Ringling), Edwin Jerome (Mr. King, of the YMCA), Charles Wilson (Capt. Conroy), Frank Spelvin (Civilian Officer), Lt. Paul Schultz (German Officer), Col. Edmund Loewe (Major Von Stoch), Lt. Hans (German Sergeant), Capt. Herman Lehmann (Brinkerhoff), Charles Peters (M.P.), Harry Von Zynde, Carl Worms (German Guards)

HISTORY: Opened September 24, 1928, at the National Theatre. 80 performances.

SUMMARY: A young Jewish songwriter leaves behind his terminally ill mother and pregnant sister to serve overseas in World War I, where he is imprisoned in a German prison camp.

NOTE: According to *The War Song*'s program notes, some of the soldiers seen in the prison camp scenes in Act Two were themselves veterans, "supplied through courtesy of U.S. Veterans' Bureau."

REVIEWS: "*The War Song* ... is an exceedingly interesting entertainment and an effective theatrical invention."—*New York Times*, 9/25/28 / "[This] is what may seem a terrible play, sight unseen, but each role has been given to a thorough player."—*Time*, 10/8/28

Claire Adams (1929)

CREDITS: A play by Daniel N. Rubin. Produced by Tom Weatherly; staged by Priestly Morrison.

CAST: Mildred MacLeod (Claire Adams), Charles Starrett (Gene Adams), Buford Armitage (Clyde Price), Earl McDonald (Jack), Thelma [Shirley] Booth (Leah), Edward Broadley (Cramer), Charles Ritchie (Ted Roper), E.M. Johnstone (Doyle), Frank Charlton (Brent), Jack McGann (Vincent)

HISTORY: Opened November 19, 1929, at the Biltmore Theatre. 7 performances.

SUMMARY: A melodrama about a bored wife who persuades her writer husband to relocate from Texas to Greenwich Village, then stirs up trouble when their new life doesn't prove as stimulating as she'd hoped. When the unfaithful Claire compels her lover to stab a former boyfriend, husband Gene is left to write up his wife's downfall for the newspaper where he now works.

NOTES: Shirley reverted to her given name of Thelma in being billed for this obscure production, which opened and closed in less than a week. The show was originally announced as *Undertow*. On the day that the show played its final performance, she married Ed Gardner.

REVIEWS: "One of the most tragic things about Mr. Daniel Rubin's tragedies is that they make people laugh."—*The New Yorker*, 11/30/29 / "It is a sordid, ordinary tragedy, conceived and acted without much imagination."—*Time*, 12/2/29

School for Virtue (1931)

CREDITS: A comedy in three acts by Arthur Ebenhack. Opened April 21, 1931, at the Longacre

Theatre. Produced by Edward Casey; staged by Victor Morley.

CAST: Buford Armitage (Bud Heasley), Evelyn Wade (Clarinda Robbins), Shirley Booth (Marg), William Atlee (Ron Sinton), Clarence Rock (Ray Graylen), Robert W. Craig (Tom Raydon), Barbara Graft (Mrs. Taylor), J.C. Osborne (Bill), Leopold Badia (Grocery Boy), Ruth Baumon, Elma Mirian, Merry Wagner, Betty Worth (Ladies of the Evening)

HISTORY: Opened April 21, 1931, at the Longacre Theatre. 7 performances.

SUMMARY: This obscure comedy was billed as "a comedy of love pedagogy," concerning a young woman who falls in with the fast crowd in Greenwich Village, and the man who tries to mend her ways.

NOTE: *School for Virtue* was first tried in an amateur production at Greenwich Village's Cherry Lane Theatre prior to this Broadway production.

REVIEW: "A vague and nasty little comedy [that] makes for a thoroughly dull and dispiriting evening in the theatre.... Although not all of them were sure of their lines, [the cast] did what they could for the play in their acting."—*New York Times*, 4/22/31

The Camels Are Coming (1931)

CREDITS: A comedy in three acts by Don Mullally; staged and produced by Mullally.

CAST: J. Anthony Hughes (Terry Tracy), Shirley Booth (Bobby Marchante), Earl Simmons (Jim Waldrone), Joseph Greenwald (Milton Markowitz), Gita Zucker (Sylvia Markowitz), Clyde Stone (Bell Boy), Guido Alexander (Manny Manoff), Rose Mary King (Alice Buckley), Lionel Dante (Eddie Collins), Bill Vaughn (Glenn Thomas), Caroline Humphries (Millicent Bryant), Anthony Pawley (William Wallace), Thomas McQuillan (Matty Wolfe), Edward Marr (Clay Farrell), Jack Reed (Charlie Evans), Joe Gerson (Frank Smith)

HISTORY: Opened October 2, 1931, at the President Theatre. 11 performances.

SUMMARY: An aspiring playwright, commissioned by a rich businessman to write a play to order, struggles to reconcile his own creative instincts with the realities of the theatrical world, and the vagaries of his sponsor.

REVIEW: "Except for the fact that it is dull and obvious, Mr. Mullally's drama ... appears to be quite all right. It is acted in much the same spirit by a troupe of adequate performers."—*New York Times*, 10/3/31

Coastwise (1931)

CREDITS: A play in three acts by H.A. Archibald and Donn Mullally. Produced by Edward F. Gardner; staged by Mullally.

CAST: Shirley Booth (Annie Duval), Richard Stevenson (Alan Farquahar), Lucia Moore (Mrs. Farquahar), Gordon Hamilton (Nelson), Thomas McQuillan (Marty), Charles Gibney (Alec MacDonald), Priscilla Knowles (Minnie), Alexander Campbell (Roberts)

HISTORY: Opened November 30, 1931, at the Provincetown Theatre. 37 performances.

SUMMARY: In a remote section of British Columbia, a woman of easy virtue impulsively marries an Englishman from a socially prominent family.

NOTES: In preliminary announcements, *Coastwise* was titled *Two Shall Be Born*, and also *Coastwise Annie*, after Shirley's character. It reverted to the latter title after its first few performances. This was the first of two shows for which then-husband Ed Gardner served as Shirley's producer.

REVIEWS: "The producer of *Coastwise* has assembled a professional cast.... But they cannot hide the fact that *Coastwise* is a singularly tatterdemalion piece of writing."—*New York Times*, 12/1/31 / "Judgment of the cast probably unfair, because of the play, which Donn Mullally, co-author, did not direct well.... Shirley Booth may do in a better play."—*Variety*, 12/8/31

The Mask and the Face (1933)

CREDITS: A comedy in three acts by Luigi Chiarelli, adapted from the Italian by W. Somerset Maugham. Produced by the Theatre Guild (production committee, Theresa Helburn and Helen Westley); staged by Philip Moeller.

CAST: Judith Anderson (Savina Grazia), Stanley Ridges (Count Paolo Grazia), Leo G. Carroll (Cirillo Zanotti), Humphrey Bogart (Luciano Spina), Shirley Booth (Elisa Zanotti), Donald McClelland (Giorgio Alamari), Dorothy Patten (Marta Setta), Alice Reinheart (Wanda Sereni), Ernest Cossart (Marco Milotti), William Lovejoy (Giacomo), Joan Marion (Teresa)

HISTORY: Opened May 8, 1933, at the Guild Theatre. 40 performances.

NOTE: This was Shirley's first role for the Theatre Guild, a connection that would eventually lead to her being cast in *Come Back, Little Sheba*. For the second time, she played opposite future film star Bogart.

REVIEWS: "The acting of the cast raises *The Mask and the Face* above what properly appeared to be a not high level." *New York Times*, 5/9/33 / "*The Mask and the Face* is terrible."—*The New Yorker*, 5/20/33

After Such Pleasures (1934)

CREDITS: A comedy by Edward F. Gardner, based on the book by Dorothy Parker. Produced by A.L. Jones; directed by Gardner.

CAST: Vernon Biddle, Shirley Booth, Henriette Caperton, Kathleen Chase, Mary Farrell, Taylor Gordon, Enid Markey, Blossom McDonald, Lea Penman, Ackland Power, Al Reiser, Lee Reiser, Don Shelton, Felicia Sorel (Ensemble)

HISTORY: Opened February 7, 1934, at the Bijou Theatre. 23 performances.

SUMMARY: Based on the writings of Dorothy Parker, the show consisted of seven vignettes, mostly concerning male-female relationships: "A Young Lady from Paris," "Dusk Before Fireworks," "Here We Are," "Impressions of a Supper Club," "You Were Perfectly Fine," "Glory in the Daytime," and "The Mantle of Whistler."

REVIEW: "...a categorical drubbing of womanhood and all its works from A to Z."—*Time*, 2/19/34

Three Men on a Horse (1935)

CREDITS: A comedy by John Cecil Holm and George Abbott. Produced by Alex Yokel; directed by George Abbott.

CAST: William Lynn (Erwin Trowbridge), Sam Levene (Patsy), Shirley Booth (Mabel), Joyce Atling (Audrey Trowbridge), Teddy Hart (Frankie), James Lane (Harry), Millard Mitchell (Charlie), Fleming Ward (Clarence Dobbins), Edith Van Cleve (Gloria), Garson Kanin (Al), Frank Camp (Mr. Carver), Nick Wiger (Delivery Boy), J. Ascher Smith (Tailor), Margaret Smithers (Motel Maid)

HISTORY: Opened January 30, 1935, at the Playhouse Theatre. Produced by Alex Yokel; directed by George Abbott. 835 performances.

SUMMARY: A meek suburbanite with an unexpected talent for predicting the outcomes of horse races becomes involved with a trio of dubious characters hoping to profit from his skill.

NOTES: One of Broadway's longest-running shows, *Three Men on a Horse* played for almost two years, closing in January 1937. It was revived on Broadway in 1942, 1969-70, and in 1993. A film version was released by Warner Brothers in 1936, with Joan Blondell assuming Shirley's role as Mabel.

REVIEWS: "Shrewd and jocular horseplay ... lively performances..."—*New York Times*, 1/31/35 / "A rowdy, immensely funny farce.... William Lynn, Sam Levene, and Shirley Booth are some of the people who help."—*The New Yorker*, 2/9/35

Excursion (1937)

CREDITS: A comedy in three acts by Victor Wolfson; produced by John C. Wilson; staged by Worthington Miner.

CAST: Whitford Kane (Obediah Rich), J. Hammond Dailey (Jonathan Rich), Shirley Booth (Mrs. Loschavio), William H. Malone (Gilchrist), Jackie Grimes (Mike Geasling), Irene Cattell (Mrs. Geasling), Marilyn Erskine (Eileen Loschavio), Connie Gilchrist (Martha), Flora Campbell (Lee Pitman), Richard Kendrick (Mr. Pitman), Conway Washburne (Mac Colman), William H. Chambers (Pat Sloan), Henry Clark (Mr. Boomer), Kathryn Grace (Mrs. Boomer), John L. Kearney (Matson), Frances Fuller (Lollie), Fred Stewart (Stevens), Robert Williams (Red Magoon), Nellie Thorne (Miss Dowdie), Jennie Moscowitz (Mrs. Fitchel), James R. Waters (Mr. Fitchel), Anthony Ross (Woods), Sylvia Leigh (Tessie), Joseph Olney (Tony), Lester Wald (Candy Boy), Robert Thomsen (Aiken), Dorothy Brackett, Mae Grimes, Julie Lawrence, John O'Shaughnessy, Billy Redfield, Eric Walz, Sylvia Weld (Passengers)

HISTORY: Opened April 9, 1937, at the Vanderbilt Theatre. 116 performances.

SUMMARY: A varied assortment of passengers takes the farewell voyage of the *S.S. Happiness* to Coney Island, unaware that their skipper has decided to transport them instead to a remote Caribbean island.

NOTES: Director Worthington Miner later produced the acclaimed television anthology series *Studio One* (CBS, 1948–58).... This play reunited Shirley with actor J. Hammond Dailey, who helped her get her start in show business in the late 1910s.

REVIEWS: "Nothing quite so refreshing as *Excursion* has turned up in this neighborhood since Spring settled down over Broadway."—*New York Times*, 4/10/37 / "...if *Excursion* isn't a hit, it should be. It is fresh and warming, and much needed in these parts.... We should all be grateful to Messrs. Wolfson and Wilson for giving such a sparkling, clean taste to the end of the season."—*The New Yorker*, 4/17/37 / "...a comedy compassionate, tender, and wise ... a large, excellent, and largely indistinguishable cast...."—*Time*, 4/19/37

Too Many Heroes (1937)

CREDITS: A drama in three acts by Dore Schary. Produced by Carly Wharton; staged by Garson Kanin.

CAST: James Bell (Job Williams), Elspeth Eric (Nora Williams), Shirley Booth (Carrie Nolan), Thomas Fisher (Tommy Potter), Lew Eckles (John Nolan), Clyde Franklin (Mr. McMillan), Francis Pierlot (Mr. Halsey), James Backus (Cosgrove), Jean Barrere (Danny Parker), Richard Keene (Harry Halsey), Francis Pierlot (Mr. Halsey), Leslie Bingham (Mrs. Halsey), Joseph Sweeney (Sheriff Bailey), Robert Reed (Captain Miller), Ernest Woodward (Peters), Lawrence Forsythe (Hartman), Jack Lee (Lassiter), Charles McClelland (Burton), Rex Williams (Andrews), Bjorn Koefoed (Nielson), Randolph Wade (Ranger), Marion Willis (First Deputy), John

Huntington (Second Deputy), Herschel Cropper (Third Deputy), Royal C. Stout (Fourth Deputy)

HISTORY: Opened November 15, 1937, at the Hudson Theatre. 16 performances.

SUMMARY: A grim story of a lynching in a small Southwestern town, and its aftermath.

NOTES: The play's original title was *Violence*.... Playwright Schary later became an executive at MGM, and wrote the critically acclaimed play *Sunrise at Campobello*.

REVIEWS: "As the wife of one of the lynch victims, Shirley Booth gives the most lucid performance in the cast, catching all the anguish of the character in the dull hatred of her acting."—*New York Times*, 11/16/37 / "...this melodrama, one of the grimmest in years, is a real job in casting, direction, and presentation.... James Bell as the unfortunate Job, Elspeth Eric as his wife, and Shirley Booth as the widow are featured, and stand out." *Variety*, 11/17/37 / "Elspeth Eric and Shirley Booth do nobly by the two miserable women involved."—*The New Yorker*, 11/27/37

The Philadelphia Story (1939)

CREDITS: A comedy in three acts by Phillip Barry. Produced by the Theatre Guild (production committee, Theresa Helburn and Lawrence Langner); staged by Robert B. Sinclair.

CAST: Katharine Hepburn (Tracy Samantha Lord), Van Heflin (Macaulay "Mike" Connor), Joseph Cotten (C.K. Dexter Haven), Dan Tobin (Alexander "Sandy" Lord), Vera Allen (Margaret Lord), Shirley Booth (Liz Imbrie), Frank Fenton (George Kittredge), Philip Foster (Edward), Lorraine Bate (Elsie), Owen Coll (Thomas), Nicholas Joy (Seth Lord), Lenore Lonergan (Dinah Lord), Forrest Orr (William "Willy" Tracy), Hayden Rorke (Mac), Myrtle Tannehill (May)

HISTORY: Opened March 28, 1939, at the Shubert Theatre. 417 performances.

SUMMARY: Socialite Tracy Lord and her family gather for a weekend to celebrate her upcoming marriage. The presence of a journalist and photographer from *Destiny* magazine, as well as Tracy's ex-husband, threatens to upset the applecart.

NOTE: *The Philadelphia Story* was adapted by MGM as a film, released in 1940. Ruth Hussey played Shirley's stage role of photographer Liz Imbrie.

REVIEW: "...a spirited and gossamer dance of comedy with just enough idea to season it pleasantly.... Shirley Booth ... help[s] to round out a joyful evening."—*New York Times*, 3/29/39

My Sister Eileen (1940)

CREDITS: A comedy by Joseph Fields and Jerome Chodorov, based on the stories of Ruth McKen-

ney. Produced by Max Gordon; directed by George S. Kaufman.

CAST: Shirley Booth (Ruth Sherwood), Jo Ann Sayers (Eileen Sherwood), Morris Carnovsky (Mr. Appopolous), Richard Quine (Frank Lippencott), Bruce MacFarlane (Chic Clark), William Post, Jr. (Robert Baker), Tom Dillon (Lonigan), Gordon Jones (The Wreck), Joan Tompkins (Helen Wade), Effie Afton (Violet Shelton), Charles Martin (Captain Fletcher), Helen Ray (Mrs. Wade), Donald Foster (Walter Sherwood), George Cotton (Jensen), Joseph Callini (The Consul), Benson Spring (Cossack), Eda Heinemann (Prospective Tenant), Eric Roberts, Robert White (Street Arabs)

HISTORY: Opened December 26, 1940, at the Biltmore Theatre. 864 performances.

NOTES: Shirley's longest-running Broadway show, this lasted just slightly longer than *Three Men on a Horse*. She remained in the cast until *Eileen* closed in January 1943.... Based on stories published in *The New Yorker* by Ruth McKenney, this much-adapted hit later became a Columbia Pictures release in 1942, casting Rosalind Russell as Ruth. Musicalized in 1954 by Leonard Bernstein, Betty Comden and Adolph Green as *Wonderful Town*, that show was followed by a film musical version of *My Sister Eileen* (Columbia, 1955), with Betty Garrett as Ruth. A television sitcom, *My Sister Eileen*, aired on CBS-TV from 1960 to 1961, with theater veteran Elaine Stritch in the role Shirley originated onstage.

REVIEW: "*My Sister Eileen* ... is a fine and generous farce.... Shirley Booth and Jo Ann Sayers, as the harassed sisters, and Morris Carnovsky, as their landlord ... have most to do, and they do it very competently indeed."— *The New Yorker*, 1/4/41

Tomorrow the World (1943)

CREDITS: A drama by James Gow and Arnaud D'Usseau. Produced by Theron Bamberger; staged by Elliott Nugent.

CAST: Ralph Bellamy (Michael Frame), Shirley Booth (Leona Richards), Skippy [Skip] Homeier (Emil Bruchner), Kathryn Givney (Jessie Frame), Edith Angold (Frieda), Nancy Nugent/Joyce Van Patten (Patricia Frame, alternating), Richard Taber (Fred Miller), Paul Porter, Jr. (Tommy), Walter Kelly (Dennis), Richard Tyler (Butler)

HISTORY: Opened April 14, 1943, at the Ethel Barrymore Theatre. 500 performances.

SUMMARY: An American college professor takes custody of his 12-year-old nephew, who has been raised in Germany under Nazi rule, and tries to reform his hate-filled outlook on life.

NOTES: A film version of this show, with the same title differently punctuated (*Tomorrow, the World!*) was released by United Artists in 1944, with Betty Field replacing Shirley as Leona....

Mr. Appopolous (Morris Carnovsky) shows off his creative side to Ruth (Shirley, center) and Eileen (Jo Ann Sayers) in *My Sister Eileen.*

During the show's original Broadway run, Shirley married second husband William H. Baker.

REVIEWS: "Because of the sincere approach to a major problem, and the treatment it gives to it, *Tomorrow the World* is not a play that can be forgotten on the way up the aisle at the end of a performance.... Shirley Booth, who never does otherwise, contributes an understanding performance as the college professor's fiancée."—*New York Times*, 4/15/43 / "*Tomorrow the World* turns an appalling postwar problem into interesting theater."—*Time*, 4/26/43

Hollywood Pinafore; or, The Lad Who Loved a Salary (1945)

CREDITS: A musical comedy in two acts. Book and lyrics revised by George S. Kaufman; music by Sir Arthur Sullivan. Supervised by Arnold Saint Subber; directed by George S. Kaufman.

CAST: Victor Moore (Joseph W. Porter), William Gaxton (Dick Live-Eye), George Rasely (Mike Corcoran), Gilbert Russell (Ralph Rackstraw), Shirley Booth (Louhedda Hopsons), Annamary Dickey (Brenda Blossom), Diana Corday (Gloria Mundi), Mary Wickes (Miss Hebe), Russ Brown (Bob Beckett), Ella Mayer (Little Miss Peggy), Pamela Randell (Beverly Wilshire), Ernest Taylor (Guard), Daniel De Paolo (Doorman), Jackson Jordan, Drucilla Strain (Secretaries), Sally Billings, Mary Alice Bingham, Eleanor Boleyn, John Butler, Dean Campbell, Ronald Chetwood, Harold Cole, Jack Collins, Helene Constantine, Charles S. Dubin, Silas Engum, Florence George, Jane Hansen, Barbara Heath, Stanley Herbertt, Lucy Hillary, Howard Hoffman, Barry Kent, Josephine Lambert, James Mate, John Mathews, Margaret McKenna, Virginia Meyer, Candace Montgomery, Ann Newland, Jeanne North, Shaun O'Brien, Regis Powers, Jack Purcell, Annette Sorell, Larry Stuart, Jeffrey Warren, Mary Williams (Ensemble)

SUMMARY: A modern-day retelling of Gilbert and Sullivan's *Pinafore*, with the characters transposed to a Hollywood film studio.

HISTORY: Opened May 31, 1945, at the Alvin Theatre. 52 performances.

REVIEWS: "*Hollywood Pinafore* is one of those musicals which never seem to get fully under way ... the result is a little disappointing.... Shirley Booth is funny as a columnist...."—*New York Times*, 6/1/45 / "...the show sadly lacks the bounce, pace, bodily movement that should go with a musical ... Shirley Booth [shows] comic poise."—*Time*, 6/11/45

Land's End (1946)

CREDITS: A drama by Thomas Job, based on the novel *Dawn in Lyonesse* by Mary Ellen Chase. Presented by Paul Feigay in association with George Somnes; staged by Robert Lewis.

CAST: Shirley Booth (Susan Pengilly), Amena Romano (Lize), Helen Craig (Ellen Pascoe), Fred Stewart (Mr. Trevetna/Fourth Fisherman), Frieda Altman (Miss Penrose), Mabel Acker (Mrs. Bond), Diane de Brett (Miss Clark), Clement Brace (Mr. Brooks), Xenia Bank (Mrs. Brooks), Joseph Foley (Mr. Brigstocke/First Fisherman), Sydney Boyd (Mr. Derby/Second Fisherman), Ross Chetwynd (Mr. Harris/Third Fisherman), Theodore Newton (The Professor), Merie Maddern (Mrs. Tregonny), Minnie Dupree (Grandmother Tregonny), Michael Feigay (Kitchen Boy), Jay Barney (The Rector)

HISTORY: Opened December 11, 1946, at the Playhouse. 5 performances.

SUMMARY: A young woman living in Cornwall sees parallels between the Tristan and Isolde legend and her own engagement to a local fisherman. Shirley plays a barmaid who becomes involved with her best friend's fiancée, with tragic results.

REVIEW: "*Land's End* is forever reaching after exalted moods that lie beyond its grasp.... Since the actors are doing ... what they have been told to do, they must not be held to account for trying to deliver more than the script contains."—*New York Times*, 12/12/46

The Men We Marry (1948)

CREDITS: A comedy in three acts by Elizabeth Cobb and Herschel Williams. Presented by Edgar F. Luckenbach; directed by Martin Manulis.

CAST: Shirley Booth (Maggie Welch), Doris Dalton (Leda Mallard), Marta Linden (Julie Madison), Neil Hamilton (Dr. Alan Lambert), David Anderson (Phillip), John Williams (Mark Kennicott), Anne Sargent (Mary), John Hudson (Peter Sterling), Robert Willey (Warren Throckmorton), Margaret Hamilton (Gwennie), Joseph Allen, Jr. (Ned Synder)

HISTORY: Opened January 16, 1948, at the Mansfield Theatre. 3 performances.

SUMMARY: Middle-aged Maggie Welch and her friends, cynical about love and marriage from their own experiences, try to prevent her daughter from marrying the young man she loves.

NOTE: This is Shirley's shortest-lived Broadway show.

REVIEWS: "The only remarkable thing about *The Men We Marry* is that anyone should have thought that it is good enough to put on the stage."—*New York Times*, 1/17/48 / "...boasts a cast of fine players who run around in circles for three acts looking for a play ... one of the worst plays of the season."—*Daily Mirror*, 1/17/48 / "Several actors whose reputations have hitherto been untarnished appear in these punishing proceedings ... the decent thing is to say no more about them."—*New York Post*, 1/17/48

Goodbye, My Fancy (1948)

CREDITS: A comedy by Fay Kanin. Produced by Michael Kanin; directed by Sam Wanamaker.

CAST: Madeleine Carroll (Agatha Reed), Conrad Nagel (James Merrill), Sam Wanamaker (Matt Cole), Shirley Booth (Grace Woods), Joseph Boland (Claude Griswold), Ralph Bunker (Prof. Dingley), Lillian Foster (Prof. Birdeshaw), Lulu Mae Hubbard (Ellen Griswold), Bethel Leslie (Ginny Merrill), Lenore Garland (Jo), Eda Heinemann (Miss Shackleford), George Mitchell (Dr. Pitt), Betty Lou Holland (Carol), Patty Pope (Susan), Gerianne Raphael (Clarice), Tom Donovan (Telephone Man), Andrew George, John Ware (Janitors)

HISTORY: Opened November 17, 1948, at the Morosco Theatre. 446 performances.

SUMMARY: Congresswoman Agatha Reed, returning to the college she once attended to receive an honorary degree, is reunited with her former lover, now the college president.

NOTES: The film version of *Goodbye, My Fancy*, released by Columbia in 1951, starred Joan Crawford as Agatha Reed, with Eve Arden in Shirley's stage role as Agatha's sardonic secretary "Woody."... After Miss Carroll left the show, Shirley continued as Woody opposite her replacement, Ruth Hussey.... In 1949, Shirley received her first Tony Award, as Best Supporting or Featured Actress, for her performance as Grace Woods.

REVIEWS: "Shirley Booth, given a plethora of salty and amusing lines as the secretary, capitalizes them into some of the season's heartiest and most welcome laughs."—*Daily Mirror*, 11/18/48 / "...a pungent, intelligent comedy.... Shirley Booth is immensely funny..."—*Daily News*, 1/18/48 / "Fortunately for everyone on both sides of the footlights, Shirley Booth is on hand to play a worldly secretary with a two-edged weariness that is hilarious."—*New York Times*, 1/18/48

Love Me Long (1949)

CREDITS: A comedy by Doris Frankel. Directed by Margaret Perry and Brock Pemberton.

CAST: Shirley Booth (Abby Quinn), George Keane (Ike Skinner), Russell Hardie (Jim Kennedy), Anne Jackson (Margaret Anderson), Harry Bannister (Mr. Sharp), Daniel Reed (Cleotus P. Anderson), Jennifer Howard (Louise Ulmer), William Sharon (Moving Man), Heywood Hale Broun (Phone Man), Carl Low (A Caller)

HISTORY: Opened November 7, 1949, at the 48th Street Theatre. 16 performances.

SUMMARY: Abby Quinn and her ex-husband, both now in new relationships, quarrel over the rights to occupy the New York apartment they once shared. When both couples take up residence simultaneously, some question arises as to which man will figure in Abby's future.

NOTE: The quick failure of this show freed Shirley to take *Come Back, Little Sheba* to Broadway, a show she had played in tryouts weeks before *Love Me Long* opened.

REVIEWS: "Shirley Booth deserves high marks for gallantry, playing Abby for all she is worth, which is not a great deal."—*New York World-Telegram*, 11/8/49 / "Shirley Booth, who has brightened numerous plays with her deft and incisive playing, has no material and no chance in *Love Me Long*.... The writing ... is self-conscious, the situations are trite, [and] the characters are more than a little silly ... a futile evening upon the stage."—*New York Sun*, 11/8/49 / "Even Miss Booth can carry a vehicle only so far, and the author has put much too heavy a burden upon her."—*New York Post*

Come Back, Little Sheba (1950)

CREDITS: A drama by William Inge. Produced by the Theatre Guild (Theresa Helburn, Lawrence Langner, administrative directors); directed by Daniel Mann.

CAST: Shirley Booth (Lola Delaney), Sidney Blackmer (Doc Delaney), Joan Lorring (Marie), Lonny Chapman (Turk), Olga Fabian (Mrs. Coffman), Robert Cunningham (Bruce), Wilson Brooks (Ed Anderson), Paul Krauss (Elmo Huston), Daniel Reed (Postman), John Randolph (Milkman), Arnold Schulman (Messenger)

HISTORY: Opened February 15, 1950, at the Booth Theatre. 190 performances.

SUMMARY: Frumpy, amiable housewife Lola Delaney and her beaten-down husband "Doc," a chiropractor struggling with alcoholism, have their humdrum lives thrown into chaos when a pretty young college student rents a room in their house.

REVIEWS: "As for the always reliable Miss Booth, she demonstrates that she is as fine at straight characterization as she has long been at slightly sardonic comedy ... her performance is one of the true acting achievements of the season."—*New York Post*, 2/16/50 / "Shirley Booth soars histrionically in a role that could dismay most actresses.... She portrays a pure simpleton, without resort to tricks, guile, or angles."—*New York World-Telegram*, 2/16/50

NOTES: Shirley originated the role of Lola in a production of *Sheba* at the Westport Country Playhouse in September 1949.... She was named Best Actress in a Play at the 1950 Tony Awards.

"Love Is the Reason" was Shirley's show-stopping song in *A Tree Grows in Brooklyn*. Onlookers are Marcia Van Dyke and Johnny Johnston.

A Tree Grows in Brooklyn (1951)

CREDITS: Book by Betty Smith and George Abbott, based on the novel by Betty Smith. Music by Arthur Schwartz; lyrics by Dorothy Fields; musical director, Max Goberman. Produced by George Abbott, in association with Robert Fryer; directed by George Abbott.

CAST: Johnny Johnston (Johnny Nolan), Shirley Booth (Aunt Cissy), Nomi Mitty (Francie), Marcia Van Dyke (Katie), Nathaniel Frey (Harry), Albert Linville (Swanswine), Claudia Campbell

(Annie), Celine Flanigan (Maudie), Alan Gilbert (Hick), Janet Parker (Florence), Jordan Bentley (Aloysius), Bruno Wick (Max), Ruth Amos (Mae), Roland Wood (Moriarty), Harland Dixon (Old Clothes Man/Judge), Donald Duerr (Edgie), Howard Martin (Junior), Art Carroll (Salesman), Beverly Purvin, Jane Copeland, Marta Beckett, Mary Statz, Dorothy Hill (Girls in Mae's Place), Doris Wright, Oleg Briansky, Val Buttignol, Donn Driver, Dick Price (Dancers), Elaine Barrow, Jeanne Grant, Beverly Jane Welch, Eleanor Williams, Delbert Anderson, Johnny Ford, James McCracken, John Mooney, Feodore Tedick, Kenneth Utt (Singers), John Connoughton, Buzzie Martin, Patti Milligan (Children)

HISTORY: Opened April 19, 1951, at the Alvin Theatre. 267 performances.

SUMMARY: Musical adaptation of Betty Smith's classic novel about a young girl's devotion to her charming but weak-willed father. Shirley played free-wheeling, fun-loving Aunt Cissy.

NOTE: Columbia Records released the original cast album (OL-4405) in 1951.

REVIEWS: "There are two shows within the stage version of *A Tree Grows in Brooklyn*, and by far the better one is Shirley Booth singing and carrying on as a somewhat faded good time girl."— *New York Herald Tribune*, 4/20/51 / "On the plus side there is the incomparable performance of Shirley Booth as Aunt Cissy. While she is aboard, which is almost all the time, there is no concern with what it's all about or why. She simply dominates the proceedings, speaking and singing."—*New York Journal-American*, 4/20/51 / "The jewel of the evening, as rumor had suggested, is Shirley Booth's miraculous handling of the salty life and loves of Cissy. If you think Miss Booth reached the top of her form with *Come Back, Little Sheba*, just wait till you see this."—*New York World-Telegram*, 4/20/51

The Time of the Cuckoo (1952)

CREDITS: A play by Arthur Laurents. Produced by Robert Whitehead and Walter Fried; directed by Harold Clurman.

CAST: Shirley Booth (Leona Samish), Dino DiLuca (Renato Di Rossi), Lydia St. Clair (Signora Fiora), Geraldine Brooks (June Yaeger), Donald Murphy (Eddie Yaeger), Silva Gaselli (Giovanna), Jose Perez (Mauro), Jane Rose (Mrs. McIlhenny), Daniel Reed (Mr. McIlhenny), Ruggero Romor (Vito)

HISTORY: Opened October 15, 1952, at the Empire Theatre. 263 performances.

SUMMARY: American tourist Leona Samish, vacationing in Venice, becomes involved in a romantic intrigue with a charming, but married, shopkeeper.

NOTES: This performance won Shirley the 1953

The original playbill for *The Time of the Cuckoo* not only gives the usual credits, but also provides an explanation of the show's title.

Tony Award as Best Actress in a Play.... *Summertime*, the 1955 United Artists film starring Katharine Hepburn, was adapted from *Time of the Cuckoo*.

REVIEWS: "Arthur Laurents has written a lovely play for Shirley Booth ... she gathers all the goodwill, emotional turbulence and chagrin of the character in an immensely dramatic performance that is warm, easy-going, and lovable."— *New York Times*, 10/16/52 / "Arthur Laurents has written an adult and incisive comedy-drama and Shirley Booth and her supporting cast play it to perfection.... [She] has never been given a greater perimeter for her established talents."—*Journal-American*, 10/16/52 / "Miss Booth play[s] the spinster with the touching beauty we have come expect of her...."—*New York Post*, 10/16/52

By the Beautiful Sea (1954)

CREDITS: A musical in two acts. Book by Herbert and Dorothy Fields; music by Arthur Schwartz;

lyrics by Dorothy Fields. Produced by Robert Fryer and Lawrence Carr; directed by Marshall Jamison.

CAST: Shirley Booth (Lottie Gibson), Wilbur Evans (Dennis Emery), Mae Barnes (Ruby Monk), Anne Francine (Flora Busch), Cameron Prud'-Homme (Carl Gibson), Richard France (Mickey Powers), Carol Leigh (Baby Betsy Busch), Cindy Robbins (Molly Belmont), Robert Jennings (Half-Note), Busch), Edith True Case (Mrs. Koch), Mary Harmon (Cora Belmont), Gloria Smith (Lillian Belmont), Larry Howard (Lenny/Ensemble), Warde Donovan (Willie Slater/Ensemble), Paul Reed (Mr. Curtis), Cindy Robbins (Molly Belmont), Rex Cooper, Ray Kirchner (Acrobats), Gaby Monet (Viola), Eddie Roll (Sidney), Larry Laurance (Burt Mayer), Thomas Gibson (Diabolo), Cathryn Damon, Dorothy Donau, Lillian Donau, Pat Ferrier, Bob Haddad, Arthur Partington, Victor Reilly, Sigyn (Dancers), Suzanne Easter, Lola Fisher, Colleen O'-Connor, Pat Roe, Jean Sincere, Libi Staiger, John Dennis, Ray Hyson, Franklin Kennedy, George Lenz, Reid Shelton (Singers)

HISTORY: Opened April 8, 1954, at the Majestic Theatre. 270 performances.

SUMMARY: In the summer of 1907, Lottie Gibson, owner of a theatrical boarding house, falls in love with Shakespearean actor Dennis Emery. Their perilous financial straits, and the unexpected presence of Dennis' ex-wife, become obstacles to their romance.

NOTE: The original cast album was released by Capitol Records (S 531).

REVIEWS: "If you want to know what really being a star is, see Shirley Booth in *By the Beautiful Sea.*"—*New York World-Telegram*, 4/9/54 / "As for Shirley Booth ... there remains little more to be said except that she's awfully good.... She is a superbly effortless professional, and the notion of setting her in the Coney Island of the early 1900's is smart showmanship."— *The Nation*, 4/24/54 / "Shirley Booth may not be to musicomedy what Ethel Merman or Mary Martin is, but she is one of the wonders of show business. Her personal warmth almost seems to constitute (or render superfluous) a style of acting...."— *Time*, 4/19/54

The Desk Set (1955)

CREDITS: A comedy by William Marchant. Produced by Robert Fryer and Laurence Carr; directed by Joseph Fields.

CAST: Shirley Booth (Bunny Watson), Dorothy Blackburn (Peg Costello), Byron Sanders (Richard Sumner), Frank Milan (Abe Cutler), Clarice Blackburn (Sadel Meyer), Frank Roberts (Mr. Bennett), Anne-Marie Gayer (Ruthie Saylor), Louis Gossett (Kenny), Harry Ellerbe (Man in Shirt-Sleeves), Mary Gildea (Lady in the Blue Suit), Joyce Van Patten (Elsa), Elizabeth Wilson (Miss Warriner), Doris Roberts (Miss Rumple), Wayne Carson (Reporter), Sterling Jensen (Photographer), Mike Steen (Elsa's Friend)

HISTORY: Opened October 24, 1955, at the Broadhurst Theatre. 297 performances.

SUMMARY: The female head of a television company's research department clashes with an efficiency expert sent to automate the unit's operations.

NOTES: The film version of *The Desk Set*, released by 20th Century–Fox in 1957, cast Katharine Hepburn in Shirley's role, opposite Spencer Tracy as Richard Sumner. Of the original Broadway cast, only supporting player Harry Ellerbe appeared in the film.... In June 1956, Audrey Christie replaced Shirley in the New York company, while Miss Booth took the show on a nationwide tour. The Broadway production closed in early July.

REVIEWS: "All those people who swore they'd go to see Shirley Booth read the telephone book now have their opportunity.... Miss Booth is, of course, a black magician with a line."—*New York Herald Tribune*, 10/25/55 / "No gentleman would be boorish enough to notice that Shirley Booth's new play is inadequate.... Miss Booth radiates humor and charm all evening. She can do no wrong."—*New York Times*, 10/25/55

Miss Isobel (1957)

CREDITS: A play in three acts by Michael Plant and Denis Webb. Produced by Leonard Sillman and John Roberts; directed by Cedric Hardwicke.

CAST: Shirley Booth (Mrs. Ackroyd), Kathleen Maguire (Ellen), Nancy Marchand (Miriam Ackroyd), Edith King (Mrs. Ling), Peter Lazer (Robin), John Randolph (Howard), Dinnie Smith (Nurse), Robert Duke (Andrew McNeil)

HISTORY: Opened December 26, 1957, at the Royale Theatre. 53 performances.

SUMMARY: A middle-aged widow and mother unexpectedly develops a mental condition that causes her to revert to childhood.

REVIEWS: "Although [Booth] is normally one of the actresses most easy to believe, she cannot make this part anything but maudlin and embarrassing.... As the nurse, Dinnie Smith has the best part in the play: she doesn't have to speak a line."—*New York Times*, 12/27/57 / "With scarcely a sign of talent, the authors of *Miss Isabel* [sic] have tackled a stage subject that might make genius stumble ... with a look, a gesture, an intonation, [Booth] can be remarkably eloquent; but in the end the play, and even the part, is too much for her. Having taken on *Miss Isabel* [sic] after the hardly less piffling *The Desk Set*, she should next time try something more than the audience's patience."—*Time*, 1/6/58

Juno (1959)

CREDITS: A musical in two acts. Book by Joseph Stein, based on *Juno and the Paycock* by Sean O'-Casey. Music and lyrics by Marc Blitzstein; dances and musical numbers staged by Agnes de Mille. Staged by José Ferrer.

CAST: Shirley Booth (Juno Boyle), Melvyn Douglas ("Captain" Jack Boyle), Monte Amundsen (Mary Boyle), Jack MacGowran (Joxer Daly), Tommy Rall (Johnny Boyle), Jean Stapleton (Mrs. Madigan), Nancy Andrews (Mrs. Brady), Sada Thompson (Mrs. Coyne), Clarice Blackburn (Mrs. Tancred), Liam Lenihan ("Needle" Nugent), Betty Low (Mrs. Dwyer), Loren Driscoll (Jerry Devine), Gemze de Lappe (Molly), Earl Hammond (Charlie Bentham), Tom Clancy (I.R.A. Man), Frank Carroll (Furniture Removal Man), Rico Froehlich (Sullivan/Policeman), Julian Patrick (Paddy Coyne), Robert Rue (Michael Brady), Chuck Bennett, Sharon Enoch, Mickey Gunnerson, Pat Heyes, Curtis Hood, Scott Hunter, Rosemary Jourdan, Gene Kelton, Annabelle Lyon, James Maher, Enrique Martinez, Howard Parker, Jim Ryan, Glen Tetley, Marjorie Wittmer, Jenny Workman (Dancers), Anne Fielding, Ted Forlow, Cleo Fry, Pat Huddleston, Gail Johnston, Barbara Lockard, Pat Ruhl, Diana Sennett, Joanne Spiller, James Tushar (Singers)

HISTORY: Opened March 9, 1959, at the Winter Garden Theatre. 16 performances.

SUMMARY: Living in a Dublin slum in 1921, hardworking Juno Boyle tries to keep her troubled family afloat, with scant help from her shiftless husband Jack.

NOTE: The original cast album of *Juno* was released by Columbia Masterworks (OL 5380).

REVIEWS: "Many good people have been trapped in this encounter.... It is a big, bleeding shame — so much talent, so much money, and so little fun." — *Journal-American*, 3/10/59 / "Miss Booth still hasn't found a show to fit her genius." *New York World-Telegram*, 3/10/59 / "Shirley Booth, in the title role, gives a finely outlined characterization to Juno." — *New York Daily News*, 3/10/59

A Second String (1960)

CREDITS: A play by Lucienne Hill, adapted from a novel by Colette. Produced by Leonard Sillman, Carroll Masterson, and Harris Masterson; directed by Raymond Gerome.

CAST: Shirley Booth (Fanny), Jean-Pierre Aumont (Farou), Nina Foch (Jane), Cathleen Nesbitt (Clara), Carrie Nye (Inez), Ben Piazza (Paul)

HISTORY: Opened April 13, 1960, at the Eugene O'Neill Theatre. 29 performances.

SUMMARY: A philanderer's wife realizes that he is having an affair with his live-in secretary. Eventually the two women join forces to achieve their common aims.

NOTE: This production's original title, taken from the book that was its source, was *The Other One*.

REVIEWS: "In skill at portraiture, in subtlety of perception, this is Miss Booth's finest acting since *The Time of the Cuckoo* in 1952. But that is all *A Second String* has to offer. The rest is trite and thin." — *New York Times*, 4/14/60 / "Whatever wit or wisdom the original Colette story possessed has been all but boiled out of it.... With a sturdy cast ... somehow acting in a mild jingle of keys, an always thin story becomes a largely tedious one." — *Time*, 4/25/60

Look to the Lilies (1970)

CREDITS: A musical based on *Lilies of the Field* by William E. Barrett. Book by Leonard Spigelgass; music by Jule Styne; lyrics by Sammy Cahn. Presented by Edgar Lansbury and Max J. Brown; directed by Joshua Logan.

CAST: Shirley Booth (Mother Maria), Al Freeman, Jr. (Homer Smith), Taina Elg (Sister Albertine), Virginia Craig (Sister Elizabeth), Patti Karr (Juanita), Carmen Alvarez (Rosita), Titos Vandis (Juan Archuleta), Anita Sheer (Lady Guitarist), Richard Graham (First Policeman/Monsignor O'Hara), Joe Benjamin (Second Policeman/Judge), Marc Allen III (Bartender), Don Prieur (District Attorney/Poker Player), Ben Laney (Defense Attorney), Paul Eichel (Courtroom Guard/Poker Player), Michael Davis (Courtroom Guard/Poker Player)

HISTORY: Opened March 29, 1970, at the Lunt-Fontanne Theatre. 25 performances.

SUMMARY: An ex-convict on the lam crosses paths with a group of nuns whose Mother Superior believes he has been sent to build them a church.

REVIEWS: "Miss Booth, with a German accent you could strain sauerkraut through, is a delight as the totalitarian Mother Superior..." — *New York Times*, 3/30/70 / "Shirley Booth is one of the first ladies of the American stage, and she is a pillar of strength to *Look to the Lilies*." — *New York Post*, 3/30/70 / "Shirley Booth returned to Broadway with this show after too many years of waste — if financial security — in television. She is still a wonderful actress and plays the Mother Superior with vast sensitivity and a characterization that is consistent right down to posture." — *Women's Wear Daily*, 3/30/70

Hay Fever (1970)

CREDITS: A comedy by Noël Coward. Presented by Leonard Sillman; directed by Arvin Brown.

CAST: Shirley Booth (Judith Bliss), John Williams (David Bliss), Marian Mercer (Myra Arundel), Carole Shelley (Jackie Coryton), Sam Waterston (Simon Bliss), Sudie Bond (Clara), Roberta Maxwell (Sorel Bliss), Michael McGuire (Richard Greatham), John Tillinger (Sandy Tyrell)

HISTORY: Opened November 9, 1970, at the Helen Hayes Theatre. 24 performances.

SUMMARY: A revival of Coward's 1925 comedy about a tempestuous weekend at the English country home of a famous leading lady and her family, each of whom has invited a guest.

REVIEWS: "Shirley Booth is such a wonderful actress that it seems strange to say that she is slightly miscast as a great star. But, while she hasn't quite the style for the role of a temperamental bully, it is fine to see her again."—*New York Post*, 11/10/70 / "Miss Booth, who must be everybody's darling, plays the part with her familiar skill. Unfortunately, though, her forthright and resolutely American manner is ill-suited to the capricious nature of this airy creature. She is always winning but the characterization lacks an essential panache."—*New York Daily News*, 11/10/70 / "Miss Booth can be an effective and moving performer but she isn't nearly versatile enough to play high comedy and will just never have the looks, the speech, the gush, the manner of a grande-dame of the British theatre."—*Women's Wear Daily*, 11/10/70

Appendix B:
Radio Log

Given the ephemeral nature of radio performances, which were usually done live in the 1930s and 1940s, it is well-nigh impossible to be a completist in documenting an actor's radio career. While Shirley Booth is no exception to this rule, her key radio roles that can be traced are listed here. A number of the programs described are still available, at least in part, from Old Time Radio (OTR) collectors and vendors. Others were not recorded for posterity, but have been documented from program listings in contemporary newspapers. In instances where this was the source of information (as noted below), it is possible that the live broadcast varied from what was announced in advance.

SERIES ROLES

Strictly Business. NBC Blue, May 31–August 23, 1940. Easily Shirley's least-known radio credit, this obscure show concerned the adventures of a press agent. Shirley played his assistant, though her character name is unknown. One of the few clues to its content comes from a brief item in *The Charleston Gazette* (July 5, 1940), which said, "The correct title for the broadcasts should be 'Strictly Monkey Business' since it is a comedy relief featuring Shirley Booth, Peggy Conklin and Lawson Zerbe." Radio and TV historian Vincent Terrace describes it, in his *Radio Programs 1924–1984: A Catalog of Over 1800 Shows*, as "a weekly drama about a sophisticated press agent ... and his slightly wacky assistant." Most OTR reference sources do not list it at all.

Duffy's Tavern. CBS and NBC, 1941–43. Shirley was a featured regular, as Miss Duffy, in this popular series, opposite her then-husband, series creator and star Ed Gardner (Archie). She left the show at the conclusion of the 1942-43 season, after her divorce from Gardner, leaving her role to be recast multiple times during the remainder of the

series' run. This series is discussed fully in Chapter 3.

While numerous episodes of this series are available from OTR collectors, the great majority of them are from later in the show's run, after Shirley left the cast. However, two of Shirley's episodes are widely distributed: the broadcast of March 23, 1943, with guest stars Susan Hayward and Frank Buck, and the June 15, 1943, segment, with Clifton Fadiman.

Hogan's Daughter. NBC, June 21–September 14, 1949. Shirley starred as Phyllis Hogan in this 30-minute summer replacement comedy series, sponsored by Philip Morris. Her initial supporting cast consisted of Howard Smith as her father, Tom Hogan, Betty Garde as mother Kate, and Everett Sloane as Phyllis' boyfriend Marvin Gaffney. Garde also voiced the smaller role of Phyllis' friend LaVerne. In later broadcasts, Ethel Owen replaced Garde as Kate Hogan. See Chapter 5 for a discussion of this program.

The episodes of July 12, 1949, and July 26, 1949, are available from OTR vendors.

GUEST APPEARANCES AND OTHER ROLES

The shows below are listed chronologically. The notation "Available" indicates that copies of the show can (as of this writing) be obtained from OTR collectors and vendors.

[Untitled]. WOR radio (Newark, N.J.), November 19, 1925. According to radio listings in the *Hartford Courant,* this 15-minute afternoon program, apparently heard only in the metropolitan New York area, presented "Shirley Booth, co-star of *Laff That Off,* in songs." It may have been Shirley's radio debut. She was heard again on the December 4, 1925, broadcast.

The Royal Gelatin Hour. NBC Red, December 17, 1936. Shirley is a guest of Rudy Vallee's popular variety show, along with Edgar Bergen with Charlie McCarthy (making their radio debut), and hostess Elsa Maxwell. Available.

Sunday Night Party. NBC, June 13, 1937. "Five Minutes from the Station." Shirley co-starred with Henry Hull in this adaptation of a short play by her friend Elaine Carrington, and hosted by James Melton. The story concerns a young couple, Bert and Carrie, entertaining the husband's boss for dinner, in hopes that Bert will be awarded a promotion. "Five Minutes from the Station" was filmed as a Vitaphone short subject in 1930. (*Washington Post*)

I've Got the Tune. CBS, October 24, 1937. An original music play composed by Marc Blitzstein. According to Blitzstein's biographer, Eric A. Gordon, the show told the story of Mr. Musiker, a composer. Shirley was cast as his secretary, Beetzie, who "represent[s] both the inanity and brutalization of the working class and at the same time its honest pragmatism and common sense." Blitzstein and Booth later re-teamed for the unsuccessful 1959 Broadway musical *Juno.*

This Is New York. CBS, January 8, 1939. Shirley was a guest, along with George Jessel, on this short-lived show produced by her husband, Ed Gardner.

Star Spangled Vaudeville. NBC, August 30, 1942. "Master of Ceremonies Walter O'Keefe will present Shirley Booth, Broadway and radio actress, swinging comedienne, Molasses and January, blackface comedy duo, and a feminine comedy team, Nan Ray and Mrs. Waterfall." (*Chicago Tribune*)

Radio Reader's Digest. CBS, November 15, 1942. Host Conrad Nagel introduced two segments—

"The Clock Strikes," with Stanley Ridges, and "They Called Her Mousie," which starred Shirley. She would return to this show often in the late 1940s. (*Chicago Tribune*)

Comedy Caravan. CBS, February 5, 1943. "Bud Abbott and Lou Costello ... suddenly find themselves at loose ends when they encounter Shirley Booth, laughingly known to dialers as 'Miss Duffy,' when all three meet as guest artists on the laugh-loaded *Comedy Caravan.*" Also appearing were Herb Shriner, and singer Georgia Gibbs. (*Cedar Rapids Tribune*)

The Sammy Kaye Show. CBS, March 10, 1943. Shirley made "another visit" to bandleader Kaye's show, according to listings in the *Mason City* (IA) *Globe-Gazette.*

That They Might Live. NBC, May 9, 1943. "In NBC's Red Cross broadcast, [Shirley] will play an embittered young nurse who joins the Army Nurse Corps because the pay appeals to her but in a base hospital at the front learns, the hard way, that mercy means as much as efficiency to the wounded men in her care." (*San Antonio Express*)

The Cavalcade of America. NBC, December 13, 1943. Sponsored by DuPont, this "prestige" show supposedly dramatized notable events from American history. In "Check Your Heart at Home," Shirley plays Red Cross nurse Jane Goodell in an adaptation of her recently published memoir *They Sent Me to Iceland.*

Radio Hall of Fame. NBC Blue, March 12, 1944. This show was an unusual venture into radio production by the staff of the trade newspaper *Variety.* Host Deems Taylor introduced varied acts chosen for their excellence. Other guests on this installment were Groucho Marx, and singer Kenny Baker, with music furnished by the Paul Whiteman Orchestra. (*Chicago Tribune*)

Blind Date. April 17, 1944. Arlene Francis hosted this radio precursor to TV's *The Dating Game.* In this episode, "Actress Shirley Booth is the chaperone for the three winning servicemen and their gals." (*Washington Post*)

The Adventures of the Thin Man. CBS, June 4, 1944. According to a press release in the *Cedar Rapids Tribune* (June 1, 1944), Shirley guest starred in "The Case of the Amorous Corpse," opposite series star David Gothard. "While Nora is away visiting relatives, Nick and Sheriff Eb Williams enlist the services of Shirley Booth (who plays herself in the story) to help them track down the murderer impersonating a beautiful but dese-dose-and-dems dame." Parker Fennelly was featured as Sheriff Williams; Shirley was filling in for female lead Claudia Morgan, who did not appear in this episode.

Stage Door Canteen. CBS, July 21, 1944. "Jane Froman, Shirley Booth, and Joseph Cotten visit the ... Canteen" (*Washington Post*). In addition to working in the real-life Canteen, Shirley appeared occasionally on this radio version, though other specific airdates are unknown.

Silver Theatre. CBS, July 23, 1944. "The Long Engagement," hosted by Conrad Nagel. From radio listings in the *Washington Post*.

The Cavalcade of America. NBC, August 14, 1944. "The Gals They Left Behind." Shirley starred as Jo Sullivan in this drama described as "the authentic experiences of two soldiers' wives." The play was adapted by Edith Sommer, from a book by Margaret Shea, and also featured Helen Claire and Parker Fennelly. Available.

The Kate Smith Hour. CBS. Shirley introduced her Miss Duffy–like character of Dottie Mahoney during the show's 1944-45 season, and reprised it in subsequent appearances. Her first known appearance, on September 29, 1944, is available. She returned on the October 15, 1944, broadcast, with fellow guest Orson Welles.

It Pays to Be Ignorant. CBS, November 3, 1944. Shirley was a guest panelist on this popular show that parodied brainy radio quizzes like *Information Please*. She was originally announced as guest star for the October 20 broadcast: "The actress is expected to appear as a defender of womanhood in general — and [series regular] Lulu McConnell in particular!" (*Cedar Rapids Tribune*, October 19, 1944). Available.

Theater of Romance. CBS, November 21, 1944. "Bachelor Mother." This is the first of at least three guest appearances by Shirley during this series' initial season. Here she played Polly Parish in an episode derived from the 1939 film comedy which had starred Ginger Rogers. Available.

Theatre of Romance. CBS, January 23, 1945. "Ball of Fire." Shirley played the role originated by Barbara Stanwyck in a popular 1941 film.

The Kate Smith Hour. CBS, February 18, 1945. Shirley "is returning to the Kate Smith show tonight over CBS to read another entry of her hilarious "Diary of Dotty," according to the *Port*

Arthur (TX) *News*. "And if you like to laugh, you'll split your sides when Shirley Booth tells the story of getting hit by a horse-car!" promised an advertisement for the show in that day's *Washington Post*.

The Hildegarde Show (a.k.a. The Raleigh Room). February 20, 1945. Shirley was a guest with "The Incomparable Hildegarde," as were Clifton Webb and Stu Erwin.

The Kate Smith Hour. CBS, March 4, 1945. "Today this great show will tickle your funny bone with *two* comedians! The new laugh hit, Harvey Stone — plus your old favorite, Shirley Booth!" (*Washington Post* advertisement)

The Kate Smith Hour. CBS, March 18, 1945. An article in the *Hartford Courant* (March 19, 1945) stated that Shirley appeared in a segment aired live via remote hookup from the Sam Dealey Recreation Center at the Groton (CT) submarine base, in honor of its dedication. An ad in that day's *Washington Post* promised, "Today it's an all-comedy show, broadcast from the Submarine Base at New London. Featured gagsters are: comic Henny Youngman, daffy Shirley Booth, and Tom Howard in *It Pays to Be Ignorant!*"

Theatre of Romance. CBS, August 7, 1945. "My Sister Eileen." Shirley reprises her Broadway role as Ruth McKenney opposite future film star Judy Holliday's Eileen.

The Tommy Dorsey Show. NBC, September 2, 1945. A blurb in the *Port Arthur* (TX) *News* stated, "Shirley Booth will take over a regular comedy spot on the Tommy Dorsey show tonight ... Miss Booth has made popular numerous radio comedy roles and been a frequent guest on network programs."

The Raleigh Room. NBC, October 2, 1945. Another guest appearance with Hildegarde, as Dottie Mahoney. Available.

The Fred Allen Show. NBC, November 25, 1945. Shirley would be heard often on Allen's popular comedy show, ultimately making at least ten appearances in the mid– to late–1940s. Here, she took part in a Gilbert and Sullivan parody, "Brooklyn Pinafore," which also headlined baseball manager Leo Durocher. Shirley, of course, played a Dottie Mahoney type.

Theatre Guild on the Air. ABC, November 25, 1945. "Morning's at Seven." Shirley was heard often on this highbrow series, produced by the organization that mounted her career-altering production of *Come Back, Little Sheba*. The programs were broadcast to a live audience, so as to simulate the experience of a theatrical performance. In deference to its longtime sponsor, the show was also known as *The United States Steel Hour.* In her first appearance, Shirley played Myrtle in this "gay comedy of family life," with co-stars Stuart Erwin, Aline MacMahon, Jean Adair, Eda Heineman, Will Geer, Howard Smith, and Ralph Morgan. Available.

Theatre Guild on the Air. ABC, December 9, 1945. "Ned McCobb's Daughter," written by Sidney Howard, with Alfred Lunt and Anthony Ross. Shirley played Carrie, the title role, in this adaptation of a show which the Guild originally produced on Broadway during the 1926-27 season. Available.

The Danny Kaye Show. CBS, December 14, 1945. Shirley's former *Duffy's Tavern* colleague Abe Burrows was among the writers on this short-lived variety show starring the popular movie comedian. In Shirley's first appearance, she performed a Dottie Mahoney routine. According to a *New York Times* listing, she returned for another appearance on January 11, 1946.

Theatre Guild on the Air. ABC, January 6, 1946. "Three Men on a Horse," with Stuart Erwin and Sam Levene. A reprise of Shirley's hit 1930s Broadway comedy, in which she played dimwitted Mabel. Available.

The Celebrity Club. CBS, February 16, 1946. Shirley was the "special guest" in this episode, according to listings in the *Hagerstown* (MD) *Morning Herald.*

The Adventures of the Red Feather Man. April 27, 1946. A fundraising program for Community Chest initiatives. "The opening program, 'No Place Like It,' will star Josephine Hull and Shirley Booth, and will depict the variety of services rendered by the Visiting Nurse Association." (*Berkshire Evening Eagle,* April 26, 1946)

The Eddie Bracken Show. CBS, 1946-47. Some radio historians, including Frank Buxton (*The Big Broadcast,* Viking, 1972) credit Shirley with a recurring role as Betty Mahoney in this series, or its predecessor, *The Eddie Bracken Story* (NBC, 1945). However, there is no mention of Shirley, or this character, in *Variety*'s contemporary reviews of the shows, or any newspaper program listings that can be traced, and she is not heard in the few episodes that survive today. It's likely that she made at least a couple of guest appearances on the program.

The Vaughn Monroe Show. CBS, October 14, 1946. Shirley and fellow guest star Oscar Levant appeared on the series opener of this Saturday night variety program, which featured a medley of Irving Berlin songs. Shirley would return often to this show, which would also be known as *The Camel Caravan,* during the 1946-47 season.

The Victor Borge Show. NBC, November 11, 1946. Shirley was the guest on Borge's variety show, which spotlighted his piano comedy routines and also featured the Benny Goodman Orchestra. (*Chicago Tribune*)

Theatre Guild on the Air. ABC, December 28, 1946. "Broadway." Oscar winner James Dunn co-starred with Shirley in this adaptation of Philip Dunning and George Abbott's play, which ran for more than 600 performances on Broadway in the late 1920s.

The Cavalcade of America. NBC, January 6, 1947. "The Woman on Lime Rock." Program listings in the *Portland Sunday Telegram* (January 5, 1947) indicate that Shirley was to be heard in "the true story of a woman who had one of the most unusual of feminine occupations, a lighthouse keeper."

The Vaughn Monroe Show. CBS, January 31, 1947. Shirley was again the guest of the popular bandleader, along with pianist Stan Kenton. (*Iowa City Press-Citizen*). Listings in the *Wisconsin Rapids Daily Tribune* credit her with another appearance on the April 19, 1947, broadcast.

Radio Reader's Digest. CBS, May 8, 1947. "Uncle By's Two Wives." Sponsored by Hallmark, this dramatic series typically accentuated the positive, like the ubiquitous magazine on which it was based. Emceed by Les Tremayne, the series featured Shirley as the guest star in at least three episodes. Here, she played the role of Paulina. Available.

The Vaughn Monroe Show. CBS, May 10, 1947. Shirley and "The Stroud Twins" were booked, according to program listings in the *Washington Post.* Listings in the *Cedar Rapids Tribune* indicate the same guests were to be heard on the May 17 broadcast, though it's unknown whether Shirley made both appearances, or whether her May 10 appearance was canceled.

Radio Reader's Digest. CBS, October 23, 1947. "The Braddock Chest." This installment also featured Vera Allen. The story concerned an antique chest, and a woman's efforts to prove its authenticity. Available.

The Fred Allen Show. Shirley appeared often on Allen's highly rated, and widely admired show, between 1947 and 1949. Among the broadcasts in which she is credited with an appearance include October 12, 1947, January 11, 1948, March 13, 1949, and June 19, 1949. Scripts from these segments are in the collection of the American Radio Archives, at the Thousand Oaks (CA) Public Library. Radio listings in the *Amarillo* (TX) *News-Globe* credit her with an appearance on April 4, 1948.

Radio Reader's Digest. CBS, February 26, 1948. "The Woman Detective and the Stolen Jewels." Shirley played Amy Bundy, librarian who aspires to be a sleuth, and solved the mystery behind the theft of a wealthy woman's jewelry, in what was purportedly based on a true story. Available.

The Cavalcade of America. NBC, April 12, 1948. "The Man Who Took the Freedom Train." Shirley and Eddie Albert starred in this drama, according to the previous day's *Amarillo* (TX) *News-Globe*. An advertisement in the *Fresno Bee* synopsized the show: "Eddie Bullock was afraid ... afraid of visiting the Freedom Train because it would take his lunch hour; afraid of his boss; afraid of getting married; afraid of going into business for himself. One day on the Freedom Train with his girl, Marge [Shirley's role], he suddenly realized what the world would be like if other men in other times had been afraid to push ahead, to work and strive and sacrifice."

Our Miss Brooks. CBS, April 9, 1948. A sample episode of the projected comedy series, starring Shirley as heroine Connie Brooks was broadcast on April 9, 1948. After a chilly initial reception, the show was retooled, and recast with Eve Arden, becoming a hit series for her upon its debut in the summer of 1948. Available.

Ford Theatre. NBC, June 13, 1948. "My Sister Eileen." Shirley reprised yet again her early 1940s stage role, described by the announcer as "one of the gayest, craziest comedies ever to hit Broadway." Virginia Gilmore co-starred. Available.

The Fred Allen Show. April 10, 1949. According to the "Radio Spotlight" column of the *La Crosse* (WI) *Tribune*, "young Broadway comedienne Shirley Booth" was booked on that evening's program.

Theater U.S.A. ABC, April 21, 1949. According to "Today's Radio Highlights" in the *Madison* (WI) *State Journal*, this 60-minute program featured excerpts from both *My Sister Eileen* and *Hamlet* (!), with Shirley, Jo Ann Sayre [sic; Sayers], Laurence Olivier, and Phil Silvers.

Kate Smith Calls. ABC, October 29, 1949. Shirley appeared in this segment, and possibly others, of the singer's 60-minute variety show of 1949-50. She did a Dottie Mahoney routine.

Theatre Guild on the Air. NBC, December 11, 1949. "Street Scene." Recreation of the Elmer Rice play that ran three years on Broadway. Shirley played Anna Maurant; also featured were Richard Conte, Diana Lynn, and Karl Malden.

Celebrity Time. ABC, January 1, 1950. "Shirley Booth and Gene Lockhart visit Conrad Nagel, Ilka Chase, and John Daly." (*Washington Post*)

Theatre Guild on the Air. NBC, March 26, 1950. "The Milky Way." Danny Kaye and Shirley teamed for this story of a nebbishy milkman who somehow kayoes a prize fighter. The play by Lynn Root and Harry Clork ran briefly on Broadway in 1934, and was also adapted into a 1936 film vehicle for Harold Lloyd.

The Talking Magazine. WNEW radio (New York City), spring 1950. "Presented in cooperation with the Industrial Home for the Blind of Brooklyn, the half-hour show will offer digests from articles in current magazines read by stars of Broadway shows" (*New York Times*, March 26, 1950). Shirley was among the performers announced as participating in this public service program for the visually impaired, but the exact date of her appearance is unknown.

The Tex and Jinx Show. WNBC (New York City), April 10, 1950. Shirley and her stage co-star Sidney Blackmer appeared on this morning talk show, presumably to promote *Come Back, Little Sheba*. (*New York Times*)

Theatre Guild on the Air. NBC, February 4, 1951. "Come Back, Little Sheba." Gary Cooper was Shirley's leading man in this version of her Tony-winning hit play.

Theatre Guild on the Air. NBC, May 20, 1951. "Ethan Frome." Owen and Donald Davis adapted Edith Wharton's novel, with a cast headed by Shirley, Raymond Massey, and Margaret Phillips.

Answer the Call. March 1, 1953. Shirley played real-life nurse Barbara Hussey in a half-hour drama used to launch the Red Cross' 1953 fundraising campaign. The program, which also featured an address from the White House by President Dwight D. Eisenhower, was heard at various times during the evening on all four major networks (NBC, Mutual, CBS, and ABC).

Theatre Guild on the Air. NBC, April 11, 1953. "The Glass Menagerie." One of the radio series' last broadcasts. Shirley would star in another production of Tennessee Williams' classic for CBS-TV in 1966.

My Most Unforgettable Child. ABC, February 14, 1954. Shirley was one of several celebrities who narrated segments of this special program aimed at raising donations for the United Nations Children's Fund. Others were Kirk Douglas, Greer Garson, Audrey Hepburn, and Deborah Kerr. The program

Shirley tries on a Red Cross helmet in preparation for a Red Cross radio drama in March 1953. Pictured with Shirley is real-life nurse Barbara Hussey, upon whose Korean War experiences the drama was based (Michael D. Strain collection).

presented "authentic stories of children in foreign lands," according to the *New York Times* (February 11, 1954).

Stagestruck. CBS, April 4, 1954. "The Story of Spring on Broadway." This CBS series hosted by

Mike Wallace was, in the words of *Time* magazine (October 12, 1953), "dedicated to the proposition that the theater, the people in it, the magic world of the stage, are glamorous and exciting to everyone, because, deep down, we're all stage-struck too." This installment included a preview of Shirley's new Broadway musical *By the Beautiful Sea.* Available.

Stagestruck. CBS, May 2, 1954. "The Highlights of the 1953-54 Theatrical Season." Shirley is one of numerous stage stars heard in this retrospective, the last episode of the series. Available.

Salute to Eugene O'Neill. NBC, May 15, 1954. Shirley appeared alongside Helen Hayes and Geraldine Page. (*Time,* May 14, 1954)

Chase and Sanborn's 101st Anniversary Show Presents Fred Allen. NBC, November 14, 1965. Edgar Bergen hosted this retrospective of Allen's life and work. Shirley was among the celebrities heard in excerpts from Allen's 1940s radio program.

Appendix C:
Filmography

Come Back, Little Sheba (1952)

CREDITS: Directed by Daniel Mann; based on the play by William Inge; produced by Hal B. Wallis; screenplay, Ketti Frings; director of photography, James Wong Howe; original music by Franz Waxman; costume design, Edith Head; makeup supervisor, Wally Westmore; special photographic effects, Gordon Jennings; editorial supervisor, Warren Low. Paramount, released December 24, 1952; 99 minutes, B&W.

CAST: Burt Lancaster (Doc Delaney), Shirley Booth (Lola Delaney), Terry Moore (Marie Buckholder), Richard Jaeckel (Turk Fisher), Philip Ober (Ed Anderson), Lisa Golm (Mrs. Coffman), Walter Kelley (Bruce), Paul McVey (Postman), Edwin Max (Elmo Huston), Ned Glass (Man at A.A. Meeting), Kitty McHugh (Pearl Stinson)

SUMMARY: The marriage of middle-aged Doc and Lola has gone sour from years of disillusionment and disappointment. Doc, a recovering alcoholic, resents the opportunities he missed by marrying Lola, who was pregnant, and dropping out of school, and is struggling with alcoholism. Lola, who lost her baby shortly after the marriage, is lonely and bored, mothering her weak-willed husband and mourning the loss of her dog that disappeared a few months ago. The arrival in the Delaney home of pretty young college student Marie brings both excitement and trouble, stirring emotions and memories that previously lay dormant.

TAGLINE: "The sensational Theatre Guild play becomes provocative motion picture entertainment!"

REVIEWS: "Despite a couple of minor outside excursions the film is the stage play photographed, cut, and spliced — with Shirley Booth recreating her immaculate performance of a sloppy woman." — Family Circle, January 1953 / "Booth, shiftlessly waddling around and prattling away endlessly in a singsong voice, does a highly skillful job of bringing the gabby, good-natured, slatternly Lola to life." — Time, 12/29/52 / "...it is Miss Booth's immensely detailed, subtle performance that gives Come Back, Little Sheba its distinction.... Such knowledge of a human being creates compassion, the force of every human soul and the truth within all art." — Washington Post, 2/12/53

Main Street to Broadway (1953)

CREDITS: Directed by Tay Garnett; screenplay by Samuel Raphaelson, from a story by Robert E. Sherwood; director of photography, James Wong Howe; song, There's Music in You, by Richard Rodgers and Oscar Hammerstein II; co-ordinator for the Council of Living Theatre, Jean Dalrymple; production manager, Norman Cook; supervising film editor, Gene Fowler, Jr.; art direction, Perry Ferguson; orchestral arrangements and conductor, Leon Arnaud; assistant director, James Anderson; make-up artist, Lee Greenway; editorial assistant, Robert Lawrence; set decorations, Edward Boyle; rerecording, Buddy Myers; costumes, Margaret Greenway; hair stylist, Hollis Barnes; sound, John Kean; special effects, Jack Cosgrove; Miss Bankhead's gowns by Hattie Carnegie; script supervisor, Dolores Rubin; titles and optical effects, Jack Rabin. MGM, released October 13, 1953. 103 minutes, B&W.

CAST: Tom Morton (Tony Monaco), Mary Murphy (Mary Craig), Agnes Moorehead (Mildred Waterbury), Herb Shriner (Frank Johnson), Rosemary DeCamp (Mrs. Craig), Clinton Sundberg (Mr. Craig), with guest stars Tallulah Bankhead, Ethel Barrymore, Lionel Barrymore,

Good-hearted Lola is pleased to attend the Alcoholics Anonymous meeting at which husband Doc's year of sobriety is commemorated.

Gertrude Berg, Shirley Booth, Louis Calhern, Leo Durocher, Faye Emerson, Henry Fonda, Oscar Hammerstein II, Rex Harrison, Helen Hayes, Joshua Logan, Mary Martin, Elsa Maxwell, Lilli Palmer, Richard Rodgers, John van Druten, Cornel Wilde (Themselves)

SUMMARY: Aspiring young playwright Tony Monaco is assigned to write a new play for Tallulah Bankhead, who's tired of unsympathetic roles. With the encouragement of girlfriend Mary, Tony tries to write the play as instructed, but can't. While Tony holes himself up to work, Mary finds herself growing interested in another man. When the completed play, *Calico and Lust,* is rejected, despondent Tony throws all but one copy off the Brooklyn Bridge. Director John van Druten reads the last copy of Tony's play, and persuades Miss Bankhead to take it to Broadway. Though the play's future is uncertain, the star tells Tony that the important thing is not to lower one's standards. Tony and Mary are happily reunited.

NOTE: Shirley has only a cameo appearance in this film, playing herself as the star of *Time of the Cuckoo,* and signing autographs for a group of fans as she leaves the Empire Theatre.

TAGLINE: "A Love Story of Show Business!"

REVIEWS: "*Main Street to Broadway* is notably inferior in the qualities of photography, sound and music. It was two years in the making and shows it.... It will captivate neither Main Street nor Broadway." —*Los Angeles Times,* 8/15/53 / "With the very best of intentions but with a casual surrender of the trust of their own and the theatre's reputations, some two or three dozen theatrical folk have taken part in a motion-picture project that is unworthy of either the theatre or the screen ... a cheap and badly slipshod 'all-star' show." —*New York Times,* 10/14/53

About Mrs. Leslie (1954)

CREDITS: Directed by Daniel Mann; produced by Hal B. Wallis; screenplay, Ketti Frings and Hal Kanter, from the novel by Viña Delmar; costumes, Edith Head; music score by Victor Young; assistant director, Richard McWhorter; makeup supervision, Wally Westmore. Paramount; released June 27, 1954. 104 minutes, B&W.

Mrs. Leslie (Shirley) sends away Pixie's troublemaking friends in *About Mrs. Leslie*.

CAST: Shirley Booth (Vivien Keeler), Robert Ryan (George Hendersall), Marjie Millar (Nadine Rowland *a.k.a.* Alice), Alex Nicol (Lan McKay), Henry [Harry] Morgan (Fred Blue), Eilene Janssen (Pixie Croffman), Philip Ober (Mort Finley), Maidie Norman (Camilla), Gale Page (Marion King), Ellen Corby (Mrs. Croffman), Ike Jones (Jim), Ian Wolfe (Mr. Pope), James Bell (Mr. Poole), Virginia Brissac (Mrs. Poole), Mabel Albertson (Mrs. Sims)

SUMMARY: Vivien, known to friends and neighbors as Mrs. Leslie, is a former New York nightclub singer. Now the middle-aged owner of a Beverly Hills rooming house, her tenants include aspiring performers Nadine and Lan, as well as elderly Mr. and Mrs. Poole, whose daughter is ill. During the course of an eventful day for her tenants, Vivien reminisces about a man she knew as George Leslie, and the unconventional romantic relationship they enjoyed until his untimely death.

TAGLINE: *"About Mrs. Leslie ... and the man she never quite married!"*

QUOTE: VIVIEN: For 46 weeks I could live somehow, because I knew when January came, I'd be there.

REVIEW: "As for Shirley, *About Mrs. Leslie* should suggest to her that Hollywood cannot always be trusted to provide the best employment for her remarkable acting talents."—*Time*, 7/5/54 / "...a soppy, or soapy, melodrama of dubious worth wrong out with all the strength of her particular genius by its star.... Shirley Booth is what matters, not the story, and it is she who gives *About Mrs. Leslie* what stature it has."—*Washington Post*, 7/22/54 / "Miss Booth provides the role with humor, humanness, and warmth."—*Chicago Tribune*, 8/4/54

The Matchmaker (1958)

CREDITS: Directed by Joseph Anthony; screenplay by John Michael Hayes, from the play by Thornton Wilder; director of photography, Charles Lang, Jr.; art direction, Hal Pereira and Roland Anderson; special photographic effects, John P. Fulton; set decoration, Sam Comer and Robert Benton; dialogue coach, William Ross; costumes, Edith Head; edited by Howard Smith; assistant director, C.C. Coleman, Jr.; makeup supervision, Wally Westmore; hair style supervision, Nellie Manley; sound recording by Gene Merritt and Winston Leverett; music score by

Adolph Deutsch. Paramount, released August 12, 1958. 103 minutes; B&W.

CAST: Shirley Booth (Dolly Levi), Anthony Perkins (Cornelius Hackl), Shirley MacLaine (Irene Molloy), Paul Ford (Horace Vandergelder), Robert Morse (Barnaby Tucker), Perry Wilson (Minnie Fay), Wallace Ford (Malachi Stack), Russell Collins (Joe Scanlon), Rex Evans (August), Gavin Gordon (Rudolph), Torbin Meyer (Maitre D')

SUMMARY: In 1890s Yonkers, New York, widowed Dolly Levi is playing matchmaker for irascible, 60-year-old merchant Horace Vandergelder. Both Vandergelder and his young chief clerk, Cornelius, are smitten with Irene Molloy, who operates a hat shop in New York City. Dolly schemes to aid and abet the romance of Cornelius and Irene, while setting her own cap for the well-to-do Vandergelder.

REVIEWS: "Miss Booth is no less than superb, draining [her] part of comedic possibilities.... One of the most engaging comedies of the season." — *Variety*, 5/7/58 / "Shirley Booth takes over the role of the Yonkers matchmaker that Ruth Gordon made so famous on Broadway and, considering her gentle quality, does very well with it ... an undeniably lively movie show." — *Saturday Review*, 8/16/58 / "Shirley Booth is a little too heavy in the key role of the matchmaker. She tries too hard to dig too deeply into the character, as though she were fighting the very conventions of the medium. As a result, she throws some of the situations off balance." — *Films and Filming*, November 1958

Hot Spell (1958)

CREDITS: Directed by Daniel Mann; produced by Hal B. Wallis; screenplay by James Poe, based upon a play by Lonnie Coleman; associate producer, Paul Nathan; director of photography, Loyal Griggs; music score, Alex North; art direction, Hal Pereira, Tambi Larsen; special photographic effects, John P. Fulton; process photography, Farciot Edouart; set decoration, Sam Comer, Arthur Krams; editorial supervision, Warren Low; costumes, Edith Head; makeup supervision, Wally Westmore; hair style supervision, Nellie Manley; assistant director, Michael D. Moore; sound recording, Harold Lewis, Winston Leverett. Paramount; released September 17, 1958. 86 minutes; B&W.

CAST: Shirley Booth (Alma Duval), Anthony Quinn (John Henry Duval), Shirley MacLaine (Virginia Duval), Earl Holliman (Buddy Duval), Eileen Heckart (Alma's Friend), Clint Kimbrough (Billy Duval), Warren Stevens (Wyatt Mitchell), Irene Tedrow (Essie Mae), Anthony Jochim (Preacher)

SUMMARY: In New Orleans, fortyish Alma Duval chooses to ignore the mounting evidence that husband Jack is seeing another woman, and can't accept the idea that her children are now young adults. Instead, Alma idealizes the early days of her marriage, when she and Jack lived in the small town of New Paris, and dismisses her friend Fen's more cynical view of men. Alma's daughter Virginia is involved with a pre-med student whose attentions may or may not be honorable, while headstrong

10349-5

Shirley in one of her favorite movie roles — as Dolly Levi in *The Matchmaker* (Paramount, 1958).

The stars of *Hot Spell* (left to right): Anthony Quinn, Shirley Booth, Earl Holliman, Shirley MacLaine, Clint Kimbrough.

son Buddy rebels against his father's refusal to acknowledge him as an equal. When Alma finds perfume and lipstick on Jack's shirt, and can no longer deny the truth about her marriage, a chain of events is set into motion that turns things upside down for every member of the Duval family.

REVIEWS: "...a sensitively observed and breathingly real tragedy of family life ... the acting in all the major roles is wonderfully full and natural...." — *Time*, 6/23/58 / "What distinguishes the Paramount film is the generally superior acting and that by Miss Booth.... There is heartbreak here." — *Los Angeles Times*, 6/12/58

The Smugglers (1968)

CREDITS: Produced and directed by Norman Lloyd; teleplay by Alfred Hayes, based on the novel *Package Deal* by Elizabeth Hely; director of photography, John F. Warren; assistant director, Edward K. Dobbs; original music, Lyn Murray; film editor, Douglas Stewart; makeup, Bud Westmore. Universal; aired December 24, 1968, on NBC-TV.

CAST: Shirley Booth (Mrs. Hudson), Carol Lynley (Jo Hudson), Kurt Kasznar (Willi Raben), Emilio Fernandez (Inspector Cesare Brunelli), Donnelly Rhodes (Antoine Cirret), David Opatoshu (Alfredo Faggio), Charles Drake (Harry Miller), Michael J. Pollard (Piero), Ilka Windish (Anna), Gayle Hunnicutt (Adrianna), Ralph Manza (Batisto), Albert Szabo (Anton)

SUMMARY: American tourist Mrs. Hudson, vacationing in Austria with her stepdaughter, becomes involved with a crook who tricks her into smuggling contraband across the Italian border. Once in Italy, the two American women take up residence at the secluded castle where the smuggler's accomplices carry out their work — and deal harshly with anyone who interferes.

NOTE: This "World Premiere" TV-movie was filmed in the fall of 1966, shortly after Shirley concluded her run in *Hazel,* but did not receive its initial airing until more than two years later.

REVIEW: "...strictly grade B international crime stuff. Despite the presence of Shirley Booth and Carol Lynley — in roles far beneath their talents — the story wandered ... and every time the action lagged, a few more corpses turned up." — Cynthia Lowry, Associated Press, 12/26/68

Appendix D:
Hazel Episode Guide

CREDITS: Executive producer, Harry Ackerman; produced by James Fonda; created by Ted Key, based on the *Saturday Evening Post* character; script consultants, William Cowley and Peggy Chantler; directed by William D. Russell (except where noted); director of photography, Frederick Gately; art directors, Ross Bellah, Malcolm C. Bert; film editors, Tom Biggart, Asa Clark, Eda Warren; set decorators, Louis Diage, Darrell Silvera, Alfred E. Spencer; music supervision, Ed Forsyth, Irving Friedman; makeup supervision, Ben Lane; assistant directors, Harold Lewis, William P. Owens, R. Robert Rosenbaum, Herb Wallerstein; production supervisor, Seymour Friedman; post-production supervisor, Lawrence Werner; music editor, Emil Cadkin; title song, Howard Greenfield, Jack Keller; sound effects, Fred J. Brown, Jack Kirschner; color by Pathé. Screen Gems Productions; 154 episodes.

CAST: Shirley Booth (Hazel Burke), Don DeFore (George Baxter, seasons 1–4), Whitney Blake (Dorothy Baxter; seasons 1–4), Bobby Buntrock (Harold Baxter), Ray Fulmer (Steve Baxter, season 5), Lynn Borden (Barbara Baxter, season 5), Julia Benjamin (Susie Baxter, season 5)

HISTORY: Aired Thursdays at 9:30 P.M. on NBC-TV (1961–1965); Mondays at 9:30 P.M. on CBS-TV (1965-1966).

FIRST SEASON (1961-62)

Pilot: Dorothy's Birthday

WRITTEN BY: William Cowley and Peggy Chantler
CAST: Edward Andrews (George Baxter), Joan Banks (Jane Edwards), Deirdre Owen (Agnes Collins), Hal Smith (Barney), Kenny Jackson (Fred), Ollie O'Toole (Charlie)
SUMMARY: Hazel works hard on her day off serving a last-minute luncheon for Dorothy and her friends. George tries to repay her by taking his wife and son out to dinner that night, but Hazel is unhappy being left at home alone on Dorothy's birthday.
NOTES: This pilot episode, filmed in early 1961 and never aired, has a different actor in the role of George Baxter, though Whitney Blake and Bobby Buntrock are on hand as Dorothy and Harold. Much of the footage from the pilot will be recycled when this script is reused for episode #23. Actor Hal Smith, known to fans of *The Andy Griffith Show* (CBS, 1960–68) as Otis Campbell, appears briefly as mailman Barney, a character played in the series by Robert B. Williams. Joan Banks, who plays a snooty friend of Dorothy's, had a recurring role as Sylvia on the 1950s sitcom *Private Secretary*. The instrumental theme used in the closing credits, attributed to Fred Steiner, is different from what was ultimately used in the series.

1. Hazel and the Playground

AIR DATE: September 28, 1961
WRITTEN BY: William Cowley and Peggy Chantler
CAST: Donald Foster (Herbert Johnson), Norma Varden (Harriet Johnson), Maurice Manson (Mr. Pruett), Lurene Tuttle (Mrs. Pruett), Hal Smith (Milton, the TV Announcer), Francis DeSales (Osborn Bailey)
SUMMARY: Hazel decides that the neighborhood

kids need a playground, and that half of the nearby botanical garden would make the perfect spot. Her petition campaign, which she plugs during a TV appearance with her bowling team, attracts the attention of George's new client, whose family founded the garden.

NOTES: Hal Smith, previously cast as mailman Barney in the pilot, returns here as the announcer who hosts the local TV coverage of the city bowling championship, which Hazel wins. The Baxters' lovably goofy neighbors the Johnsons make their debut here. Actor Donald Foster, cast in the recurring role of Herbert, co-starred with Shirley in the early 1940s Broadway hit *My Sister Eileen.*

2. Hazel Makes a Will

AIR DATE: October 4, 1961
WRITTEN BY: William Cowley and Peggy Chantler
CAST: Maudie Prickett (Rosie), Robert B. Williams (Barney), Wright King (Leroy Burke), Queenie Leonard (Mert)
SUMMARY: Hazel and George are gearing up to negotiate her annual raise when she trips and falls over the step he neglected to repair. When she sends for her lawyer nephew, George concludes that he's about to be sued.
NOTES: This episode introduces Maudie Prickett as Hazel's friend and fellow maid Rosie Hamecker, and mailman Barney, as played by recurring actor Robert B. Williams.

3. Hazel Plays Nurse

AIR DATE: October 12, 1961
WRITTEN BY: William Cowley and Peggy Chantler
CAST: Howard Smith (Harvey Griffin), Henry Hunter (Dr. Summerfield), Hal Baylor (Gordy), Molly Dodd (Miss Scott)
SUMMARY: George has an important meeting with a client, but Hazel puts him to bed when she realizes he's come down with a cold. Mr. Griffin, who's also sick, thinks this is a poor excuse for missing a meeting, until he encounters Hazel.
NOTES: George's frequent client Harvey Griffin is introduced. Actor Howard Smith was previously a featured player in Shirley's 1949 radio series *Hogan's Daughter,* playing her father. Two other minor recurring characters, the Baxters' family doctor and George's legal secretary Miss Scott, are seen for the first time as well.

4. A Matter of Principle

AIR DATE: October 19, 1961
WRITTEN BY: Louella MacFarlane
CAST: Vinton Hayworth (Mr. Sutherland), Lewis Martin (Judge Rosencrantz), Larry Haddon (Prosecutor), John Lasell (Officer Dietrich), Victor French (Bailiff)
SUMMARY: Hazel ropes George into defending her

in court against a $2 ticket she received for an expired parking meter.
NOTES: Like a number of the guest players in this series, Vinton Hayworth had acted onstage with Shirley. They co-starred in the unsuccessful 1947 play *Heartsong,* which closed out of town. TV viewers know him for his recurring role as General Winfield Schaeffer in the later years of *I Dream of Jeannie* (NBC, 1965–70). He will reprise the role of Ralph Sutherland in several *Hazel* segments. The first script not attributed to Cowley and Chantler is the work of Louella MacFarlane, who will be credited with more than 20 *Hazel* segments, including the series finale in 1966.

5. Dorothy's New Client

AIR DATE: October 26, 1961
WRITTEN BY: William Cowley and Peggy Chantler
CAST: Joan Banks (Francesca Kettering), Mary Jackson (Flora Duncan), Maudie Prickett (Rosie), Robert B. Williams (Barney), Alice Backes (Della), Queenie Leonard (Mert), Kay Stewart (Mrs. Wagner)
SUMMARY: Dorothy needs a decorating job to pay for the chair she bought George. Hazel enlists the help of the Sunshine Girls to persuade a new neighbor to hire Dorothy instead of an unscrupulous rival.
NOTES: Hazel's circle of friends, the Sunshine Girls, is introduced in this episode. Actress Joan Banks, who had earlier appeared in the *Hazel* pilot, plays another disagreeable character here.

6. "What'll We Watch Tonight?"

AIR DATE: November 2, 1961
WRITTEN BY: William Cowley and Peggy Chantler
CAST: Walter Kinsella (Thornton), John Graham (Jerry Burns), Annelle Hayes (Margaret Burns), Maudie Prickett (Rosie), Queenie Leonard (Mert)
SUMMARY: Tired of having Hazel interfere with his TV viewing, George agrees to replace the set in her room. Instead of buying another small black-and-white set, however, Hazel uses George's money to make a down payment on a color set. Friends and neighbors crowd the Baxter house to experience the wonders of TV in color.
NOTES: The only color episode of the first season, this is little more than a 30-minute commercial for color television sets, though a pleasant enough outing. Another NBC series already airing in color, *The Perry Como Show* (1948–63), is plugged liberally.

7. A Dog for Harold

AIR DATE: November 9, 1961
WRITTEN BY: Ray Allen and Jim Allen

CAST: Lou Krugman (Mr. Roberts), John Graham (Bob Waters), Raymond Guth (Chuck)
SUMMARY: When George refuses to let Harold keep the stray dog he brought home, Hazel and Dorothy scheme to make him reconsider. Their discussion of a local burglary scare prompts not the acquisition of a dog, but instead a burglar alarm.
NOTE: Harold's dog Smiley is introduced.

8. George's Niece

AIR DATE: November 16, 1961
WRITTEN BY: William Cowley and Peggy Chantler
CAST: Cathy Lewis (Deirdre Thompson), John Washbrook (Eddy Burke), Davey Davison (Nancy Thompson), Larry Blake (Tom Forbes)
SUMMARY: George's chilly sister Deirdre announces that she and her family, including daughter Nancy, will be moving into town from Boston. Deidre, whose relationship with Nancy is strained, can't conceal her displeasure when the teenager accepts a date with Hazel's nephew Eddy.
NOTES: The series' head writers introduce another pivotal recurring character. Cathy Lewis, whose credits included a starring role in the 1950s sitcom *My Friend Irma* (both on radio and television), provides an excellent sparring partner and counterpoint to Booth's character. Lewis will be one of the few guest players on this series to be given her own solo billing card in the closing credits, usually reading, "And Cathy Lewis as Deirdre." This is the last episode to feature the lyrics to the show's theme song, performed by the Modernaires. Subsequent episodes will use an instrumental version of the theme.
QUOTE: DEIRDRE *(to Dorothy)*— Until I started talking to Hazel, I was fine! Why you and George persist in keeping that woman, I'll never understand!

9. Everybody's Thankful but Us Turkeys

AIR DATE: November 23, 1961
WRITTEN BY: William Cowley and Peggy Chantler
SUMMARY: While cooking an enormous Thanksgiving dinner for the Baxters, Hazel finds time to solve the marital problems of George's sister Phyllis, cure his mother's loneliness, and keep tabs on the Johnsons' dinner as well.
CAST: Donald Foster (Herbert Johnson), Norma Varden (Harriet Johnson), Harriet MacGibbon (Mother Baxter), Beverly Tyler (Phyllis Burkett), Charles Cooper (Bob Burkett), Maida Severn (Phoebe), William Bakewell (Tom)
NOTES: More Baxter relatives are introduced, including another sister. Although last week's episode showed Deirdre and her family planning to settle nearby, no mention of them is made here. The endearingly goofy Johnsons are seen

for the first time since the series opener. Mention is made of Hazel's sister Jenny, though she's unseen.

10. Winter Wonderland

AIR DATE: December 7, 1961
WRITTEN BY: Louella MacFarlane
CAST: William Zuckert (Johnny Manson), Maudie Prickett (Rosie), Florence Sundstrom (Minna), Sally Mansfield (Pat Bergstrom)
SUMMARY: Hazel is looking forward to a family trip to a ski lodge, but she has to stay home when George is delayed by business. Dorothy encourages Hazel to use any method possible — including Rosie's yodeling — to get George to put his business aside and join the vacation.
NOTES: The actor who plays Hazel's partner in a dog-sled race is mistakenly billed as having played Joe, rather than Johnny. Actress Sundstrom, who plays Hazel's rival here, will later return to the series as one of the Sunshine Girls. Thanks to a real-life mishap in his home workshop, Don DeFore shot several first-season episodes with his hand bandaged. Because the episodes aired out of sequence, his injury comes and goes from week to week. It's visible here.

11. Hazel's Winning Personality

AIR DATE: December 14, 1961
TELEPLAY BY: William Cowley and Peggy Chantler
STORY BY: Ray Allen and Jim Allen
CAST: George Mitchell (Zeke), Dee J. Thompson (Laura), Chet Stratton (Mr. Goodheart), Louise Lorimer (Mrs. Osborne), Fred Downs (Charles Perkins)
SUMMARY: Hazel and her shy friend Laura attend a night class, "You and Your Dynamic Personality." The instructor recommends a steady diet of compliments, but Hazel's application of the technique goes awry.
NOTE: George's freeloading cousin Charlie, introduced in this episode, introduces what will become a running theme on *Hazel* — lazy, deadbeat Baxter relatives. Along with his snobbish sister Deirdre, George's family isn't presented in a very flattering light. Like so many players seen on this show, Downs had worked with Shirley onstage — he appeared in *By the Beautiful Sea.*

12. Hazel's Christmas Shopping

AIR DATE: December 21, 1961
WRITTEN BY: William Cowley and Peggy Chantler
CAST: Byron Foulger (Larry), Maudie Prickett (Rosie), Dan Tobin (Mr. Brubaker), Hope Cameron (Saleslady), Robert B. Williams (Barney), Bert Whaley (Store Detective), Eleanor Audley, Hope Spring (Customers)
SUMMARY: Hazel takes a seasonal job at Masterson's Department Store to pay for her Christmas

present to Dorothy. Her unorthodox approach to customer service almost gets her fired, until she helps nab the shoplifter who's been plaguing the store.

NOTES: Dan Tobin, who plays the department store floorwalker, was one of Shirley's co-stars in the 1939-40 Broadway production of *The Philadelphia Story*. Veteran character actress Eleanor Audley makes the first of her several *Hazel* appearances. Among other roles, she played Oliver Douglas' mother on *Green Acres* (CBS, 1965–71).

13. Dorothy's Obsession

AIR DATE: December 28, 1961
WRITTEN BY: Robert Riley Crutcher
CAST: Frances Helm (Peggy Baldwin), Lauren Gilbert (Phil Baldwin), Hal Taggart (Mr. Burton), Roy Wright (Pete), Don Rhodes (Joe)
SUMMARY: Dorothy visits an estate sale and buys not only an antique desk for her friend Peggy, but a piano for the Baxter house. She and Hazel scheme to convince George he wants a piano before the delivery men arrive.
NOTES: Actor Lauren Gilbert, who plays Peggy's exasperated husband, will later return to *Hazel* in a recurring role as George's law partner, Harry Noll. Much is made in this script of how good the piano looks in the living room, and how much more suitable for a certain corner it is than the chair they were using there. Nonetheless, in subsequent episodes, the piano will be nowhere in sight, and the chair back in its usual place ... This is the first *Hazel* episode penned by Robert Riley Crutcher, who will contribute more than three dozen scripts to the series over its five-year run.

14. Hazel's Dog Days

AIR DATE: January 4, 1962
WRITTEN BY: Robert Riley Crutcher
CAST: Wendell Holmes (Mr. Wagner), Kay Stewart (Louise James), Jennifer Gillespie (Sandra Wagner), Dan Sheridan (Mr. Harris), Jean Jory (Miss Miller), Don Kennedy (Dog Trainer)
SUMMARY: When the Baxters take Harold's dog Smiley to obedience school, the staff recognizes him as the dog stolen from one of their other clients. Hazel tries to find a solution that will prevent Harold from losing his beloved pet.

15. Replacement for Phoebe

AIR DATE: January 11, 1962
TELEPLAY BY: James Allardice
STORY BY: James Fonda
CAST: Donald Foster (Herbert Johnson), Norma Varden (Harriet Johnson), Tamar Cooper (Agnes), Elvia Allman (Gertrude), Frank Milan (Mr. Sprague), Claire Carleton (Elizabeth)

SUMMARY: When the Johnsons' maid quits, Hazel promises to find them a new one. George's patience is tested as each candidate for the job is given a trial run at the Baxters' house.
NOTES: This is the only *Hazel* script contributed by James Allardice, better known for writing the host's witty introductions on *Alfred Hitchcock Presents* (CBS, 1955–65). Elvia Allman (1904–1992), who plays militaristic martinet Gertrude, had a recurring role as Selma Plout on *Petticoat Junction* (CBS, 1963–70), and was the forewoman of Kramer's Kandy Kitchen in the iconic *I Love Lucy* episode "Job Switching." Actor Frank Milan, who plays the demanding Mr. Sprague, was a friend and occasional escort of Shirley's dating back to their Broadway hit *The Desk Set*.

16. Hazel's Famous Recipes

AIR DATE: January 18, 1962
WRITTEN BY: Robert Riley Crutcher
CAST: Harry Ellerbe (Mr. Fenton), Maudie Prickett (Rosie), Robert B. Williams (Barney), Jack Daly (Mr. Hathaway)
SUMMARY: Hazel has been trying to find a publisher for her cookbook, "Hazel's Handy Recipes," but eight publishers have rejected the manuscript. But when George finds a publisher willing to take it on, the Baxters and Hazel herself are taken aback by the idea of her leaving her job for an extended publicity tour.
NOTE: Actor Harry Ellerbe, who plays Hazel's prospective publisher, appeared opposite Shirley Booth in the Broadway production of *The Desk Set*.
QUOTE: DOROTHY—George, you like Hazel, don't you? You like her very much. I mean, you're very fond of her, aren't you? GEORGE: Why, of course I am! If I weren't, I'd have fired her for keeps years ago!

17. Hazel's Tough Customer

AIR DATE: January 25, 1962
WRITTEN BY: Louella MacFarlane
CAST: Howard Smith (Harvey Griffin), Robert B. Williams (Barney), Norman Leavitt (Charley), Charles Tannen (Gus), Molly Dodd (George's Secretary)
SUMMARY: Spurned by Barney in favor of a "dishwater blonde," Hazel worries that she's losing her appeal to men, until an unlikely suitor appears on the horizon. Grouchy Mr. Griffin buys a house in the neighborhood, and proposes marriage to Hazel.
NOTE: Hazel's long-ago boyfriend Gus is seen in a dream sequence here. The actor's face is hidden, because it doesn't match the photo seen at her bedside in previous episodes. Gus resurfaces for real in #67.

18. Hazel's Secret Wish

AIR DATE: February 1, 1962
TELEPLAY BY: William Cowley, Peggy Chantler, and Louella MacFarlane
STORY BY: Louella MacFarlane
CAST: Kathryn Givney (Mrs. Forbes-Craigie), Jean Engstrom (Mrs. Camden), Betty Lou Gerson (Mrs. Willoughby), Maxine Stuart (Louise), Peg LaCentra (Edith Stone), Danielle Aubry (Anna)
SUMMARY: Dorothy's magazine-editor friend offers Hazel a free two-week vacation at Rancho Verde, an exclusive resort. Afraid her wealthy clients will be offended, the resort owner asks Hazel not to tell other guests she's a maid.
NOTE: Actress Kathryn Givney, who plays one of the resort's wealthy guests, co-starred with Shirley Booth on Broadway in *Tomorrow the World.* She plays similarly well-heeled characters in episodes #95, 136, and 151.

19. Hazel, the Tryst-Buster

AIR DATE: February 8, 1962
WRITTEN BY: William Cowley and Peggy Chantler
CAST: Kathie Browne (Trudy Garson), Walter Reed (Fred Garson), Sheila Bromley (Mrs. Arnold)
SUMMARY: George's old girlfriend Trudy seeks him out after a fight with her husband. Dorothy isn't worried by this, but Hazel is convinced that Trudy means to have George for herself.
NOTE: Browne, a frequent TV guest star during this period, was later the real-life wife of actor Darren McGavin, from 1969 until her death in 2003. She returns to *Hazel* in #115.

20. The Investment Club

AIR DATE: February 15, 1962
TELEPLAY BY: William Cowley, Peggy Chantler, and James Fonda
STORY BY: James Fonda
CAST: Frederick Downs (Charlie Parkins), Dee J. Thompson (Laurie), John Astin (Hal Gordon), J. Edward McKinley (Howard Porter), Gertrude Flynn (Hilda), Skip Torgerson (Ralph)
SUMMARY: George wants no part of advising the Sunshine Girls on their investments, until he sees them about to fall victim to some shady dealers who use subliminal suggestion to sell worthless stock.
NOTES: George's deadbeat cousin Charlie makes his second appearance, his name having changed slightly since episode #11. A young and clean-shaven John Astin, pre–*Addams Family,* is featured in this episode. Although the Sunshine Girls figure prominently in this episode, Maudie Prickett's Rosie is inexplicably absent.

21. Hazel's Mona Lisa Grin

AIR DATE: March 1, 1962
WRITTEN BY: Robert Riley Crutcher

CAST: Cathy Lewis (Deirdre Thompson), Mario Siletti (Charlie), Ralph Clanton (Mr. Williams), Howard Wendell (Mr. Bowles)
SUMMARY: George's sister Deirdre just spent a small fortune having her new house decorated by an exclusive designer from New York. So how come she has a picture of Hazel over the mantel?
NOTE: Character actor Mario Siletti, seen here as the proprietor of a junk shop, is recognizable to *I Love Lucy* fans as knife-wielding Professor Falconi from the classic 1953 episode "Lucy Tells the Truth." He will reprise his role as Charlie in several later *Hazel* episodes.

22. Hazel and the Gardener

AIR DATE: March 8, 1962
WRITTEN BY: William Cowley and Peggy Chantler
CAST: O.Z. Whitehead (Ernie Talbott), Joan Tompkins (Florence Gurney), Henry Beckman (Pitchman), Molly Dodd (Miss Scott)
SUMMARY: George threatens to fire Ernie, the gardener, whose work has suffered since he was dumped by his girlfriend. Hazel takes it upon herself to rekindle his interest in life — and save his job.
NOTES: A new opening title sequence makes its debut with this installment. It shows Hazel standing at the front door to welcome the Baxters home from a trip, waving as they get out of the car, and then running out to the curb to embrace them. Guest player Joan Tompkins appeared opposite Shirley in Broadway's *My Sister Eileen.*

23. Dorothy's Birthday

AIR DATE: March 15, 1962
WRITTEN BY: William Cowley and Peggy Chantler
CAST: Joan Banks (Jane Edwards), Deidre Owen (Agnes Collins), Robert B. Williams (Barney), Sam Edwards (Fred), Ollie O'Toole (Charlie)
SUMMARY: Hazel works hard all day serving a luncheon in honor of Dorothy's birthday. George tries to repay her by taking his wife and son out to dinner that night, but Hazel is unhappy being left at home alone.
NOTES: This episode is a revamped version of the series pilot, with minor script changes. It contains footage retained from the version shot with Edward Andrews as George, though all of George's scenes have been redone with Don DeFore. Shirley isn't wearing her usual *Hazel* wig here, so that the new footage will match scenes shot for the pilot.

24. Number, Please?

AIR DATE: March 22, 1962
WRITTEN BY: William Cowley and Peggy Chantler
CAST: Dub Taylor (Mitch Brady), Vinton Hayworth

(Mr. Sutherland), Fay Baker (Madeleine), George Lambert (Tom)

SUMMARY: Tired of sales calls, George signs up the Baxters for an unlisted phone number. The plan backfires when an important client needs to call George from overseas, but has been given the phone number of a local cab company instead of the Baxters' new number.

NOTES: Vinton Hayworth reprises his role as George's client Mr. Sutherland from episode #4, while Dub Taylor makes the first of several appearances as Hazel's occasional date Mitch Brady. Mention is made here that the Baxters live on Marshall Road.

25. Them New Neighbors Is Nice

AIR DATE: March 29, 1962
WRITTEN BY: William Cowley and Peggy Chantler
CAST: John Newton (Stan Blake), Paul Engle (Don Blake), Charles Tannen (Whit), Fred Graham (Bob)

SUMMARY: Over George's objections, Hazel gets chummy with the new neighbors, a widower and his teenage son. The boy develops an immediate crush on Dorothy, and Hazel unwittingly encourages him to make his feelings known.

NOTES: The Blake family, introduced here, will appear occasionally for the remainder of this season, with one final appearance midway through Season 2.

26. Hazel's Pajama Party

AIR DATE: April 5, 1962
WRITTEN BY: William Cowley and Peggy Chantler
CAST: Brenda Scott (Linda Blake), Paul Engle (Don Blake), Ann Marshall (Mary Selby)

SUMMARY: Hazel organizes a pajama party for boy-crazy neighbor Linda. George and Dorothy try to prevent her feelings from being hurt when it turns out that the teenagers don't want Hazel to attend the party.

NOTES: Paul Engle reprises his role as teenage neighbor Don. Don's sister Linda, mentioned but not seen in the previous installment, appears also. Two younger Blake children are discussed but not seen.

27. Three Little Cubs

AIR DATE: April 12, 1962
WRITTEN BY: Louella MacFarlane
CAST: Alix Talton (Anne Kingsley), Henry Hunter (Dr. Bruce Kingsley), Scott Lane (William Kingsley), Rickie Sorenson (Sid), Mary Treen (Nurse), Donnie Carter (David), Allen Gerard (Tom)

SUMMARY: Hazel decides that joining Harold's Cub Scout troop would be just the ticket for a snobbish and overprotected little boy.

NOTES: Alix Talton co-starred in the CBS sitcom *My Favorite Husband* (1953–55). Scott Lane was the juvenile lead in the NBC sitcom *McKeever and the Colonel* (1962-63). *TV Guide* critic Gilbert Seldes, reviewing *Hazel* in the magazine's April 26, 1962 issue, disliked the message he took away from this episode, saying that "it pains me to hear Hazel razzing the parents of a bright schoolboy because he isn't a Cub Scout," and complaining that the writers devalued the importance of education.

28. Bringing Out the Johnsons

AIR DATE: April 19, 1962
WRITTEN BY: Louella MacFarlane
CAST: Donald Foster (Herbert Johnson), Norma Varden (Harriet Johnson), Howard Smith (Harvey Griffin), Deirdre Owen (Precinct Worker)

SUMMARY: The Johnsons want to become more involved in the community, and offer their home as a polling place for a special election. Poll workers Hazel, George, and Dorothy make a bet with Mr. Griffin as to the outcome of the vote.

29. Hazel Quits

AIR DATE: April 26, 1962
WRITTEN BY: Keith Fowler and Phil Leslie
CAST: John Litel (Mr. Wheeler), Donald Foster (Herbert Johnson), Norma Varden (Harriet Johnson), Charles Seel (Chet Cooper), Larry Thor (TV Announcer), Paul Barselow (Mr. Blick)

SUMMARY: Hazel speaks out on TV against the draining of a local lake, unaware that the man who bought the property is George's client. George refuses to give in to Mr. Wheeler's demand that his outspoken maid be fired, but she decides to help her boss by temporarily leaving the Baxters to fill in for the Johnsons' vacationing maid Agnes.

NOTES: This plot is reminiscent of the series opener. Once again, Hazel's stance on a civic issue puts her at odds with a Baxter client. Having mastered the art of plugging in the TV set on last week's show, this week Mr. Johnson learns to use the vacuum cleaner.

30. Hazel the Matchmaker

AIR DATE: May 3, 1962
WRITTEN BY: Edward Kirsch
CAST: John Newton (Stan Blake), Doris Singleton (Mimi Andrews), Renee Godfrey (Miss Lewis), Maudie Prickett (Rosie), Paul Engle (Don Blake), Kim Tyler (Stevie), Judy Erwin (Mavis), Brenda Scott (Linda), Vici Raaf (Manicurist)

SUMMARY: George objects when Hazel and Dorothy try to pair neighbor Stan with Harold's teacher. But when Stan shows an interest in being fixed up, George has his own idea as to a woman who would suit him. Hazel correctly guesses that George's candidate isn't cut out to be a stepmother to four children.

NOTES: Widower Stan Blake returns, this time with all four of his children seen. Doris Singleton is best known for her recurring role as Caroline Appleby on *I Love Lucy*. Renee Godfrey is mistakenly billed as having played Miss Johnson. The character's name may have been changed during filming so as to avoid confusion with the Baxters' other neighbors. Maudie Prickett returns as Rosie after an absence of several weeks.

31. Rock-a-Bye Baby

AIR DATE: May 10, 1962
WRITTEN BY: Peggy Chantler
CAST: Donald Foster (Herbert Johnson), Norma Varden (Harriet Johnson), Mary Grace Canfield (Miss Simmons), Don Dorrell (David Watson), Pat McNulty (Angela Watson)
SUMMARY: The Johnsons are taking care of her niece's baby while the young couple is away. Guess who pitches in to help when the baby nurse proves unsuitable?
NOTE: Mary Grace Canfield, who plays the inflexible baby nurse, is better known to sitcom fans as the female half of the inept carpentry team of Alf and Ralph Monroe on *Green Acres* (CBS, 1965–71).

32. The Burglar in Mr. B's P.J.'s

AIR DATE: May 17, 1962
WRITTEN BY: William Cowley
CAST: Alan Hale (Peter)
SUMMARY: While the Baxters are out at a dance, Hazel takes it upon herself to lend a helping hand to the down-on-his-luck man who broke into the house in search of food.
NOTE: Alan Hale had already starred in the syndicated series *Biff Baker, U.S.A.* (1952-53) and *Casey Jones* (1957-58), but hadn't yet been cast in his famous role as the Skipper on *Gilligan's Island* (CBS, 1964–67). He will return to *Hazel* in episode #74.

33. Heat Wave

AIR DATE: May 24, 1962
WRITTEN BY: Louella MacFarlane
CAST: Virginia Gregg (Mrs. Merryweather), Maudie Prickett (Rosie), Mario Siletti (Charlie), Robert B. Williams (Barney), Howard Wright (Mr. Butterworth), Jean Owens (Mrs. Butterworth)
SUMMARY: Hazel is envious when Rosie's employers, the Craigs, install central air conditioning. When George refuses to do the same, Hazel

schemes to get her hands on the used window air conditioner the Craigs sold to her junk dealer friend.
NOTES: In this episode, George is made a partner in his law firm. Two days before this episode was first telecast, Shirley Booth won her first Emmy for the role of Hazel. Veteran character actress Virginia Gregg makes the first of several *Hazel* appearances, which will include two as Harold's schoolteacher Miss Tilcy. A longtime radio stalwart, she was one of the actresses whose voice was used to depict Norman Bates' mother in *Psycho* (1960).

34. George's Assistant

AIR DATE: May 31, 1962
WRITTEN BY: Robert Riley Crutcher
CAST: Don Spruance (Alan Merrick), Howard Smith (Harvey Griffin), Maggie Pierce (Gail Sanders), William Beckley (Jack), Ken Wales (Phil), Nesdon Booth (Mr. Merrick)
SUMMARY: George is exhausted from working on Mr. Griffin's account, and Hazel decides he needs an assistant. She thinks her friend's son, who just graduated from law school, fits the bill perfectly. But Mr. Griffin has a candidate of his own to recommend.

35. Hazel's Day

AIR DATE: June 7, 1962
WRITTEN BY: Peggy Chantler
CAST: Cathy Lewis (Deirdre Thompson), Dub Taylor (Mitch Brady), Walter Woolf King (Judge Farley), Robert P. Lieb (Harry Thompson), Theodore Newton (Dr. Carroll), George Mather (Photographer)
SUMMARY: Harold suggests that Hazel be honored with her own day like Mother's Day or Father's Day. When the planned date conflicts with Deirdre's dinner party, at which she intended to introduce George to an influential judge, Deidre can't believe which event takes precedence.
NOTES: Dub Taylor reprises his role from episode #24. Robert P. Lieb makes his debut as Deirdre's husband Harry. Though listed in some reference sources as a *Hazel* regular, he actually appears in fewer than ten of the show's 154 episodes. This episode reveals that Dorothy's maiden name is Webster.

SECOND SEASON (1962-63)

36. Hazel's Cousin

AIR DATE: September 13, 1962
WRITTEN BY: Robert Riley Crutcher

CAST: Rosemary DeCamp (Susie), Jean Engstrom (June Lowell), John Archer (John Lucius), Robert B. Williams (Barney), Harold Gould (Mr. Prior), Addison Myers (Camera Operator)

SUMMARY: Hazel's cousin Susie is now the enormously successful cosmetics queen Lady Sybil, who's about to marry a well-known society figure. When Susie's social secretary learns that Hazel is a maid, she decides to preserve the "gracious and refined social occasion" she's planned by excluding the bride's cousin.

NOTES: Rosemary DeCamp co-starred in the popular sitcom *The Bob Cummings Show* (NBC/CBS, 1954–59) and later played Marlo Thomas' mother on *That Girl* (ABC, 1966–71). Jean Engstrom, previously seen in episode #18, makes her second guest appearance on *Hazel*. This season's new competitor in the 9:30 P.M. Thursday slot was ABC's *McHale's Navy,* another sitcom starring an Oscar winner (Ernest Borgnine).

37. Rosie's Contract

AIR DATE: September 20, 1962
WRITTEN BY: Peggy Chantler
CAST: Maudie Prickett (Rosie), Richard St. John (Dr. Craig), Frank Creig (Carpenter), Joane Gaylord (Clerk)
SUMMARY: Rosie's boss Dr. Craig has George draw up a five-year contract for his maid. Despite Dorothy's misgivings, George and Hazel decide she needs one as well.
NOTE: In reality, Shirley Booth was under a five-year contract with Screen Gems to play Hazel.

38. We've Been So Happy Till Now

AIR DATE: September 27, 1962
WRITTEN BY: William Cowley
CAST: Steven Geray (Zoltan), Jonathan Hole (Fulton), Queenie Leonard (Mert), Frank Kreig (Monty), Barbara Bell Wright (Arlene)
SUMMARY: The morning after attending a party, George and Dorothy aren't speaking. The neighborhood grapevine soon has them ripe for a divorce. When Hazel learns that their argument concerned her, she decides it's her duty to set things right.
NOTE: With this episode, a new opening titles sequence was introduced. It shows Hazel sitting in the Baxters' convertible clutching a football and being showered with confetti. George and Dorothy step outside and laugh at the sight of Harold tossing confetti down from his perch on a tree limb, and their maid surrounded by little boys in football uniforms, with a banner identifying her as "Our Coach."
QUOTE: HAZEL (to the Baxters)—Boy, if you two don't start talkin' to each other, I'm gonna have a conniption fit!

39. How to Lure an Epicure

AIR DATE: October 4, 1962
WRITTEN BY: Robert Riley Crutcher
CAST: Alan Hewitt (Mr. Templeton), Peter Mamakos (Mr. Tonetti), Harry Ellerbe (Mr. Williams), Pat Michon (Marie), Queenie Leonard (Mert), Florence Sundstrom (Flo)
SUMMARY: George's friend Mr. Tonetti pins his hopes for the success of his new restaurant on a review by the acerbic critic of *Templeton's Restaurant Guide.* When Mr. Templeton fails to be impressed by Tonetti's cuisine, Hazel staffs his kitchen with Sunshine Girls to produce a meal he'll never forget.
NOTES: Harry Ellerbe plays a publisher for the second time on *Hazel,* though not the same one he played in episode #16. Busy character actor Alan Hewitt later played Detective Bill Brennan on *My Favorite Martian* (CBS, 1963–66). He returns to *Hazel* in #94.

40. Barney Hatfield, Where Are You?

AIR DATE: October 11, 1962
WRITTEN BY: Louella MacFarlane
CAST: Robert B. Williams (Barney), Irwin Charone (Mr. Cranston), Jamie Farr (Counterman), Judd Foster (Young Mailman), Cyril Delevanti (Elderly Man), Corinne Cole (Boo-Boo Bedoux), Darlene Fields (Stripper)
SUMMARY: Longtime mailman Barney calls in sick, but can't be located at his apartment. Using her only clue, a warmly inscribed photograph of a burlesque dancer, Hazel sets out to find her missing friend.
NOTE: Actor Jamie Farr, who later achieved fame as Corporal Klinger on *M*A*S*H* (CBS, 1972–83), appears briefly in this episode. He will return to *Hazel* with a more substantial role in #98.

41. A Four-Bit Word to Chew On

AIR DATE: October 18, 1962
WRITTEN BY: William Cowley
CAST: Howard Smith (Harvey Griffin), Bert Whaley (Bob)
SUMMARY: Mr. Griffin, who came from a poor family to become a successful executive, hires George to set up an educational foundation for disadvantaged youth. But George and Hazel's ongoing game of trying to stump each other with vocabulary words irks Mr. Griffin, who thinks George is mocking his lack of formal education.

42. Hazel's Tax Deduction

AIR DATE: October 25, 1962
WRITTEN BY: Robert Riley Crutcher
CAST: Maurice Manson (Mr. Floyd), Howard

Smith (Harvey Griffin), Robert Cornthwaite (Mr. Perkins), Viola Harris (Grace Fowler)

SUMMARY: When Internal Revenue agents question some of George's tax deductions, he's counting on Mr. Griffin to verify how much he uses his home for business purposes. But Mr. Griffin, who's getting ready to propose to a woman friend, is too preoccupied to help until Hazel steps in.

NOTES: Mention is made here of Mr. Griffin's previous marriage proposal to Hazel, which occurred in episode #17. Mr. Griffin fires George as his attorney for the second week in a row.

43. Mr. B on the Bench

AIR DATE: November 1, 1962
WRITTEN BY: William Cowley
CAST: Willis Bouchey (Arnold Winters), Maudie Prickett (Rosie), Robert B. Williams (Barney), Queenie Leonard (Mert), Bert Whaley (Bob), Florence Sundstrom (Flo)
SUMMARY: George is on the shortlist of candidates to replace a retiring Municipal Court judge. Proud Hazel can't wait to share the news with the neighborhood, not realizing that the breach of confidentiality will force her boss to make a difficult choice.

NOTE: Thanks to Hazel's eagerness to spread the news, this episode features virtually the entirety of her social network — mailman Barney, baker Bob, Rosie, and two other Sunshine Girls.

44. License to Wed

AIR DATE: November 8, 1962
WRITTEN BY: Louella MacFarlane
CAST: John Washbrook (Eddy Burke), Davey Davison (Nancy Thompson), Robert P. Lieb (Harry Thompson), Molly Dodd (Miss Scott)
SUMMARY: For once, Deirde and Hazel agree on something — neither of them thinks Eddie and Nancy are ready to get married. But while Deidre dissolves into hysterics, Hazel applies a little psychology to the situation.

NOTES: Seen in this episode is yet another variation on the show's opening titles, one of the most commonly used. This shorter version incorporates the footage of George and Dorothy laughing and waving from the doorway, and Harold throwing confetti. Hazel is seen taking a bag of groceries from the car and looking through them, replacing the footage of her with Harold's football team. As per this script, Hazel's opposition to Eddy getting married pertains to the scholarship he just won, and his chance to become the first member of the Burke family ever to attain a distinguished professional career. Clearly the writers have forgotten her other nephew, the lawyer, seen in episode #2.

45. Genie with the Light Brown Lamp

AIR DATE: November 15, 1962
WRITTEN BY: Robert Riley Crutcher
CAST: Frederic Downs (Charlie Parkins), Mario Siletti (Charlie), Virginia Gregg (Miss Tilcy), Paul Smith (Harrison)
SUMMARY: While on a family trip far from home, Harold's dog Smiley gets lost. After Hazel reads Harold a story about genies and magic lamps from the *Arabian Nights,* he buys a gravy boat from Charlie's antique shop that he thinks will help him get his dog back.

46. The Natural Athlete

AIR DATE: November 22, 1962
WRITTEN BY: William Cowley
CAST: William Zuckert (Jack Ballard), Bing Russell (Alex)
SUMMARY: George decides to give champion bowler Hazel, who's won the weekly bowling competition for several weeks in a row, a little competition. He signs up for lessons, using an assumed name, to polish his rusty bowling skills, but does so well that Hazel is warned the mysterious newcomer could unseat her as champion.

NOTES: Though Shirley convincingly plays a gifted bowler, she clearly isn't doing the actual bowling herself, as the camera cuts away from her every time she prepares to throw. Don DeFore, on the other hand, is seen several times bowling a strike without the aid of a double.

47. New Man in Town

AIR DATE: December 6, 1962
WRITTEN BY: Peggy Chantler
CAST: Robert Lowery (Pablo Rivera), Dub Taylor (Mitch Brady), Maudie Prickett (Rosie), Robert B. Williams (Barney), Florence Sundstrom (Flo)
SUMMARY: Hazel and Rosie vie for the attentions of a handsome new chauffeur in the neighborhood, and Hazel casts aside old standby Mitch Brady on the eve of the Sunshine Girls' Picnic.

NOTE: Guest player Lowery was Shirley's leading man in the 1957 *Playhouse 90* segment "The Hostess with the Mostes'."

48. Herbert for Hire

AIR DATE: December 13, 1962
WRITTEN BY: William Cowley
CAST: Donald Foster (Herbert Johnson), Norma Varden (Harriet Johnson), Howard Smith (Harvey Griffin), Eleanor Audley (Violet Totter), Joan Tompkins (Miss Adams), Maida Severn (Roberta Crawford)
SUMMARY: The Johnsons' investments in companies like United Harness and Saddle aren't producing the dividends they once did, causing a potential financial crisis for the couple. George

and Hazel try to persuade Mr. Griffin that he should employ Mr. Johnson, whose main credential is his degree in dead languages.

NOTES: This is the first appearance of the Johnsons in season 2. Actress Maida Severn, who played their maid Phoebe in episode #9 (and was said in episode #15 to have resigned), appears here as their latest domestic help, with no mention of the more agreeable Agnes who took Phoebe's place.

49. *Hazel and the Lovebirds*

AIR DATE: December 20, 1962

WRITTEN BY: Peggy Chantler

CAST: John Washbrook (Eddy Burke), Davey Davison (Nancy Thompson), Robert P. Lieb (Harry Thompson), Robert Hogan (Bud Donovan), Susan Silo (Gabriella)

SUMMARY: Deirdre allows Nancy to move back home from a snooty private school she hates, provided that she date boys other than Hazel's nephew Eddy. Meanwhile, the Johnsons welcome a new young maid, recently emigrated from Italy.

NOTES: The ongoing story of the romance between Hazel's nephew and Deirdre's daughter is, surprisingly, dropped after this installment. Guest player Susan Silo, cast as the Johnsons' maid, went on to a successful career as an actress and cartoon voice talent. Asked about this early role, and working with Shirley, Ms. Silo commented, "I was *very* young when I did the show and all I remember is how kind she was to me and so warm and helpful as a fellow actor! It was a joy to be on the same set with her!" (e-mail to the author, July 8, 2007)

50. *Top Secret*

AIR DATE: December 27, 1962

WRITTEN BY: Robert Riley Crutcher

CAST: Larry Gates (Senator Sterling), John Newton (Stan Blake), Judy Erwin (Mavis Blake), Helen Wallace (Miss Talbert), Stuart Nisbet (Herbert Andrews), Sam Edwards (Eddie), Jack Bernardi (Mr. Fox)

SUMMARY: While George is away on a business trip with neighbor Stan, Hazel takes Stan's daughter Mavis to meet a visiting senator. The senator takes a shine to Hazel, but when he realizes Mavis accidentally walked out with some highly classified documents, he doesn't know how to find them.

NOTE: This is the final appearance of the Blake family.

51. *The Sunshine Girls Quartette*

AIR DATE: January 3, 1963

WRITTEN BY: Louella MacFarlane

CAST: Jean Willes (Pauline Dunbar), Dub Taylor (Mitch Brady), Maudie Prickett (Rosie), Howard Smith (Harvey Griffin), Lauren Gilbert (Bill), Linda Leighton (Myra)

SUMMARY: Hazel, Rosie, and two other Sunshine Girls have teamed with Mitch to form a musical group, and are eager to audition for a talent scout passing through town. But a surprise birthday party for Mr. Griffin prevents Hazel from keeping the audition appointment.

NOTES: Van Alexander is credited with the arrangements for the Quartette's renditions of "Down by the Riverside" and "For He's a Jolly Good Fellow". In an early scene, the actresses who play the Sunshine Girls convincingly harmonize as poorly as the script dictates. Later, when they're supposed to sound good, they are rather obviously dubbed by professional singers.

52. *A Good Example for Harold*

AIR DATE: January 10, 1963

WRITTEN BY: Norm Liebmann and Ed Haas

CAST: Philip Ober (Mr. Boyle), Maudie Prickett (Rosie), Robert B. Williams (Barney), Teru Shimada (Mr. Isaka), Shigeko Tsunehiro (Shigeko Isaka)

SUMMARY: After reading Harold the story of George Washington and the cherry tree, Hazel and the Baxters agree to observe a policy of telling the truth at all costs. Unfortunately, Hazel's relentless honesty causes a quarrel with Rosie, and endangers a business deal for George.

NOTES: The scene in which Hazel gives her frank opinion of Rosie's new hat is strongly reminiscent of a classic moment from the 1953 *I Love Lucy* episode "Lucy Tells the Truth," as is much of the basic plot of this episode. Speaking of *I Love Lucy*, guest player Philip Ober was, in real life, the ex-husband of *Lucy* co-star Vivian Vance (Ethel). Ober was also featured in two of Shirley's movies, *Come Back, Little Sheba* and *About Mrs. Leslie*.

53. *Hazel's Highland Fling*

AIR DATE: January 17, 1963

WRITTEN BY: Robert Riley Crutcher

CAST: Katherine Henryk (Angie Campbell), Howard Smith (Harvey Griffin), James Doohan (Gordon MacHeath), Larry Blake (Murphy), Claire Carleton (Beauty Operator)

SUMMARY: Tired of Mr. Griffin inviting himself to dinner, Hazel and the Baxters plot to resolve his dissatisfaction with his own cook. When Hazel learns that the young Scottish woman came to America only in hopes of finding her longtime boyfriend, the effort to locate the missing man is underway.

NOTE: *Star Trek* regular James Doohan puts his "Scotty" accent to good use in this early role as Angie's beau from her homeland.

54. Ain't Walter Nice?

AIR DATE: January 24, 1963
WRITTEN BY: William Cowley
CAST: Frank Aletter (Walter Burke), Howard Smith (Harvey Griffin), William Giorgio (Stew), Kay Stewart (Secretary)
SUMMARY: Hazel is thrilled by a visit from her nephew Walter, who describes himself as a "promoter." But when he announces his intentions of soliciting a large investment from Mr. Griffin, George and Hazel are worried that Walter is just a scam artist.
NOTES: Walter is said to be the son of Hazel's brother Steve. Frank Aletter, a familiar face on TV during this period, was a regular on three unsuccessful CBS sitcoms—*Bringing Up Buddy* (1960-61), *The Cara Williams Show* (1964-65), and *It's About Time* (1966-67).

55. Mr. Griffin Throws a Wedding

AIR DATE: January 31, 1963
WRITTEN BY: Peggy Chantler
CAST: Howard Smith (Harvey Griffin), Carolyn Kearney (Maggie), Dick Sargent (Pete), John Graham (Harry)
SUMMARY: Maggie, a young stenographer in George's office, is engaged to marry Mr. Griffin's nephew Pete, who's an aspiring writer. When Mr. Griffin takes it upon himself to plan the wedding, buy the couple a home, and find Pete a new career, only Hazel can stop the steamroller in his path.
NOTE: Dick Sargent was, of course, Darrin #2 on *Bewitched* (ABC, 1969–72).

56. Hazel and the Stockholders' Meeting

AIR DATE: February 7, 1963
WRITTEN BY: Louella MacFarlane
CAST: Max Showalter (Gerald Starkey), Byron Foulger (Mr. Zimmerman), James Bell (Ralph Davidson), Walter Coy (Chairman), William Lally (Mr. Merryweather), Arlene Harris (Mrs. Mott)
SUMMARY: When Hazel's new vacuum cleaner proves to be a lemon, she invades the stockholders' meeting of the company to get satisfaction.
NOTES: Max Showalter was a friend of Shirley Booth, dating back to their time as co-stars in Broadway's *My Sister Eileen*. He returns as a different character in episode #58. The premise of this episode is reminiscent of the 1953–55 Broadway hit *The Solid Gold Cadillac,* in which a woman uses her ownership of a few shares of stock to assume a leadership role in a large corporation. In the mid–1950s, Shirley's film producer Hal Wallis tried unsuccessfully to buy the film rights to the Howard Teichman — George S. Kaufman comedy as a vehicle for her.

57. Hazel's Day Off

AIR DATE: February 14, 1963
WRITTEN BY: Louella MacFarlane
CAST: James Westerfield (Joe Arden), William Schallert (Kemper), Percy Helton (Cyrano), Elizabeth Talbot-Martin (Waitress)
SUMMARY: Cantankerous Mr. Arden, who's always in a hurry, will only donate land for a new city playground if George draws up the contract on a Sunday afternoon. But when Arden arrives at George's office, he runs afoul of a certain opinionated maid.
NOTES: William Schallert, who plays Arden's lawyer, is better known as the loving father of ABC's *The Patty Duke Show* (1963–66) and *The Nancy Drew Mysteries* (1977-78). Actor Westerfield will make three appearances in season 5 playing a similar character, Steve's client J.B. Turner.

58. I've Been Singing All My Life

AIR DATE: February 21, 1963
WRITTEN BY: William Cowley
CAST: Cathy Lewis (Deirdre Thompson), Max Showalter (Mr. Blackpoole), Maudie Prickett (Rosie), Eleanor Audley (Loretta Greene), Roxane Brooks (Nurse)
SUMMARY: George's sister plans a talent show as a fundraiser for the local children's hospital. Auditions for "An Evening with Deirdre and Her Friends" make it clear to Hazel and Rosie that maids are not wanted on the program, but a last-minute revelation causes Deirdre to reconsider.
NOTE: Shirley sings "Bye, Bye, Blackbird."

59. The Fire's Never Dead While the Ashes Are Red

AIR DATE: February 28, 1963
WRITTEN BY: Robert Riley Crutcher
CAST: Vaughn Taylor (Professor Jeremy Webster), Lurene Tuttle (Celeste Morgan), Lauren Gilbert (Harry Noll), Sue England (Marie)
SUMMARY: George's former law professor has written a bestselling novel based on his own life. When Hazel learns that the proprietor of a local bookstore is the woman he loved and lost many years earlier, she resolves to bring them together.
NOTES: Actor Lauren Gilbert seems to be playing his recurring role as George's friend and partner Harry in this episode, and that's how he's billed. But Don DeFore, playing George, calls him Howard throughout their scenes together. Gilbert will be seen often as Harry during seasons 3 and 4.

60. Hazel's Navy Blue Tugboats

AIR DATE: March 7, 1963
WRITTEN BY: Louella MacFarlane
CAST: Donald Foster (Herbert Johnson), Norma

Varden (Harriet Johnson), Margarita Cordova (Senora Villanova), Marlene Delamater (Anna Villanova), Robert Tafur (Senor Villanova), Ronald Long (Shoe Salesman), Harry Jackson (Joe), Hal Baylor (Officer Anderson), Don Spruance (Young Father)

SUMMARY: George lends Hazel his car to attend a shoe sale, on the condition that she returns by noon. En route to the sale, she encounters the Johnsons with their new bicycles, an expectant father needing a ride to the hospital, and a lost little girl who speaks no English, but still makes it to the sale and back in time.

61. The Hazel Walk

AIR DATE: March 14, 1963
WRITTEN BY: Norm Liebmann and Ed Haas
CAST: Howard Smith (Harvey Griffin), Hugh Sanders (Mr. Stettner), Ed Prentiss (Mr. Cormack), Walter Reed (Mr. Murray), Guy Raymond (Sheriff)
SUMMARY: Hazel doesn't want a new highway built through the scenic Pocono Trail, while George and Mr. Griffin prefer that to the alternative — having their golf course razed. But a weekend hiking trip down the once-scenic trail gives everyone a new perspective.

62. Hazel Digs a Hole for Herself

AIR DATE: March 21, 1963
WRITTEN BY: Louella MacFarlane
CAST: Louise Lorimer (Mrs. Baxter), Cathy Lewis (Deirdre Thompson), Vinton Hayworth (Ralph Sutherland), Tyler McVey (Salesman)
SUMMARY: George's mother has been bored and restless ever since Deirdre moved her out of her longtime home and into a small apartment. With Hazel's encouragement, Mrs. Baxter launches a late-in-life career as a gardener, which may come to a halt when her snooty daughter finds out.
NOTES: Seen for the first time since episode #9, George's mother is now played by a different actress, probably because Harriet MacGibbon, who originated the role, is busy playing Mrs. Drysdale on *The Beverly Hillbillies* (CBS, 1962–71). For reasons unexplained, Deirdre's hair is silvery-gray, rather than its usual brown, in this segment.

63. Hazel Sounds Her "A"

AIR DATE: April 4, 1963
WRITTEN BY: Robert Riley Crutcher
CAST: Torin Thatcher (Sir Horace), Doris Singleton (Lady Hobart), Vincton Hayworth (Ralph Sutherland), Ann Doran (Mrs. Waverly), Deirdre Owen (Librarian), Hedley Mattingly (Mr. Bankhead), John Zaremba (Mr. Handcock)
SUMMARY: The new conductor of the town's symphony orchestra refuses to work with female

musicians, and has fired the violinist daughter of Hazel's friend. But when Hazel bones up on the conductor's life story at the library, she uncovers some information that may play to her advantage.
NOTES: Doris Singleton makes her second *Hazel* appearance (see episode #30), while Vinton Hayworth appears for his second episode in a row as George's client (and, here, opera patron), Mr. Sutherland. Torin Thatcher, who plays the pompous conductor, was a veteran film and stage actor whose credits included the Broadway production of *The Miracle Worker* and the 1957 film adaptation of *Witness for the Prosecution.*

64. Hazel's Luck

AIR DATE: April 11, 1963
WRITTEN BY: John McGreevey
CAST: Henry Hunter (Dr. Summerfield), Raymond Guth (Manager), Eddie Quillan (Attendant)
SUMMARY: George thinks Hazel's belief in superstitions is a bad influence on Harold, so she agrees to destroy a chain letter she received. But when the family's trip to watch Hazel compete in the regional ladies' bowling championship is plagued with problems, she believes they're paying the price for breaking the chain.

65. Oh, My Aching Back!

AIR DATE: April 18, 1963
WRITTEN BY: William Cowley
CAST: Henry Hunter (Dr. Summerfield), Jack Bryan (Carl)
SUMMARY: Sick of hearing Hazel say "I told you so," whether the subject is baseball or household repairs, George tries to hide the fact that he sprained his back lifting a heavy pile of newspapers. But George's deception gets out of hand when he has to explain why the family doctor made a house call.

66. Maid of the Month

AIR DATE: April 25, 1963
WRITTEN BY: Robert Riley Crutcher
CAST: Richard St. John (Mr. Anderson), Howard Smith (Harvey Griffin), Mary Scott (Miss Sharpe), Virginia Gregg (Secretary)
SUMMARY: Hazel receives a telegram telling her she's been named *American Elegance* magazine's "Maid of the Month." Mr. Griffin, who's an investor in the magazine, secretly suggested Hazel for the award as a tribute. But the snobbish reporter sent to interview Hazel for the feature resents the assignment, and makes her feel unworthy of the honor.

67. So Long, Brown Eyes

AIR DATE: May 2, 1963
WRITTEN BY: Peggy Chantler

CAST: Patrick McVey (Gus Jenkins), Robert B. Williams (Barney)

SUMMARY: Gus Jenkins, the only man Hazel ever loved, visits and wants to resume their relationship. Hazel has to make a choice between the life she's made for herself, and the new one she's being offered by gadabout Gus.

NOTE: Like Shirley, guest player Patrick McVey was a veteran of a successful William Inge play, having been featured in *Bus Stop* during its original 1955-56 run on Broadway.

THIRD SEASON (1963-64)

68. Pot Luck a la Mode

AIR DATE: September 19, 1963

WRITTEN BY: Ted Sherdeman and Jane Klove

CAST: Phil Ober (Addison Sudley), Russell Collins (Charles Butterworth), Virginia Gregg (Lydia Sudley), Helene Heigh (Mrs. Butterworth), Chuck Webster (Chauffeur), Robert Johnson (Waiter)

SUMMARY: A prospective client and his wife are rumored to be so persnickety that, when they accept an invitation to the Baxters' house for dinner, George's boss suggests he get rid of Hazel for the evening. But a scheduling mix up finds Hazel at home alone when the Sudleys arrive.

NOTES: Don DeFore and Whitney Blake's credit in the opening titles changes this season, from "co-starring" to "also starring." Actor Philip Ober, billed here as "Phil," played a similar character in #52. Writers Sherdeman and Klove also contributed scripts to other Screen Gems series, including *Bewitched* and *The Flying Nun*, and will write for *Hazel* throughout the show's last three seasons. *Variety*'s annual review of the *Hazel* season opener, in the October 2, 1963 issue, was mostly a pan, as usual, but there were some grudging words of praise for the show's star: "Miss Booth playing Hazel is roughly tantamount to John Barrymore playing Henry Aldrich, but probably no one could play it better."

69. An Example for Hazel

AIR DATE: September 26, 1963

WRITTEN BY: William Cowley

CAST: Linda Watkins (Grace Baxter), Robert B. Williams (Barney Hatfield), Jack Bernardi (Smitty), Herb Vigran (Mickey)

SUMMARY: George's second cousin Gracie is an extremely timid and proper middle-aged woman who comes to stay with the Baxters after the death of her father. George hopes Hazel might acquire a little refinement courtesy of Gracie, but things don't quite work out that way.

NOTES: This is the first of several third season episodes to credit a producer other than James Fonda. Here, longtime writer Cowley fills in as producer. Linda Watkins reprises this role in the two-parter that airs as #85 and #86. George sarcastically refers to Hazel, who's leading a group sing-along, as "Mitch Miller." Miller was at this time the host of the popular *Sing Along with Mitch* (1961–66), which followed *Hazel* on NBC's Thursday night schedule.

70. Dorothy Takes a Trip

AIR DATE: October 3, 1963

WRITTEN BY: William Cowley

CAST: Maudie Prickett (Rosie), Gene Blakely (Jack Spencer), Lauren Gilbert (Harry Williams), Bek Nelson (Dr. Phyllis Gordon), John Graham (Phil)

SUMMARY: Dorothy is called away to tend to her sister Barbara, who sprained her ankle. Thanks to Rosie, Hazel worries that George will become involved with another woman, but he's more interested in the game of poker he's rounding up.

NOTES: Whitney Blake appears in only the prologue to this episode, and will not be seen in #71 and #72, while Dorothy is said to be out of town. Produced by William Cowley. Lauren Gilbert's recurring character of Harry is seen here. At this point, his character is named Harry Williams; later, he will become Harry Noll.

71. You Ain't Fully Dressed Without a Smile

AIR DATE: October 10, 1963

WRITTEN BY: Robert Riley Crutcher

CAST: Ellen Corby (Minnie Smith), Louise Lorimer (Mrs. Baxter), Mario Siletti (Charlie), Nelson Olmstead (Mr. Wilcox), Eddie Quillan (Mover)

SUMMARY: Hazel convinces George to act as attorney to elderly Minnie Smith, who is threatened with losing the fix-it shop she owns and operates. Grateful Minnie presents George with a rickety antique desk that he doesn't much appreciate, until he thinks it's a historic artifact that once belonged to Abraham Lincoln.

NOTES: Whitney Blake does not appear in this episode, as Dorothy is still said to be away. Ellen Corby's character owns a shop very much like the one owned by Miss Elsie in #84. Corby (1911–1999), best-known for her later gig as Grandma on *The Waltons* (CBS, 1972–81), appeared opposite Shirley in *About Mrs. Leslie,* playing the overly indulgent mother of spoiled Pixie. She returns to *Hazel,* as a different but not dissimilar character, in #130.

72. Cheerin' Up Mr. B

AIR DATE: October 17, 1963

WRITTEN BY: William Cowley

CAST: Lauren Gilbert (Harry Williams), Howard Smith (Harvey Griffin), Maudie Prickett (Rosie)

SUMMARY: With Dorothy still out of town, Hazel tells Rosie that it's her responsibility to keep George from moping. Although George is looking forward to a quiet Saturday, he's interrupted by Rosie, Harry, and Mr. Griffin, all of whom are following Hazel's instructions to keep her boss busy.

NOTE: For viewers who thought George would never tell Hazel off, this episode must have been surprising, as he calls her "an interfering busybody" and makes her cry.

QUOTE: HAZEL (talking to Mr. Griffin on the telephone)—How are you? ... Oh, well, that's probably because you don't eat enough greens ... Well, greens and lots of liquids oughta help!

73. Piccolo Mondo

AIR DATE: October 24, 1963
WRITTEN BY: John McGreevey
CAST: Gregory Morton (Enzo Martelli)
SUMMARY: Hazel attends night school to study Italian so that she can translate some recipes. While there, she meets a handsome man who's still working on his English, and they both pitch in to help when the Baxters entertain a dinner guest who speaks no English.
NOTES: Produced by Peter Kortner ... This episode introduces Hazel's Italian boyfriend, who will return in #118 and #135.

74. Hazel Scores a Touchdown

AIR DATE: October 31, 1963
WRITTEN BY: Robert Riley Crutcher
CAST: Alan Hale (Coach Murphy), Vinton Hayworth (Mr. Wheeler), Willis Bouchey (Mr. Dempsey), John Archer (Mr. Johnson), Jon Arnett (Gus)
SUMMARY: Hazel's favorite football team, the Bulldogs, is about to be sold because of its poor performance. But she believes the coach could lead the team to victory if she put a stop to the longstanding feud between the team's co-owners.
NOTES: Produced by Peter Kortner. This episode's guest cast is full of *Hazel* veterans, including Vinton Hayworth's first appearance *not* playing his usual character of Ralph Sutherland.

75. George's 32nd Cousin

AIR DATE: November 7, 1963
WRITTEN BY: Louella MacFarlane
CAST: Diane Ladd (Sharlene Baxter), David Whorf (Joe Cook), John Brandon (Ben Cook)
SUMMARY: George's distant cousin Sharlene is a lazy deadbeat who takes over the Baxter house and tries to hoodwink him into financing her modeling career. Enlisting the help of her two

new friends who work as house painters, Hazel sets out to kill two birds with one scheme.

NOTE: Ladd, seen here in an early TV appearance, is a three-time Oscar nominee for Best Supporting Actress, including her role as Flo in *Alice Doesn't Live Here Anymore* (1974).

76. The Baby Came C.O.D.

AIR DATE: November 14, 1963
WRITTEN BY: Robert Riley Crutcher
CAST: James Stacy (David Merrick), Oliver McGowan (Dean Evans), Mikki Jamison (Maria Merrick), Kathleen O'Malley (Nurse), Larry Barton (Manager)
SUMMARY: George is one of two candidates to deliver the annual Oliver Wendell Holmes Memorial Lectures at his law school. But when he tries to settle down and write an outline, he keeps getting interrupted by the problems of young law student David and his expectant wife.
NOTES: Produced by Peter Kortner. This episode almost seems to be an offshoot of episode #34, "George's Assistant," also written by Crutcher. Both concern young lawyers-to-be, named Merrick, and their efforts to balance their studies and their personal lives. Actor James Stacy was later the star of TV's *Lancer* (CBS, 1968–70), but was permanently disabled in 1973, after being hit on his motorcycle by a drunk driver. Oliver McGowan, who plays the dean of George's law school, will be seen often on *Hazel*, playing various authority figures, including the governor (in #101).

77. All Hazel Is Divided into Three Parts

AIR DATE: November 21, 1963
TELEPLAY BY: Peggy Chantler Dick
STORY BY: Peggy Chantler Dick and Frank Granville
CAST: Cathy Lewis (Deirdre Thompson), Douglas Dick (Gabriel Fairchild), Donald Foster (Herbert Johnson), Norma Varden (Harriet Johnson)
SUMMARY: Hazel and the Sunshine Girls are serving as foster parents to a girl in an impoverished Italian village. When she meets the Johnsons' friend, a renowned portrait painter, she sees an opportunity to raise more money for children in the village, while Deirdre sees a chance to enhance her social prestige.
NOTE: Co-head writer Peggy Chantler had recently married the actor who plays Mr. Fairchild. Mr. and Mrs. Dick would later collaborate on scripts for Screen Gems series like *Bewitched* (ABC, 1964–72).

78. The Vanishing Hero

AIR DATE: November 28, 1963
WRITTEN BY: Louella MacFarlane

CAST: Leif Erickson (Zachary King), Gloria Henry (Gloria King), Howard Smith (Harvey Griffin), Brian Johnson (Harry)

SUMMARY: Mr. Griffin wants George to entice his old schoolmate, and Olympic boxing champion, into accepting a job with Griffin Enterprises. As it happens, Mr. King is quite eager to have the job, but his longstanding rivalry with George threatens to quash the deal.

NOTES: Gloria Henry, who plays Mrs. King, co-starred in Screen Gems' *Dennis the Menace* (CBS, 1959–63). Leif Erickson was a stage and film veteran whose credits included *Tea and Sympathy* on Broadway.

79. Call Me Harve

AIR DATE: December 5, 1963
WRITTEN BY: Robert Riley Crutcher
CAST: Ann Jilliann (Laurie), Howard Smith (Harvey Griffin), Maudie Prickett (Rosie)

SUMMARY: Rosie's niece Laurie has raised sheep on a farm upstate to pay for her education, but a cold front threatens the health of her livestock. Meanwhile, George reaches the boiling point with Mr. Griffin, and resigns from his account. Griffin agrees to pay for sweaters for the sheep if Hazel can mend the rift between him and George.

NOTE: Ann Jillian, who will return to the series with a recurring role in season 5, makes her *Hazel* debut as Rosie's niece. As an adult, she was a regular on the 1980s sitcom *It's a Living.* On *Hazel,* she is billed as "Jilliann," rather than the shorter version of the name she later used.

QUOTE: GEORGE (having a disagreement with Hazel)—I don't care to discuss it! HAZEL: We ain't discussin' it, I'm just telling you.

80. The Retiring Milkman

AIR DATE: December 12, 1963
WRITTEN BY: Phil Leslie and Keith Fowler
CAST: Sterling Holloway (Claude Waters), Howard Smith (Harvey Griffin), Barbara Luddy (Ruth), Queenie Leonard (Peggy), Betty Hanna (Dee), Myrna Dell (Receptionist)

SUMMARY: The neighborhood's longtime milkman, Claude, is a friendly "old duffer" whose work is getting sloppy. When Mr. Griffin buys the Bronson Milk Company and wants all the dead wood removed, Claude is in danger of losing his job after 30 years.

NOTE: Holloway, instantly recognizable as the voice of Winnie the Pooh, even gets to proclaim his fondness for honey in this script.

81. Hazel's Nest Egg

AIR DATE: December 19, 1963

WRITTEN BY: Robert Riley Crutcher
CAST: Charles Herbert (Leslie), Howard Smith (Harvey Griffin), Paul Smith (Mr. Merrick)

SUMMARY: Harold refuses to take the test to become a Tenderfoot Boy Scout out of loyalty to his best friend Leslie, who hasn't mastered the skills needed to pass. When Mr. Griffin presents Hazel with five shares of stock in his company, she decides to share the wealth with the boys and give them an incentive to pass the test.

NOTE: Paul Smith, who appears as the scoutmaster, was later a regular on *The Doris Day Show* (CBS, 1968–73).

82. Hazel and the Halfback

AIR DATE: December 26, 1963
WRITTEN BY: William Cowley
CAST: Frank Gifford (Himself), Cathy Lewis (Deirdre Thompson), Lauren Gilbert (Harry Williams), William Zuckert (Mr. Brewster), Gregg Dunn (Leo), Linda Marshall (Miss Sterling)

SUMMARY: Frank Gifford of the New York Giants comes to dinner at the Baxters,' to discuss his possible investment in a local bowling alley. Considering bowling to be her area of expertise, Hazel sets out to convince Gifford to invest in her favorite bowling center instead.

NOTES: Produced by William Cowley. Dorothy is "away" again, so Deirdre is pitching in at the Baxter house, and is even seen uncharacteristically performing some housework. This script implies that George's law partner Harry (here still called Harry Williams) has a wife and daughter. Later episodes will depict him as a confirmed bachelor and playboy.

83. Hazel and the Model T

AIR DATE: January 2, 1964
TELEPLAY BY: Helen Spencer
STORY BY: Helen Spencer and Frank Granville
CAST: Donald Foster (Herbert Johnson), Norma Varden (Harriet Johnson), Maurice Manson (Josh Egan), Howard Smith (Harvey Griffin), William Bakewell (Fred)

SUMMARY: Wanting her own transportation, Hazel buys a Model T from Mr. and Mrs. Johnson for $25.00. The car unexpectedly provides a golden opportunity for George, when the businessman with whom he wants to negotiate a deal for Mr. Griffin proves to be an antique car buff.

NOTE: Manson reprises his role as Mr. Egan in #102, #121, and #125.

84. Hot Potato a la Hazel

AIR DATE: January 9, 1964
WRITTEN BY: Robert Riley Crutcher
CAST: Alice Pearce (Miss Elsie), Mario Siletti

(Charlie), Hope Summers (Edna), Alice Frost (Julia), Howard Wendell (Mr. Drake), Jeff Burton (Policeman)

SUMMARY: Shop owner Miss Elsie hopes to snare Hazel's friend Charlie for a husband. Hazel plans a romantic dinner for the pair, but a comedy of errors results in the two women being suspected of robbing a dress shop.

NOTE: Alice Pearce's character here is not unlike her persona as the original Gladys Kravitz on *Bewitched*, which premiered a few months after this guest appearance. Pearce was posthumously awarded an Emmy in 1966, shortly after her death from cancer.

85/86. *Scheherazade and Her Frying Pan*

Air Dates: January 16 and 23, 1964
WRITTEN BY: Louella MacFarlane
CAST: Linda Watkins (Gracie), Roland Winters (Mr. Bixby), Lou Krugman (Freddie Hobart), Edgar Stehli (Willie Gant), Joseph A. Vitale (Handsome Harry), Emile Meyer (Wheels), Baynes Barron (Detective #1), Rusty Lane (Fisherman #1), John Cliff (Guard #1), Roy Glenn (Detective #2), Ken Strange (Guard #2), Bert Remsen (Federal Man, part 2 only)

SUMMARY: In this change-of-pace two-parter, Hazel drives to California to visit her timid friend Gracie, who's working for a mysterious man named Mr. Bixby. Gracie doesn't realize that her employer is a gangster, and when Hazel infiltrates his estate during a meeting with his associates, she and Gracie find themselves held hostage.

87. *The Fashion Show*

AIR DATE: January 30, 1964
WRITTEN BY: Keith Fowler and Phil Leslie
CAST: Cathy Lewis (Deirdre Thompson), Reginald Gardiner (Mr. Montague), Douglas Fowley (Mr. Jeffries), Florence Sundstrom (Mrs. Jeffries), Anna Karen (Marietta Horne), Elizabeth Harrower (Edith)

SUMMARY: Deidre's latest charity affair is a fashion show for which Dorothy is slated to serve as a model. But when Dorothy twists her ankle, and sends Hazel to the show with a message, she's mistaken for a substitute model, and provides just the touch of variety the show needs.

NOTES: Florence Sundstrom, who played one of the Sunshine Girls in early episodes, appears here as the wife of a well-to-do client. Veteran character actor Reginald Gardiner (1903–1980), seen here as the harried fashion designer, returns to *Hazel* in #120. He was later featured in Phyllis Diller's ill-fated sitcom *The Pruitts of Southampton* (ABC, 1966-67).

88. *George's Ordeal*

AIR DATE: February 6, 1964
TELEPLAY BY: Peggy Chantler Dick
STORY BY: Peggy Chantler Dick and Frank Granville
CAST: Henry Hunter (Dr. Summerfield), Howard Smith (Harvey Griffin), Maudie Prickett (Rosie), Barbara Luddy (Ruth)

SUMMARY: George's doctor puts him on a strict 1500-calorie-per-day diet so he will lose ten pounds. Hazel and Rosie make a wager, with Rosie's new hat at stake, as to the outcome of George's diet.

NOTES: Barbara Luddy, seen as Mr. Griffin's maid in #80, reprises her role here. This is the last script contributed by Peggy Chantler, who wrote or co-wrote more than two dozen *Hazel* episodes.

89. *The Reluctant Witness*

AIR DATE: February 13, 1964
WRITTEN BY: Robert Riley Crutcher
CAST: Mabel Albertson (Miss Ramsey), John Archer (Harry Belmont), Gretchen Hale (Mrs. Osborne), Helen Wallace (Miss Welby)

SUMMARY: Dorothy's reputation as a decorator is at stake when she is threatened with a lawsuit by an unhappy client. Only one unlikely eyewitness can testify to what really happened between Dorothy and her client.

NOTES: Harry Belmont, described (but not seen) in episode #76 as the lawyer who's frequently defeated George in court, appears here. Mabel Albertson, who plays the grouchy tax assessor, is best known for her recurring role as Samantha's mother-in-law on Screen Gems' *Bewitched* (ABC, 1964–72), but also appeared with Shirley in *About Mrs. Leslie*.

90. *Democracy at Work*

AIR DATE: February 20, 1964
WRITTEN BY: Keith Fowler and Phil Leslie
CAST: Francis DeSales (Mr. Burgess), Maudie Prickett (Rosie), William Giorgio (Monte), Judd Foster (Postman)

SUMMARY: Hazel's annual campaign for a raise is put to a vote by George, who's teaching Harold about the meaning of democracy. But when Dorothy sides with George, Hazel cooks up a phony story that she's sure will result in a recount.

NOTE: Produced by William Cowley.

91. *The Countess*

AIR DATE: February 27, 1964
WRITTEN BY: Ted Sherdeman and Jane Klove
CAST: Cathy Lewis (Deirdre Thompson), Maudie Prickett (Rosie), Lester Matthews (Mr. Archibald), Russell Collins (Mr. Butterworth),

Jack Bernardi (Butcher), Robert P. Lieb (Harry Thompson)

SUMMARY: A letter from a British law firm leads Hazel to believe that she might be the Countess of Brentwood, heir to an estate. Thanks to Rosie, who quickly spreads the gossip, Deirdre plans to throw an elaborate reception for the newly crowned royalty.

92. Hazel's Midas Touch

AIR DATE: March 5, 1964
WRITTEN BY: Robert Riley Crutcher
CAST: Leo G. Carroll (William Samson Cady), Max Showalter (Mr. Barry), Richard St. John (Mr. Logan), Molly Dodd (George's Secretary), John Dennis (Policeman)
SUMMARY: George hopes to convince an eccentric millionaire he met on an airplane to donate some valuable artwork to the city museum. Too bad the "alleged crackpot" Mr. Cady threw out of his hotel room just happens to be one Hazel Burke.
NOTES: Shirley Booth's friend Max Showalter makes his third guest appearance on *Hazel*. Leo G. Carroll, who plays the irascible millionaire, went on a few months later to co-star in NBC's *The Man from U.N.C.L.E* (1964–68), and is still remembered for playing the title role in the sitcom *Topper* (CBS, 1953–55). He first acted opposite Shirley in Broadway's *The Mask and the Face*, in 1933.

93. Everybody's a Comedian

AIR DATE: March 12, 1964
WRITTEN BY: Keith Fowler and Phil Leslie
CAST: Oliver McGowan (Mr. Martindale), Howard Smith (Harvey Griffin), Molly Dodd (Helen), Jester Hairston (Marvin), Stanley Farrar (Mr. Dunn), John Dennis (Policeman)
SUMMARY: Hazel won't admit that she needs glasses, but makes a deal with George that she'll get them if her poor eyesight ever causes a problem. When she misreads a telegram and sends him to the airport to pick up Mr. Griffin five hours early, Hazel leaps into action to set things right.
NOTES: Jester Hairston, who has a small role in this episode, had running parts on *The Amos 'n' Andy Show* (CBS, 1951–53), and much later played Rolly Forbes on *Amen* (NBC, 1986–91). Along with Roy Glenn, who appeared briefly in the two-parter #85 and #86, he is one of the first African-American actors to have a speaking role on *Hazel*, bringing a welcome, if minor, touch of racial diversity to the series. Actress Molly Dodd, who's been making infrequent appearances as George's secretary since the show began, is addressed as Helen here. Actor John Dennis appears as a an unnamed police officer for the second consecutive episode.

94. All Mixed Up

AIR DATE: March 19, 1964
WRITTEN BY: Frank Crow
CAST: Howard Smith (Harvey Griffin), Maudie Prickett (Rosie), Alan Hewitt (Mr. Buckley), Richard Niles (TV Director)
SUMMARY: Hazel hits it big as the TV spokeswoman for Aunt Nora's cake mix. But when her new responsibilities have Hazel too busy to cook Mr. Griffin's favorite meals, the wealthy industrialist kicks up a fuss.
NOTE: The plot of this episode is reminiscent of #16, "Hazel's Famous Recipes."

95. Arrivederci, Mr. B

AIR DATE: March 26, 1964
WRITTEN BY: Robert Riley Crutcher
CAST: Luciana Paluzzi (Carla Carlotti), Mario Siletti (Charlie Charlotti), Kathryn Givney (Mrs. Hampton), Lauren Gilbert (Harry Noll)
SUMMARY: Hazel's friend Charlie is hiding his niece and her baby at his antique shop. The baby's American great-grandmother, who happens to be George and Harry's wealthy client, wants to take him away from the foreign-born mother she believes is unfit.
NOTES: Leading lady Paluzzi's film credits include the Bond film *Thunderball* (1965). Hazel, who wants to help her learn English, teaches her to say, "I ain't got nothing to worry about."

96. Such a Nice Little Man

AIR DATE: April 2, 1964
WRITTEN BY: Phil Leslie and Keith Fowler
CAST: Byron Foulger (Willie Gaffney), Donald Foster (Herbert Johnson), Norma Varden (Harriet Johnson), Jerry Hausner (Homer Dandridge), Owen Bush (Policeman)
SUMMARY: Hazel befriends a drifter and helps him get work doing chores for the Johnsons. But when George recognizes Willie from court, where he was the defendant in a theft case, he worries that the naive Johnsons will be victimized.
NOTE: Actor Jerry Hausner, who plays the proprietor of an antique shop, is a sitcom veteran most recognizable as Ricky Ricardo's agent Jerry on *I Love Lucy*. Byron Foulger, an accused thief here, previously was a shoplifter in episode #12.

97. Campaign Manager

AIR DATE: April 9, 1964
WRITTEN BY: Ted Sherdeman and Jane Klove
CAST: Philip Ober (Addison Sudley), James Flavin (Perry Preston), Harold Gould (TV Announcer), Maidie Norman (Lady), Sam Edwards (Make-Up Man)
SUMMARY: Hazel and Dorothy circulate a petition to protest a rezoning decision that will replace the city's picnic grounds with a factory. When

the petition fails to impress a stuffy city councilman, they persuade George to run against him in the upcoming election.

NOTES: Ober reprises his role from #68 as George's client. James Flavin, who plays the city councilman, appeared often on *The George Burns and Gracie Allen Show* (CBS, 1950–58), usually as Gracie's contact on the Beverly Hills police force. Maidie Norman, seen here as a woman who signs Hazel's petition, is a veteran African-American character actress perhaps most recognizable as Joan Crawford and Bette Davis' maid Elvira in *What Ever Happened to Baby Jane?* (1962). She was also featured in *About Mrs. Leslie.*

QUOTE: PRESTON (commenting on Hazel's petition drive)—One of the burdens of politics ... attacks from the lunatic fringe!

98. Let's Get Away from It All

AIR DATE: April 16, 1964
WRITTEN BY: Dorothy Cooper Foote
CAST: Jamie Farr (Tony Carlotti), Stuart Nisbet (Mr. Baldwin)
SUMMARY: Hazel and the Baxters are expecting to enjoy a quiet dinner at an out-of-the-way Italian restaurant. Instead, they find themselves in the thick of the action when the owner's wife goes into labor and a roomful of diners are impatient to be fed.
NOTE: The syndicated version of this show lacks the correct closing credits, and inexplicably has the credits for #45 substituted.

99. Maid for a Day

AIR DATE: April 23, 1964
WRITTEN BY: Dorothy Cooper Foote
CAST: Cathy Lewis (Deirdre Thompson), Hugh Sanders (E.J. McClaine), Harvey Korman (Max Denton), Lillian Culver (Emily Dearborne)
SUMMARY: Deirdre wants the lead role in a local play being staged for charity, even though it means she'll be cast as a maid. Spending the day working alongside Hazel doesn't do much to help her characterization, but an encounter with George's obnoxious client proves unexpectedly helpful.
NOTE: Harvey Korman, appearing here as the playwright, was then a regular on CBS' *The Danny Kaye Show* (1963–67).

FOURTH SEASON (1964-65)

---

100. Never Trouble Trouble

AIR DATE: September 17, 1964

WRITTEN BY: Robert Riley Crutcher
CAST: Frederick Downs (Fred Baxter), Harold Gould (Mr. Wheeler), Mark Dymally (Franklin)
SUMMARY: Instead of the loan Cousin Fred wants, George gives him a stern lecture about being self-reliant and getting an honest job. When the Baxters are robbed, and a note left behind implies that the burglar is someone George knows, he's forced to consider the possibility that his relative is a thief.
NOTES: Seen for the first time since episode #45, Downs seems to be playing the same deadbeat cousin who's been George's longtime nemesis, but the character's name has changed. This lapse in continuity, while common in many sitcoms, is unusual for *Hazel.* This is the second time the Baxters' house has been burglarized (see episode #7), though there's no mention made here of the burglar alarm installed in that episode. Competing against this season opener was the first Thursday installment of ABC's new prime time serial *Peyton Place,* which would soon pose serious competition to *Hazel.*

101. Luncheon with the Governor

AIR DATE: September 24, 1964
WRITTEN BY: Phil Leslie and Keith Fowler
CAST: Oliver McGowan (Gov. Willard McGuire), Lois Roberts (Marge Logan), Douglas Dick (Tom Jennings), Maudie Prickett (Rosie), William Cort (Jim Logan), Virginia Christine (Mrs. McGuire), Larry Thor (TV Reporter)
SUMMARY: When word gets out that the Baxters will be hosting a luncheon for the governor at their home, the married students at the local university organize a picket to fight for affordable student housing. Hazel, who's been forbidden by George to say anything other than "yes," "no," and "maybe" to the governor, finds a way to win his sympathy for the cause.
NOTE: Virginia Christine, who plays the First Lady, was known to a generation of TV viewers as Mrs. Olsen in a long-running series of coffee commercials.

102. Ain't That a Knee Slapper?

AIR DATE: October 1, 1964
WRITTEN BY: William Cowley
CAST: Howard Smith (Harvey Griffin), Maurice Manson (Josh Egan)
SUMMARY: Mr. Griffin has reluctantly agreed to a merger with a longtime rival. But when George invites both men to dinner in hopes of signing the contract, their disdain for each other threatens to kill the deal.
NOTE: Maurice Manson reprises his role from episode #83.

103. Marriage Trap

AIR DATE: October 8, 1964
WRITTEN BY: Robert Riley Crutcher
CAST: Ken Berry (Phil Merrick), Linda Marshall (Linda Sterling), Lauren Gilbert (Harry Noll), Gene Blakely (Stanley Wilson), Carol Byron (Harriet Wilson), Monty Margetts (Mrs. Logan), Max Mellinger (Justice of the Peace)
SUMMARY: George's young secretary is giving her boyfriend the cold shoulder after an argument. But when she impulsively accepts a marriage proposal from George's flirtatious partner Harry, Hazel steps in to make sure she doesn't marry the wrong man.
NOTE: George describes Linda as "the best secretary I've ever had" in this script, with no mention of Miss Scott, played by Molly Dodd in several previous episodes. Even so, Dodd's character returns in #114.

104. The Flagpole

AIR DATE: October 15, 1964
WRITTEN BY: Robert Riley Crutcher
CAST: Lauren Gilbert (Harry Noll), Frank Cady (Mr. Pincus), Allyson Ames (Harry's Girlfriend), Sally Hughes (Secretary), Breland Rice (Policeman)
SUMMARY: George is presented with a large American flag as thanks for some legal work he did in Washington. But when he learns that Harry has been too busy romancing a new lady friend to finish some important contracts, the resulting argument has George too distracted to buy the huge iron flagpole Hazel wants.
NOTE: Frank Cady, who appears in this episode, is best known as Hooterville shopkeeper Sam Drucker on CBS' *Petticoat Junction* (1963–70) and *Green Acres* (1965–71).

105. Welcome Back, Kevin

AIR DATE: October 22, 1964
WRITTEN BY: William Cowley
CAST: Michael Callan (Kevin Burkett), Richard Niles (Bill Kincaid), Margaret Bly (Helen Burkett), Joan Patrick (Gloria Kincaid)
SUMMARY: George's nephew Kevin, a soldier, arrives for a visit depressed because his wife asked for a divorce while he was stationed overseas. Trying to plan a surprise party with all of Kevin's friends, Hazel learns that there's more to the story than the version she heard from him.
NOTE: Michael Callan, who appeared in the original Broadway production of *West Side Story,* was under long-term contract to Columbia at this time, being groomed as a leading man. That contract subsequently resulted in his starring role in the unsuccessful Screen Gems sitcom *Occasional Wife* (NBC, 1966-67).

QUOTE: HAZEL— You see, Mr. B, I got this terrific understanding of psychology!

106. Mind Your Own Business

AIR DATE: October 29, 1964
WRITTEN BY: Phil Leslie and Keith Fowler
CAST: Howard Smith (Harvey Griffin), John Graham (Bob Yates), Francine York (Monica Yates), Rowena Burack (Gypsy Fortuneteller)
SUMMARY: George lays down the law when Hazel butts into once too often. But having agreed to stay out of her boss' affairs, Hazel refuses to bend when Mr. Griffin wants her opinion on a new disposable skillet he may manufacture.
QUOTE: HAZEL— Oh, come on, Mr. B! You make it sound as if I go around buttin' into all kinds of stuff. I don't do that!

107. High Finance Hits a New Low

AIR DATE: November 5, 1964
TELEPLAY BY: Louella MacFarlane
STORY BY: Rik Vollaerts
CAST: Donald Foster (Herbert Johnson), Norma Varden (Harriet Johnson)
SUMMARY: Hazel persuades George to take on the unenviable task of acting as the Johnsons' financial adviser. Things go from bad to worse when a packet full of negotiable bonds belonging to the couple disappears from George's desk.

108. Just Me, Harold, and the Universe

AIR DATE: November 12, 1964
WRITTEN BY: Frank Crow
CAST: Woodrow Parfrey (Lester Morton), Jane Van Deusen (Miss Dart), Peggy Rea (Louise Masters), Sue England (Mrs. Plunkett), Kevin Tate (Eddie Masters), Garland Thompson (Messenger)
SUMMARY: Hazel enters a "Housekeeper of the Month" contest, with the first prize being a trip to the New York World's Fair that she hopes to share with Harold. When she ties for first place with a widow who's new to the neighborhood, both women are entered into a bakeoff to pick the winner.

109. Mix-Up on Marshall Road

AIR DATE: November 19, 1964
WRITTEN BY: Robert Riley Crutcher
CAST: Lauren Gilbert (Harry Noll), Karen Steele (Rita Noll), Ross Elliott (Howard North), Gene Blakely (Bill Murphy)
SUMMARY: Hazel helps the Baxters' neighbor sell his house so that he can accept a job in California. When Harry comes home from a trip newly married, Hazel thinks George's partner and his wife would make the perfect buyers.
NOTES: Ross Elliott, who makes his only appearance

as this previously unseen neighbor, was a popular character actor. He's perhaps best remembered for playing the director whose demands for repeated rehearsals get Lucy Ricardo plastered on Vitameatavegamin in the classic *I Love Lucy* episode "Lucy Does a TV Commercial" ... Karen Steele (1931–1988), introduced here as Harry's new wife Rita, a former actress, reprises the role in episodes #112 and 114. A frequent TV guest star in the 1960s, Steele was also featured in the movie classic *Marty* (United Artists, 1955).

110. Lesson in Diplomacy

AIR DATE: November 26, 1964
WRITTEN BY: John McGreevey
CAST: Oscar Homolka (Pozega), Willis Bouchey (Mayor), Douglas Henderson (Courtney Hicks), Stuart Nisbet (Reporter)
SUMMARY: As chair of the mayor's welcoming committee, George is asked to entertain a visiting dignitary from behind the Iron Curtain. He and his family are unaware that the man who's taking part in their Thanksgiving dinner is a phony, sent to test whether the Baxters can handle a visitor who may be difficult.
NOTE: Guest player Homolka, though often cast as Russian characters, was in fact Austrian by birth. However, casting directors saw in him a resemblance to Leonid Brezhnev (1906–1982), who came into power in the Soviet Union shortly before this episode aired.

111. To Build or Not to Build

AIR DATE: December 3, 1964
WRITTEN BY: Ted Sherdeman and Jane Klove
CAST: Lauren Gilbert (Harry Noll), Guy Raymond (Clyde Clifton)
SUMMARY: Hazel and Dorothy try a variety of methods, including subliminal suggestion while George sleeps, to persuade him the kitchen should be remodeled. But when the estimate he receives from the contractor Harry recommended is sky-high, George puts Dorothy in charge of the project.

112. Better to Have Loved and Lost

AIR DATE: December 10, 1964
WRITTEN BY: Robert Riley Crutcher
CAST: Lauren Gilbert (Harry Noll), Karen Steele (Rita Noll), Carol Byron (Susan Standish)
SUMMARY: Harry and his new wife are settling in next door to the Baxters, and Mrs. Noll wants their marriage to be just as successful. Things are going fine until Hazel innocently gives Rita a negligee Harry threw out, not knowing it belongs to his secretary.
NOTE: The exterior views of the Nolls' new house seem to have been shot on the same standing set

at Screen Gems that represented Sam and Darrin's home on *Bewitched.*

113. Hazel Squares the Triangle

AIR DATE: December 17, 1964
WRITTEN BY: Louella MacFarlane
CAST: Cathy Lewis (Deirdre Thompson), Robert P. Lieb (Harry Thompson), Henry Hunter (Dr. Summerfield), William Bakewell (Clerk), Peter Forster (Doorman)
SUMMARY: When Deirdre finally pushes her long-suffering husband Harry too far, he rebels, saying he'll retire to Bora Bora instead of taking the promotion he's been offered. Though Harry's staying temporarily at his club — women not allowed — Hazel manages to infiltrate his hideaway with a message from his recalcitrant wife.

114. Just 86 Shopping Minutes to Christmas

AIR DATE: December 24, 1964
WRITTEN BY: Louella MacFarlane
CAST: Lauren Gilbert (Harry Noll), Karen Steele (Rita Noll), Molly Dodd (Miss Scott), Lindsay Workman (Credit Manager)
SUMMARY: Sick of Christmas commercialism, George decrees no gift exchange among the adult Baxters and their friends. Harry, on the other hand, plans to give his wife a mink coat, which he asks George to hide at his house.
NOTE: The Nolls make their final appearance here.
QUOTE: HAZEL — I never thought that Mr. B'd turn out to be a Scrooge!

115. Champagne Tony

AIR DATE: January 7, 1965
TELEPLAY BY: Robert Riley Crutcher
STORY BY: James Fonda
CAST: Tony Lema (Himself), Kathie Browne (Mrs. "Baby" Gollard), Don Briggs (Bill Gollard), Alice Backes (Miss Logan), Hal Baylor (Policeman)
SUMMARY: Golfer Tony Lema is to stay with the Baxters while he competes in a local tournament. Thanks to a mixup involving two lookalike cars, Hazel accidentally loses his prized clubs.
NOTE: Guest star Lema, along with real-life wife Betty, was killed in a plane crash on July 24, 1966, at the age of 32. He had won ten PGA tour events in the last four years of his life.

116. It's a Dog's Life

AIR DATE: January 14, 1965
WRITTEN BY: Ted Sherdeman and Jane Klove
CAST: Lee Patrick (Mrs. Durham), Hardie Albright (Ashton Durham), Robert B. Williams (Barney), Orville Sherman (Nurseryman)
SUMMARY: The Baxters are stuck with entertaining a client, his wife, and their obnoxiously spoiled dog Rodney. Fed up with waiting hand

and foot on Rodney, Hazel devises a scheme to end the Durhams' stay.

NOTE: Lee Patrick, who plays Rodney's overprotective owner, was a veteran character actress who appeared in numerous Warner Bros. classics like *The Maltese Falcon* and *Mildred Pierce*, and was featured in the TV sitcom *Topper* (CBS, 1953–55). She also appeared with Shirley in the touring production of *The Desk Set*.

117. Love 'em and Leave 'em

AIR DATE: January 21, 1965
WRITTEN BY: Robert Riley Crutcher
CAST: Vickie Cos (Zelda Warren), Virginia Gregg (Miss Tilcy), Greger Vigen (Ted), Anne Bellamy (Mrs. Warren)
SUMMARY: Harold trades his autographed football for a date with his classmate Zelda. Hazel and the Baxters try to accept the idea of their little boy growing up, until events suggest that the worry may be a bit premature.

118. Temper, Temper

AIR DATE: February 4, 1965
WRITTEN BY: John McGreevey
CAST: Gregory Morton (Enzo Martelli), Barbara Shelley (Bianca Bellina), Vinton Hayworth (Mr. Sutherland)
SUMMARY: The local symphony has hired a talented but temperamental singer to perform the lead in its current production. The only person who can keep the demanding diva happy is Hazel's Italian boyfriend, which leads to complications when opening night conflicts with her bowling banquet.
NOTE: British-born Barbara Shelley was well-known to horror movie fans for her roles in a number of Hammer Films productions, and also appeared in the classic *Village of the Damned* (MGM, 1960).

119. Bonnie Boy

AIR DATE: February 11, 1965
WRITTEN BY: Fredric M. Frank
CAST: Willis Bouchey (Mayor Dixon), Florence Sundstrom (Matilda), Arthur Peterson (Salvation Army Leader), Robert B. Williams (Barney), Molly Dodd (Miss Scott), Hank Grant, Joseph Finnigan, Robert Johnson (Newsmen), Pat Rosson (Newsboy), George Mather (Cameraman), Edward Colebrook (Collection Man)
SUMMARY: Hazel buys a sweepstakes ticket as a last-minute birthday present for George, not knowing that the mayor just appointed him to a committee investigating illegal gambling in the community. When a damaging headline ("Anti-Gambling Official Draws Sweepstakes Horse") appears on the front page, Hazel owns up to her mistake, but won't divulge the name of the friend who sold her the ticket.

NOTE: Guest player Arthur Peterson had a lengthy career that ranged from a lead role in the radio serial *The Guiding Light* in the late 1930s to his comic turn as Jessica Tate's loony father "The Major" on *Soap* (ABC, 1977–81).

120. Stop Rockin' Our Reception

AIR DATE: February 18, 1965
WRITTEN BY: Ted Sherdeman and Jane Klove
CAST: Reginald Gardiner (Mr. Gilbert), William Bramley (Mr. Camden), David Bailey (Bruce Camden), Morgan Jones (Electrician)
SUMMARY: Harold's new friend down the block is a short-wave radio enthusiast. The friendship between the two boys is jeopardized when George blames the short-wave equipment for the problems he's having with his TV reception.
NOTES: For the purposes of this plot, there's no mention made of the color television set that Hazel acquired for her room in episode #6. Actor Reginald Gardiner plays a high-faluting television repairman who bills himself as "Gilbert the TV Doctor," balks at making house calls, and employs a stethoscope to diagnose problems in TV circuitry.

121. What's Buggin' Hazel?

AIR DATE: February 25, 1965
WRITTEN BY: Robert Riley Crutcher
CAST: Paul Barselow (Gus Anderson), Maurice Manson (Mr. Egan), Parley Baer (Mr. Rowland), Jonathan Hole (Mr. Wilson)
SUMMARY: George's latest client, Mr. Egan, is a department store owner whose office has been bugged by a rival while he's negotiating a sensitive real estate deal. When Egan sees Hazel's friend Gus listening into headphones, and learns that he works at the competing store, the resulting confusion causes Gus to lose his job on the eve of his silver wedding anniversary.
NOTES: A script oddity: when Dorothy learns that Hazel co-signed a loan for Gus, she asks George for an explanation, as she doesn't know what the term "co-signer" means. While this allows George to speak some expository dialogue that might have been thought necessary for some viewers, it's a bit implausible that a woman who operates her own part-time business has never heard of such a thing. Guest player Barselow worked often on Screen Gems' *Bewitched,* usually as the bartender serving Darrin drinks as he ponders being married to a witch.

122. Hazel's Day in Court

AIR DATE: March 4, 1965
WRITTEN BY: Louella MacFarlane

CAST: Hugh Marlowe (Donald Burton), Charles Macaulay (Phil Grantson), Lewis Martin (Judge), John Cliff (Policeman), Arthur Adams (Clerk)

SUMMARY: Frustrated by the city's lack of response to her request for a needed crosswalk, Hazel takes matters into her own hands with a can of paint. When she's hauled into court and charged with defacing public property, an unscrupulous newspaper reporter sees an opportunity to embarrass Mayor Dixon, whose re-election George supports.

NOTES: Guest star Hugh Marlowe (1911–1982), whose many film, TV, and stage credits include the cult favorite *The Day the Earth Stood Still* (Fox, 1951), spent his later years as patriarch Jim Matthews on the NBC soap opera *Another World*, a role he assumed in 1969. This is actor Lewis Martin's second stint as a judge on *Hazel* — he previously appeared in #4, and was similarly employed in several early 1960s episodes of TV's *Perry Mason.*

QUOTE: HAZEL (to George, who's representing her) — Ain't you gonna put me on the stand? GEORGE: Heaven forbid!

123. Hazel's Inquisitive Mind

AIR DATE: March 11, 1965
WRITTEN BY: William Cowley
CAST: Aki Aleong (Mike Shiga), Howard Wendell (Malcolm P. Denton), Maudie Prickett (Rosie), Howard Smith (Harvey Griffin), Alice Nunn (Hildegarde), Queenie Leonard (Marybelle), Ruth Clifford (Mrs. Denton)

SUMMARY: George hopes to be retained as the lawyer for a wealthy industrialist who's moved into the neighborhood. He's counting on Mr. Griffin, who's friendly with the man, to recommend him, but Hazel tries a different approach — convincing Rosie and the other Sunshine Girls to induct Mr. Denton's Japanese houseboy as an honorary member.

NOTES: This is Howard Smith's final appearance as Mr. Griffin. Actor-musician Aleong was a veteran of Broadway's *Teahouse of the August Moon,* and later served on the board of the Screen Actors Guild, and as executive director of the nonprofit organization Asians in Media.

124. George's Man Friday

AIR DATE: March 18, 1965
WRITTEN BY: Keith Fowler and Phil Leslie
CAST: Paul Hartman (Al DeWitt), Harold Gould (Judge Winston), Molly Dodd (Miss Scott), Ivan Bonar (Mr. Lyons), Arthur Adams (Bailiff), Benjie Bancroft (Motorcycle Cop)

SUMMARY: When George successfully defends an itinerant horse-player against a theft charge, the grateful man decides to adopt the Baxters as his

family. Unfortunately, Al does nothing but cause problems when he tries to express his gratitude with stunts like handing out George's business cards on the courthouse steps. Knowing he's a confirmed bachelor, Hazel decides to scare him off by putting the moves on him.

NOTES: Guest star Paul Hartman had a long show business career, but is probably best known as Emmett Clark on *The Andy Griffith Show* (CBS, 1960–68) and its spinoff, *Mayberry RFD* (1968–71). Character actor Harold Gould, known to TV fans as the father to Valerie Harper's *Rhoda* (CBS, 1974–78) and Miles Webber on *The Golden Girls* (NBC, 1985–92), is almost unrecognizable (less gray and without his trademark mustache) in this early appearance. Arthur Adams once again plays an officer of the court, as he did in episode #122. Mention is made here of Hazel's boyfriend Enzio, seen in episode #118.

125. The Investor

AIR DATE: March 25, 1965
WRITTEN BY: Louella MacFarlane
CAST: John Banner (Mr. Mueller), Maurice Manson (Mr. Egan), Jill Hill (Sally Lou), Frank Puglia (Signor Angelo)

SUMMARY: Hazel's nephew has sent her $1000, and George wants her to invest it wisely so as to save for her retirement. But when she sees that the owner of Mueller's Bakery is having trouble staying afloat since his wife left him, she decides to invest in the business and help him out.

NOTES: This is the final episode to feature Don DeFore and Whitney Blake as George and Dorothy Baxter. Actor John Banner would soon be cast in his most famous role, as Sgt. Schultz on *Hogan's Heroes* (CBS, 1965–71). Maurice Manson reprises his role from episode #121 as department store owner Mr. Egan.

FIFTH SEASON (1965-66)

126. Who's in Charge Here?

AIR DATE: September 13, 1965
WRITTEN BY: William Cowley
DIRECTED BY: E.W. Swackhamer
CAST: Ernest Truex (Robert Dunlap), Sylvia Field (Mrs. Dunlap), Maudie Prickett (Rosie), Robert B. Williams (Barney), Queenie Leonard (Mert), Ann Jillian (Millie Ballard)

SUMMARY: With George and Dorothy having temporarily relocated to Baghdad so that he can work on a long-term project for Mr. Griffin, Hazel and Harold move in with George's younger brother Steve, his wife Barbara, and their small daughter Susie. Steve, a real estate agent, declares that he won't let Hazel run his life as she did his brother's.

NOTES: This episode, scripted by the series' long-time story consultant, opens in the familiar kitchen set, where Hazel is surrounded by old friends Rosie, Barney the mailman, and fellow Sunshine Girl Mert. Steve and Barbara, never previously mentioned in the series, presumably live nearby, as Hazel expects the trip to their house to take no more than an hour. This is the first episode of *Hazel* not directed by William D. Russell. Sylvia Field, who co-starred in Screen Gems' *Dennis the Menace* (CBS, 1959–63), appears with her real-life husband, character actor Ernest Truex. Also introduced here is Steve's part-time secretary, giddy teenager Millie.

127. Hazel's Second Week

AIR DATE: September 20, 1965
WRITTEN BY: William Cowley
DIRECTED BY: E.W. Swackhamer
CAST: Mala Powers (Mona Williams), Charles Bateman (Fred Williams), Maudie Prickett (Rosie)
SUMMARY: Eager to please her new employers, Hazel is working so hard that there's nothing left for Barbara to do. When even the Hollandaise sauce Barbara insists on making for dinner is subject to Hazel's improvements, Mrs. Baxter finally blows her stack.
NOTE: This episode introduces Barbara's slightly snooty friend Mona, who sounds much like the character of Deirdre when she declares Hazel "infuriating" after a brief acquaintance. Mala Powers (1931–2007), who plays Mona, enjoyed a long film and television career that began in the early 1950s, when she was a protégée of actress-director Ida Lupino.

128. How to Lose 30 Pounds in 30 Minutes

AIR DATE: September 27, 1965
WRITTEN BY: Robert Riley Crutcher
DIRECTED BY: E.W. Swackhamer
CAST: Laurence Haddon (Bill Fox), J. Edward McKinley (Mr. Bates), Lee Meriwether (Miss Wilson), Joan Shawlee (Mrs. Fox)
SUMMARY: When a salesman from Steve's real estate office teases Hazel about her figure, she resolves to lose weight. In order to raise the $250 she needs to enroll in a "Figure Contouring" class, Hazel convinces Steve to let her take a stab at generating some sales for him.
NOTE: Guest player Joan Shawlee may be best remembered for her featured role as Sweet Sue in *Some Like It Hot* (United Artists, 1959). She also made a few appearances on the classic *Dick Van Dyke Show* (CBS, 1961–66), as Buddy Sorrell's seldom-seen wife Pickles.

129. Do Not Disturb Occupants

AIR DATE: October 11, 1965
WRITTEN BY: John McGreevey
DIRECTED BY: Charles Barton
CAST: Oliver McGowan (Charles Stoneham), Edith Atwater (Edith Stoneham)
SUMMARY: Steve's new client can't find a house he likes, until he sees the Baxter home. After happily agreeing to sell the house for a $6000 profit, Steve and Barbara come to realize that they don't want to move.
NOTES: According to this script, Steve and Barbara are veteran house "flippers" who have bought, fixed up, and then re-sold several homes since they were married. Edith Atwater, who plays the client's wife, was a Broadway veteran with nearly as many shows to her credit as Shirley, among them the part of Maggie Cutler in *The Man Who Came to Dinner* (1939–41). She later played Aunt Gertrude in early episodes of TV's *The Hardy Boys* (ABC, 1977–79).

130. The Holdout

AIR DATE: October 18, 1965
WRITTEN BY: Robert Riley Crutcher
DIRECTED BY: E.W. Swackhamer
CAST: Ellen Corby (Minerva Anderson), James Westerfield (J.B. Turner), Laurence Haddon (Bill Fox), Shannon Farnon (Alice Cameron), Sharyn Hillyer (Ethel)
SUMMARY: Hazel helps persuade her friend from church to sell Steve's client the property he needs for an office building. But when Hazel learns that her friend didn't get a fair deal, she and Steve resolve to get their hands on the contract before it's delivered.

131. A-Haunting We Will Go

AIR DATE: October 25, 1965
WRITTEN BY: John McGreevey
DIRECTED BY: Charles Barton
CAST: Vaughn Taylor (Marshall Timmons), Charles Francisco (James Garrison), Dabney Coleman (Les Swanton), Richard Correll (Richie Garrison), Dick Balduzzi (Pete)
SUMMARY: A man who bought a house from Steve is threatening to sue him, claiming that the house is haunted by a noisy ghost. After Steve and Barbara spend a spooky night in the house, it's Hazel who finds an earthbound explanation for the seemingly supernatural problem.
NOTES: Actor Vaughn Taylor previously appeared as George Baxter's law professor in episode #59. Film and television star Dabney Coleman (*Nine to Five; Buffalo Bill*) appears briefly as the homeowner's attorney. Teenaged Richard Correll was a veteran of *Leave it to Beaver* (CBS and ABC, 1957–63), where he played Beaver's friend Richard.

132. *Hazel Needs a Car*

AIR DATE: November 1, 1965
WRITTEN BY: William Cowley
DIRECTED BY: Charles Barton
CAST: James Westerfield (J.B. Turner), Shannon Farnon (Alice), Mala Powers (Mona Williams), Ann Jillian (Millie), Louis Quinn (Mr. Foster)
SUMMARY: Everyone wants something from Steve — Barbara wants a mink, Millie wants a raise, and Hazel wants help buying her own car. Hazel's trip to a pet store, where she invests in a tank of rare fish expected to multiply, winds up helping not just her, but Steve, who's had a falling-out with his client Mr. Turner.
NOTES: Ann Jillian has her largest role yet in a *Hazel* segment, being prominently featured in this installment. Actors Westerfield and Farnon reprise their roles as Mr. Turner and his secretary from episode #130. This is Cowley's last *Hazel* script.
QUOTE: MILLIE (to Hazel, who's just described her latest scheme) — You wouldn't dare! HAZEL: Think that over. MILLIE (after a brief pause): You'd dare.

133. *Hazel Sits It Out*

AIR DATE: November 8, 1965
TELEPLAY BY: Robert Riley Crutcher
STORY BY: James Fonda
DIRECTED BY: Charles Barton
CAST: Malcolm Atterbury (Mr. Bullock), Mabel Albertson (Mrs. Clark), Eleanor Audley (Mrs. Hardy), Henry Hunter (Mr. Lucas), Catherine McLeod (Mrs. Lucas), Parker McCormick (Mrs. Richards)
SUMMARY: When Steve's salesman is unable to host an open house, Hazel volunteers to fill in and show the house while the rest of the family goes on a picnic. The busy afternoon brings a host of visitors, including several prospective buyers, a crabby neighbor who tries to discourage unsuitable buyers, and ultimately Steve's client, who's angry that a maid has been left in charge.
NOTE: This episode is virtually a reunion of familiar sitcom players, including Darrin's mother from *Bewitched,* Oliver Douglas' mother from *Green Acres,* and an unbilled Jack Dodson (Mayberry's Howard Sprague). Henry Hunter, who made several appearances in *Hazel*'s first format as the Baxter family doctor, appears here in a different guise.

134. *A "Lot" to Remember*

AIR DATE: November 15, 1965
WRITTEN BY: Ted Sherdeman and Jane Klove
DIRECTED BY: E.W. Swackhamer
CAST: Anne Seymour (Laura Kirkland), Harry Harvey, Sr. (J.M. Carter), John Hiestand (Auctioneer), Douglas Evans (Commissioner), Stanley Farrar (Cashier), Arthur Adams (Man in County Office)
SUMMARY: Attending a county auction with Barbara, Hazel impulsively buys a small lot. Disappointed when she sees the tiny plot of land, and frustrated by the assessments she's charged, Hazel schemes to unload her white elephant.

135. *A Bull's Eye for Cupid*

AIR DATE: November 22, 1965
WRITTEN BY: Louella MacFarlane
DIRECTED BY: Charles Barton
CAST: Mala Powers (Mona Williams), Charles Bateman (Fred Williams), Gregory Morton (Enzo Martinelli)
SUMMARY: Steve has forgotten his wedding anniversary, and planned a fishing trip with his friend Fred. To smooth things over, Steve pretends that the trip was intended for both couples to enjoy together. But when Barbara learns the truth, she gives her husband the cold shoulder.
NOTE: Hazel's off-again, on-again boyfriend Enzo appears for the first time since episode #118.

136. *The Crush*

AIR DATE: November 29, 1965
WRITTEN BY: Robert Riley Crutcher
CAST: Ann Jillian (Millie Ballard), Kathryn Givney (Miss Warren), Philip Ober (Mr. Ballard)
SUMMARY: When Steve's teenage secretary finds a romantic poem he wrote as a college student, she develops a crush on her boss. Hazel and the Baxters, conspiring with Millie's father, cook up a plot to cure the teenager of her fascination with Steve.

137. *Kindly Advise*

AIR DATE: December 6, 1965
WRITTEN BY: Robert Riley Crutcher
DIRECTED BY: Charles Barton
CAST: Cathy Lewis (Deirdre Thompson), Robert P. Lieb (Harry Thompson)
SUMMARY: Steve's sister Deirdre has taken it upon herself to instruct Barbara as to how she can be a better wife and mother. But when Deidre bullies her sister-in-law into allowing Susie to be enrolled in Miss Peterson's Elocution School, Hazel encourages Barbara to draw the line.
NOTES: Cathy Lewis, making her first appearance as Deirdre in the new format, appears in this and the next two episodes. Barbara explains to Hazel that Steve greatly respects his older sister, who "practically raised him."

138. *Noblesse Oblige*

AIR DATE: December 13, 1965
WRITTEN BY: John McGreevey
DIRECTED BY: Charles Barton

CAST: Cathy Lewis (Deirdre Thompson), Lee Patrick (Cora Pritchard), Nelson Olmsted (Everett Pritchard), Monroe Arnold (Mr. Grimes), Elizabeth Harrower (Agnes)

SUMMARY: After getting into an argument with another woman over a parking space, Hazel is later embarrassed to learn that her adversary is the socially prominent wife of a wealthy businessman Deirdre wanted Steve to meet. Making matters worse, when snooty Mrs. Pritchard walks out on the community pageant where she has traditionally played the lead, the director finds Hazel the perfect candidate to replace her.

NOTES: The gifted character actress Lee Patrick, previously seen in episode #116, contributes another strong performance here. Elizabeth Harrower, who has a small role as the pageant director's assistant, later became a soap opera writer, and was the mother of longtime *Days of Our Lives* star Susan Seaforth Hayes.

139. Hazel's Endearing Young Charms

AIR DATE: December 27, 1965
WRITTEN BY: Robert Riley Crutcher
DIRECTED BY: E.W. Swackhamer
CAST: Cathy Lewis (Deirdre Thompson), Robert P. Lieb (Harry Thompson), Alix Talton (Marge)
SUMMARY: Steve, who just lost a big real estate deal, is developing an inferiority complex from hearing Hazel's constant bragging about his successful brother. Realizing her mistake, Hazel tries to make amends by praising Steve instead. When he learns he's being manipulated, an angry Steve calls Deirdre to see if Hazel and Harold can go live with the Thompsons.
NOTE: Alix Talton, playing a friend of Barbara's, introduces herself onscreen as Marge Henry, but is billed as playing Marge Evans. She's making her first *Hazel* appearance since the show's first season (episode #27).

140. A Car Named Chrysanthemum

AIR DATE: January 3, 1966
WRITTEN BY: Louella MacFarlane
DIRECTED BY: Charles Barton
CAST: Ann Jillian (Millie Ballard), Peter Brocco (Mr. Ricci), Alvy Moore (Mr. Haverstraw), Harvey Grant (Ted Drake)
SUMMARY: Ready to invest $200 in a used car, Hazel is stymied when Steve refuses to co-sign for the dubious financing from "Wheeler the Dealer." Instead, she enlists the help of Millie's boyfriend Ted to fix up an old wreck she bought for $35 from the owner of a nursery.
NOTE: Alvy Moore, who appears as the car salesman, is most recognizable as county agent Hank Kimball on *Green Acres* (CBS, 1965–71).

141. Once an Actor

AIR DATE: January 10, 1966
WRITTEN BY: Ted Sherdeman and Jane Klove
CAST: Pat O'Brien (Jerome Van Meter), Anne Seymour (Laura Kirkland), Ann Jillian (Millie Ballard), Viola Harris (Mrs. Raymond), Hardie Albright (Mr. Raymond)
SUMMARY: Barbara's uncle is a washed-up matinee idol reduced to freeloading off the Baxters. Steve offers him a chance to train for a career in real estate, but Uncle Jerome can't resist one last chance at an acting career.
NOTES: Actor Pat O'Brien, veteran of Warner Brothers movie classics like *Angels with Dirty Faces* (1938) and *Knute Rockne, All American* (1940), also starred in an unsuccessful TV sitcom, *Harrigan and Son* (ABC, 1960–61). Anne Seymour reprises her role as wealthy Miss Kirkland from #134.

142. $285 by Saturday

AIR DATE: January 17, 1966
WRITTEN BY: Louella MacFarlane
DIRECTED BY: Charles Barton
CAST: Mala Powers (Mona Williams), Charles Bateman (Fred Williams), Ann Jillian (Millie Ballard), Alice Backes (Clara Grimaldi), Lindsay Workman (Mr. Springer), Warren Parker (Antique Dealer)
SUMMARY: After receiving a letter from George and Dorothy about an overseas missionary school that needs musical instruments for its students, Hazel takes up a collection. The owner of a music store offers to sell her an organ at a reduced price if she can raise the cash by the end of the week.
NOTES: This episode shows Hazel throwing a fundraising party and inviting all her friends. Clearly she has formed another circle like the Sunshine Girls, a group that now includes Mona and Fred Williams' maid, but Maudie Prickett's Rosie and the other Girls are nowhere to be seen.

143. Boom or Bust

AIR DATE: January 24, 1966
WRITTEN BY: Louella MacFarlane
DIRECTED BY: E.W. Swackhamer
CAST: Viola Harris (Hazel Purcell), Charles Alvin Bell (Stanton Purcell), Roy Stuart (Cliff), Walter Matthews (Pawnbroker), Jon Kowal (Assistant Manager)
SUMMARY: With business slow at the office, Steve puts the family on a strict budget. When Barbara spends her entire month's allowance on a book of tickets to a charity luncheon, Hazel devises a unique marketing scheme to unload the tickets.

NOTE: Actor Roy Stuart, who appears here as a car salesman, is most recognizable for his recurring role as Sergeant Carter's assistant, Corporal Boyle, on *Gomer Pyle, U.S.M.C.* (CBS, 1964–69).

144. Harold's Gift Horses

AIR DATE: January 31, 1966
WRITTEN BY: Robert Riley Crutcher
DIRECTED BY: Charles Barton
CAST: Anne Seymour (Miss Kirkland), James Westerfield (Mr. Turner), Anne Bellamy (Mr. Turner's Secretary), Murray Alper (Bill)
SUMMARY: Miss Kirkland has been entertaining Harold after school, giving him presents to ingratiate herself with him. When Steve's other wealthy client, Mr. Turner, learns of this, he decides to make Harold his office boy, leaving Steve and Barbara uncertain how to stop their nephew from being spoiled by the two lonely people.
NOTE: Beginning with this episode, Ray Fulmer and Lynn Borden's credit in the opening titles changes from "introducing" to "with."

145. How to Find Work Without Really Trying

AIR DATE: February 7, 1966
WRITTEN BY: Jack Sher
CAST: Victor Jory (Mr. Woods), Ann Jillian (Millie Ballard), Maudie Prickett (Rosie), Maurice Marsac (Maitre D.), Louis Mercier (Pierre Rolland), Orville Sherman (Postman), Carl Milletaire (Waiter)
SUMMARY: Hazel's prize in a newspaper contest is a dinner at ritzy Chez Gourmet, but no one's available to accompany her. She impulsively invites a man she met at the park, and tries to help him get back into the swing of working.
NOTES: Maudie Prickett makes her first appearance as Rosie since #127. Guest Victor Jory's dozens of film credits range from the sublime to the ridiculous—witness his appearances as Jonas Wilkerson in *Gone with the Wind* (1939), and as leading man to Marie Windsor in the unforgettable *Cat-Women of the Moon* (1953).

146. My Son, the Sheepdog

AIR DATE: February 14, 1966
WRITTEN BY: Ted Sherdeman and Jane Klove
CAST: Mala Powers (Mona Williams), Charles Bateman (Fred Williams), Pat Cardi (Jeff Williams)
SUMMARY: The adults are horrified when Harold and his friends grow their hair long, and form a combo called the Leaping Lizards. When the group wins the talent competition on a TV show called *Pandemonium,* Hazel, the Baxters, and their friends fight back by adopting their own beatnik look.

NOTES: This episode introduces Mona and Fred's previously unseen son Jeff. Mala Powers, as Mona, utters the line from which the episode's title is taken. Sherdeman and Klove's script parodies the short-lived mid-sixties fad for rock and roll variety shows on prime time television; NBC's version, which aired on Monday nights during the 1965-66 season, was called *Hullabaloo,* while ABC had *Shindig!* (1964–66). Seen as the drummer of the Leaping Lizards is an unbilled Keith Thibodeaux, better known as Richard Keith (Little Ricky) of *I Love Lucy* fame.

147. Please Don't Shout

AIR DATE: February 21, 1966
TELEPLAY BY: Robert Riley Crutcher
STORY BY: James Fonda and Robert Riley Crutcher
CAST: Gene Blakely (Harvey), Charles Bateman (Fred Williams), Mala Powers (Mona Williams), Charles Francisco (Jack), Jess Kirkpatrick (Mr. Hobart), Barbara Luddy (Mrs. Hobart), Emile Sitka (Mr. Miller)
SUMMARY: Steve's poker buddy Harvey is miserable in his house since the construction of a nearby thruway that causes a deafening racket day and night. With the encouragement of Barbara and Hazel, Steve agrees to take on the thankless task of selling a house no one wants.
NOTE: Mala Powers' chief contribution to this episode is a voice-over she performs as the offscreen Mona objects to having Harvey as an unexpected houseguest.

148. But Is It Art?

AIR DATE: February 28, 1966
WRITTEN BY: John McGreevey
CAST: Claude Akins (Milwaukee Ames), Cathy Lewis (Deirdre Thompson), Bill McLean (Ralph Pankhurst), Tom Palmer (Vance)
SUMMARY: A tale of two painters—the eccentric artist Deirdre wants to commission to do her portrait, and the one Hazel needs to repaint the walls of her room. Naturally, Hazel finds a way to kill two birds with one stone.
NOTES: In the pre-credits sequence, Hazel finds a unique way to remind Steve that it's his wedding anniversary. Not surprising he finds the date difficult to remember, since the Baxters already had an anniversary earlier this season, in #135. This is Cathy Lewis' final appearance as Deirdre.

149. Who Can Afford a Bargain?

AIR DATE: March 7, 1966
WRITTEN BY: Jack Sher
CAST: Mala Powers (Mona Williams), Charles Bateman (Fred Williams), Pat Cardi (Jeff Williams), Laurence Haddon (Bill Fox), Ann

Jillian (Millie Ballard), Don Douglas (Mr. Sherell), Ann Ayars (Mrs. Sherell), John Harmon (Mr. Craven)

SUMMARY: Mona falls in love with an elegant house Steve's representing. When Hazel realizes that Fred has agreed to buy the house even though it will be a financial strain, she resolves to make Mona see the error of her ways.

NOTES: According to the script, this exorbitantly expensive house is on the market for $60,000 (equivalent to about $375,000 in the mid–2000s), with a $15,000 down payment required. This episode features a rare reference to another family that employed Hazel before she went to work for Dorothy's parents.

150. Hazel's Free Enterprise

AIR DATE: March 14, 1966
WRITTEN BY: Ted Sherdeman and Jane Klove
CAST: Mala Powers (Mona Williams), Charles Bateman (Fred Williams), Ed Prentiss (Mr. Richey), Byron Foulger (Mr. Moore), Bobby Johnson (Richey Driver)

SUMMARY: To pay for the pool table Barbara bought Steve for his birthday, she and Hazel go into business bottling "Aunt Hazel's Chili Sauce." When news of the new enterprise gets out, Fred thinks the Baxters are in financial straits, while Hazel receives a visit from the health inspector.

NOTE: The premise of this episode is reminiscent of a favorite *I Love Lucy* segment, in which Lucy and Ethel try to sell "Aunt Martha's Old-Fashioned Salad Dressing." Unlike those ladies, though, Barbara and Hazel do make money from their venture.

151. Bee in Her Bonnet

AIR DATE: March 21, 1966
WRITTEN BY: Robert Riley Crutcher
DIRECTED BY: Hal Cooper
CAST: Guy Raymond (Hogan), Kathryn Givney (Mrs. Fillmore), Harry Harvey, Sr. (Muntz)

SUMMARY: En route to an appointment with a prospective client, Good Samaritan Steve stops to help a stranger who wrecked his car. Hearing Hazel's story of a friend who collected a large insurance settlement after an auto accident, the ungrateful man decides to recoup his losses by suing Steve.

152. The Perfect Boss

AIR DATE: March 28, 1966
WRITTEN BY: John McGreevey
CAST: Mala Powers (Mona Williams), Charles Bateman (Fred Williams), Ann Jillian (Millie Ballard), Alice Backes (Clara Grimaldi)

SUMMARY: With a $100 prize at stake, Hazel wants to enter a newspaper essay contest by describing Steve as "the perfect boss." He's reluctant until he learns that Fred's maid Clara will be submitting an entry as well, rousing the competitive spirit between the two men.

NOTE: Alice Backes, first seen as the Williams maid in #142, reprises that role here, though she's inexplicably missing from the episode's closing credits.

153. A Little Bit of Genius

AIR DATE: April 4, 1966
WRITTEN BY: Ted Sherdeman and Jane Klove
CAST: Mala Powers (Mona Williams), Charles Bateman (Fred Williams), Pat Cardi (Jeff Williams)

SUMMARY: Harold feels left out when his friend Jeff is transferred into a class for gifted students. Hazel decides that Harold could use a little help with his homework, while Jeff, who's becoming arrogant with all the attention he's receiving, needs a little remedial work in social skills.

154. A Question of Ethics

AIR DATE: April 11, 1966
TELEPLAY BY: Robert Riley Crutcher
STORY BY: Louella MacFarlane
CAST: John Qualen (Mr. Johansson), Alice Frost (Mrs. Johansson), Ann Jillian (Millie Ballard), Bill Zuckert (Joe Ryan), Willis Bouchey (Mr. McComer), Steve Rinaldi (Ted), Heather Woodruff (Miss Hill)

SUMMARY: Hazel's friends the Johanssons, longtime farmers, are ready to retire, and have been made an offer of $12,000 for their property. When Hazel suggests they enlist Steve's help in seeking a better price, the Johanssons' real estate agent cries foul, and files an ethical complaint against his rival.

NOTE: Millie's boyfriend Ted is presumably the same character seen in #140, but the role has been cast with a different actor.

Appendix E:
A Touch of Grace Episode Guide

CREDITS: Executive producers, Ted Bergmann, Herman Rush; producers, Saul Turteltaub and Bernie Orenstein; directed by Carl Reiner, Bill Hobin; written by Jeff Harris and Bernie Kukoff, Rick Mittleman, David Pollock and Elias Davis, Saul Turteltaub and Bernie Orenstein, George Tibbles. Adapted from the Thames TV series *For the Love of Ada,* created by Vince Powell and Harry Driver.

CAST: Shirley Booth (Grace Simpson), J. Pat O'Malley (Herbert Morrison), Marian Mercer (Myra Bradley), Warren Berlinger (Walter Bradley)

HISTORY: Aired Saturdays at 8:30 p.m. (EST) on ABC-TV.

FIRST—AND ONLY—SEASON (1973)

---

1. A Touch of Grace (Pilot)

AIR DATE: January 20, 1973 (repeated May 12, 1973)

CAST: Britt Leech (Man in Cemetery)

SUMMARY: Grace Simpson, a recent widow living with her daughter and son-in-law, shocks her family by bringing home a man she met at the cemetery, where he works as a gravedigger. When Grace gifts her new friend with a suit and gold watch that belonged to her late husband, she and daughter Myra are headed for a showdown.

2. The Weekend

AIR DATE: January 27, 1973 (repeated May 12, 1973)

CAST: John Fiedler (Desk Clerk)

SUMMARY: Herbert wins a free weekend trip for himself and his wife to a resort in Sausalito. Grace agrees to accompany him on the outing, but gets cold feet when it comes time to register as husband and wife at the hotel.

NOTE: Guest player Fiedler supplied the voice for Piglet in numerous Winnie the Pooh cartoons, and also played timid therapy patient Mr. Peterson on *The Bob Newhart Show* (CBS, 1972–78).

3. The Working Girl

AIR DATE: February 3, 1973 (repeated May 19, 1973)

CAST: Fritzi Burr (Mrs. Sherman)

SUMMARY: Walter and Myra may be leaving Oakland, so that he can accept a job out of town. Rather than tag along, Grace decides she'd rather be self-sufficient, and gets herself a job as a ladies' room attendant.

NOTE: Character actress Burr was seen often on NBC's *Sanford and Son* (1972–77), usually as a stuffy or crabby woman who aroused Fred's ire.

4. Lover's Quarrel

AIR DATE: February 10, 1973 (repeated May 26, 1973)

CAST: Roy Roberts (Bertram Garrett)

SUMMARY: Since Herbert refuses to escort Grace to a senior citizens' dance, she resolves to show her boyfriend that there are other fish in the sea. But her new beau proves to have a few quirks of his own.

NOTE: This is one of the last television appearances by actor Roy Roberts (1900–1975), who previously played Mr. Cheever on *The Lucy Show,* and

193

Darrin's father Frank on *Bewitched,* among many other roles. Back in the 1940s, as a young man, Roberts appeared opposite Shirley in Broadway's *My Sister Eileen,* replacing the actor originally cast as "The Wreck."

5. Pregnant Conversation

AIR DATE: February 17, 1973 (repeated June 2, 1973)
CAST: Florence Lake (Mrs. Fitton), Doris Packer (Mrs. Armstrong)
SUMMARY: Grace tells her friends that she's soon to be a grandmother. Now all she has to do is convince Myra and Walter it's a good idea.

6. The Apartment

AIR DATE: February 24, 1973
CAST: Zack Taylor (Richard), Amy Farrell (Annie), Sue Marrow, Gay Waters (Prospective Tenants)
SUMMARY: Walter and Myra decide to earn some extra money by renting out the ground floor of their home. They're happy with their prospective tenants—a young couple expecting their first child—until they learn that the two newcomers aren't married.

7. The Driving Lesson

AIR DATE: March 3, 1973
CAST: Stephen Hood (Gordon), Bob Duggan (Official)
SUMMARY: Frustrated when the bus company no longer provides convenient transportation to the cemetery, Grace decides the solution is to get her own driver's license. Walter is given the thankless task of acting as his mother-in-law's driving instructor.

8. Saturday Night at the Movies

AIR DATE: March 17, 1973
CAST: Gino Conforti (Ebsen), Gordon Jump (Greenwald), Bo Kaprall (Man in Cemetery)
SUMMARY: What begins as an innocent movie date for Grace and Herbert leads to embarrassment when the theater is raided for showing X-rated films.
NOTE: Gordon Jump is best-remembered for his role as radio station owner Arthur Carlson on *WKRP in Cincinnati* (CBS, 1978–82).

9. The Lodge

AIR DATE: March 24, 1973
CAST: Arte Johnson (Charlie), Tom Bosley (Preacher), Herbie Faye (Caterer), Jackie Vernon (Bartender), Christopher Connelly (Mickey)
SUMMARY: Grace helps arrange a surprise party for Herbert at his lodge, but his plans to give her a birthday party threaten to make him miss the big event.
NOTE: This episode was taped near the end of Arte Johnson's run as a regular player on *Laugh-In* (NBC, 1968–73), and just prior to Tom Bosley's being cast as father Howard Cunningham on a far more successful ABC sitcom, *Happy Days* (1974–84).

10. The Reunion

AIR DATE: March 31, 1973
CAST: Ian Wolfe
SUMMARY: The man who comes to dinner was an old Army buddy of Grace's late husband, and once saved his life, making it awkward for the family to bring his visit to a close.
NOTE: Guest star Wolfe was a veteran character actor who previously appeared in Shirley's 1954 film *About Mrs. Leslie,* playing the proprietor of a used bookstore.

11. The Commercial

AIR DATE: April 7, 1973
CAST: Milton Frome (Moorpark), Joby Baker (Dickson), Johnny Haymer (Charles), Tom Biener (Makeup Man), Brenda Elder (Secretary)
SUMMARY: Grace's on-air endorsement for Walter's grocery store proves highly effective, until it comes to light that she's his mother-in-law.
NOTE: Guest player Joby Baker was the leading man of the sitcom *Good Morning, World* (CBS, 1967-68).

12. The Accident

AIR DATE: April 14, 1973
CAST: Richard Dreyfuss (Donald), Ned Wertimer (Bushling)
SUMMARY: Grace and Herbert are riding a city bus that winds up in an accident. When the bus company offers each passenger a $400 settlement, some of them decide their "mental anguish" is worth much more.
NOTES: Future Oscar winner Dreyfuss made this guest appearance just months before a role in *American Graffiti* (1973) took his career to a new level. Ned Wertimer played doorman Ralph on *The Jeffersons* (CBS, 1975–85).

13. The Engagement

AIR DATE: April 21, 1973 (repeated June 16, 1973)
CAST: Jan Arvan (Watson)
SUMMARY: Grace decides to accept Herbert's marriage proposal, but a misunderstanding over the ring she selects may derail the wedding.
NOTE: The June 16 repeat of this final episode was *Grace*'s swan song on ABC.

Chapter Notes

Introduction

1. Brooks Atkinson, "Magnetic Lady: 'By the Beautiful Sea' Suits Miss Booth," *New York Times,* April 18, 1954.
2. Bernard F. Dick, *Hal Wallis: Producer to the Stars* (Lexington: University Press of Kentucky, 2004), 140.

Chapter 1

1. Hal McClure, "Oscar Winner Shirley Booth Thinks Award Came Too Soon," *Newport* (RI) *News,* August 24, 1956.
2. Lydia Lane, "'Hazel' Not Able-Thin," *Los Angeles Times,* November 3, 1963.
3. *Current Biography* (1942), 96.
4. "Reasons for Living on the Heights: No More Beautiful Places Anywhere Than the Morningside and Washington Hill Tops," *New York Times,* April 7, 1895.
5. "Actress," *New Yorker,* May 19, 1951.
6. Phyllis Battelle, "Facing Reality Hard Task for Top Broadway Actress," *Charleston Gazette,* May 25, 1954.
7. Robert Coughlan, "New Queen of the Drama," *Life,* December 1, 1952.
8. *Current Biography* (1942), 97.
9. Ida Jean Kain, "'Little Sheba's Star Learned Posture Secret the Hard Way," *Washington Post,* March 2, 1951.
10. "The Trouper," *Time,* August 10, 1953.
11. *The Flying Dutchman II: An Exposition of a New York City High School with Its Activities,* Erasmus Hall High School, 1911, 281.
12. Ibid, 125.
13. Coughlan, "New Queen of the Drama."
14. John McClain, "Shirley Booth a Contender for Movie Oscar in March," *Cedar Rapids Gazette,* December 21, 1952.
15. Coughlan, "New Queen of the Drama."
16. Bob Zaiman, "The Human Touch," *Hartford Courant,* March 21, 1953.

17. *Hartford Courant,* May 8, 1923.
18. Jay Kaye, "Shirley Booth: Broadway's Choice," *Coronet,* December 1953.
19. Coughlan, "New Queen of the Drama."
20. Albert J. Duffy, "Hartford Girl in 'Undertow,'" *Hartford Courant,* November 1, 1929.
21. Zaiman, "The Human Touch."
22. "Delightful Comedy at Palace Theater," *Hartford Courant,* November 26, 1918.
23. Jean Webster, *Daddy-Long-Leg.* (New York: Century, 1912), 8.
24. "'Daddy Long Legs' at Palace Theater: Popular Poli Players Will Appear in Charming Play This Week," *Hartford Courant,* November 3, 1918.
25. Ibid.
26. "Poli Players in 'Daddy Long Legs': Fine Presentation Given at Palace Theater," *Hartford Courant,* November 5, 1918.
27. "Fine Drama of New England Life: Palace Theatre Will Present 'Lavender and Old Lace' This Week," *Hartford Courant,* December 15, 1918.
28. "Shirley Booth Contented," *Troy Times Record,* September 26, 1964.
29. Ibid.
30. *Hartford Courant,* April 13, 1919.
31. 'Sis Hopkins' is Likable Comedy," *Hartford Courant,* April 5, 1919.
32. Zaiman, "The Human Touch."
33. Coughlan, "New Queen of the Drama."
34. "Poli Players Say Farewell," *Hartford Courant,* May 18, 1919.
35. Ibid.
36. Coughlan, "New Queen of the Drama."
37. Ralph Bellamy, *When the Smoke Hit the Fan* (Garden City, NY: Doubleday, 1979), 65.
38. Ibid.
39. William Lyon Phelps, *The Twentieth Century Theatre: Observations on the Contemporary English and American Stage* (Freeport, NY: Books for Libraries Press, 1967), c1918.
40. "Miss Williams Likes Palace Audiences," *Hartford Courant,* July 6, 1918.
41. "Seen and Heard," *Lowell Sun,* December 1, 1932.

42. Jean Meegan, "Doesn't Mix Stage Roles, Private Life," *Hartford Courant,* June 13, 1943.

43. "Musical Comedy at the Palace: Poli Players Will Present This week 'Oh, Lady, Lady,'" *Hartford Courant,* July 9, 1922.

44. "'Off to Paris' Musical Comedy at the Palace; Production Will Have First Presentation Here Before Going to New York Theater," *Hartford Courant,* August 6, 1922.

45. *Coshocton Tribune,* April 22, 1923.

46. "Actress," *New Yorker,* May 19, 1951.

Chapter 2

1. "Actor Shot on Stage with Wrong Pistol; Bullet Barely Misses Actress; Show Delayed," *New York Times,* February 12, 1925.

2. "Aunt Cissy from Williamsburg," *New York Times,* May 6, 1951.

3. "The Best Bets in Broadway Theatres," *Charleston Daily Mail,* November 15, 1925.

4. "Gossip of the Rialto," *New York Times*, March 14, 1926.

5. "George Jean Nathan Looks on the Drama," *Hartford Courant,* July 4, 1926.

6. Burns Mantle, *The Best Plays of 1925-26, and the Yearbook of Drama in America* (New York: Dodd, Mead, 1926), 10.

7. "In a Farce," *Chicago Tribune,* September 19, 1926.

8. Robert Coughlan, "New Queen of the Drama," *Life,* December 1, 1952.

9. Richard Maney, *Fanfare: The Confessions of a Press Agent* (New York: Harper, 1957), 278.

10. "The Footlights Lure Society Girls," *Hartford Courant,* September 9, 1928.

11. George Jessel, *So Help Me: The Autobiography of George Jessel* (New York: Random House, 1943), 96.

12. Coughlan, "New Queen of the Drama."

13. Albert, J. Duffy, "The Show Window," *Hartford Courant,* November 5, 1929.

14. "Wall St.'s Depression Still Hurting B'Way Legits, But Smashes Hold to Big Money," *Variety,* November 13, 1929.

15. "Skidding Market Skidded B'Way Legits Badly Last Week," *Variety,* November 6, 1929.

16. George A. Mooney, "Talk of the Tavern," *New York Times,* April 6, 1941.

17. Ibid.

18. Anton Remenih, "It Goes Without Saying, Duffy Has Say on Air!," *Chicago Tribune,* December 9, 1950.

19. Abe Burrows, "Ed 'Archie' Gardner." In *Duffy's First Reader* (New York: Bristol-Myers Company, 1943), 40.

20. Ibid., 43.

21. Paul Harrison, "Theatre Continues to Have a Strong Foreign Policy," *Dunkirk Evening Observer,* June 3, 1933.

22. "Equity Will Permit Recess for Actors; Coun-cil Rules Managers May Lay off Companies for Two Weeks Before Christmas," *New York Times,* November 30, 1933.

23. Burrows, "Ed 'Archie' Gardner," 44.

24. *New York Times,* February 8, 1934.

25. "New 'Sunday Nights at 9: Cast Changes in Latest Edition of Intimate Revue," *New York Times,* March 5, 1934.

26. "New Comedy Staged by Red Barn Players; Locust Valley Playhouse Has Premiere of 'The Nude in Washington Square,'" *New York Times,* August 7, 1934.

27. Mark Barron, "How Shirley Booth Won Leading Role," *Uniontown Morning Herald*, January 3, 1953.

28. Ibid.

29. Paul Harrison, "In New York," *Frederick* (MD) *Daily News,* March 8, 1935.

30. John Harkins, "Farewells Are Said for Play," *Charleston Gazette,* April 25, 1937.

31. Franklin J. Schaffner, *Worthington Miner* (Metuchen, NJ: Scarecrow Press, 1985), 102.

32. Ibid., 101.

33. Ibid.

34. Burns Mantle, *The Best Plays of 1936-37, and the Yearbook of Drama in America* (New York: Dodd, Mead, 1937), 328.

35. Carroll Carroll, *None of Your Business; Or, My Life with J. Walter Thompson (Confessions of a Renegade Radio Writer* (New York: Cowles, 1970), 63.

Chapter 3

1. Mel Heimer, "Shirley Booth Entitled to Movie Oscar," *Winona* (MN) *Republican-Herald,* January 15, 1953.

2. "New York Hick," *Time,* June 21, 1943.

3. *Variety,* June 5, 1940.

4. John Kobler, *Damned in Paradise: The Life of John Barrymore* (New York: Atheneum, 1977), 356.

5. *Current Biography* (1942), 97.

6. Ibid.

7. Milton R. Bass, "The Lively Arts," *Berkshire Eagle,* August 29, 1963.

8. John Crosby, "Duffy Back with Weird Tavern Gang," *Oakland Tribune,* October 13, 1948.

9. Abe Burrows, *Honest, Abe: Is There Really No Business Like Show Business?* (Boston: Little, Brown, 1980), 61.

10. John K. Hutchens, "A Very Fine Joint: A Salute to Duffy's Tavern, Where the Elite, Including Ed Gardner, Meet," *New York Times,* November 23, 1941.

11. John Crosby, "Nice Stuff for You on 3rd Avenoo," *Oakland Tribune,* November 28, 1947.

12. Jordan R. Young, *The Laugh Crafters: Comedy Writing in Radio and TV's Golden Age* (Beverly Hills: Past Times, 1999), 15.

13. C.B. Driscoll, "New York Day by Day," *Benton Harbor* (MI) *News-Palladium,* June 17, 1942.

14. Dick Van Patten, telephone interview with the author, September 9, 2007.

15. Larry Gelbart, *Laughing Matters: On Writing M*A*S*H, Tootsie, Oh, God!, and a Few Other Funny Things* (New York: Random House, 1998), 15–16.

16. Phyllis Battelle, "The Divine Shirley: At Age 2, Miss Booth Fell in Love with Sound of One Human Hand Smacking Against Another," *Charleston Gazette*, May 28, 1954.

17. Robert Musel, "Miss Booth Comes to Tea," *TV Guide*, December 3, 1966.

18. Hedda Hopper, "Looking at Hollywood," *Los Angeles Times*, April 10, 1943.

19. Jack Gould, "One Thing and Another," *New York Times*, July 25, 1943.

20. *Variety*, October 13, 1943.

21. Kevin Minton, "Shirley Booth: A Tribute," *Classic Images*, June 1999.

Chapter 4

1. "The Trouper." *Time*, August 10, 1953.

2. Earl Wilson, "'Broadway Still the Class Act,'" *Daily Intelligencer*, May 26, 1979.

3. Joyce Van Patten, telephone interview with the author, August 27, 2007.

4. Jean Meegan, "Doesn't Mix Stage Roles, Private Life," *Hartford Courant*, June 13, 1943.

5. James Poling, "One Touched with Genius," *Collier's*, June 16, 1951.

6. Robert Coughlan, "New Queen of the Drama," *Life*, December 1, 1952.

7. Van Patten interview.

8. "Suits Charge Fraud in $700,000 Policies," *New York Times*, October 7, 1932.

9. Dorothy Kilgallen, untitled column, *Lowell Sun*, August 27, 1943.

10. Poling, "One Touched with Genius."

11. Dorothy Kilgallen, "The Voice of Broadway," *Olean* (NY) *Times Herald*, May 20, 1944.

12. Richard K. Hayes, *Kate Smith: A Biography, with a Discography, Filmography, and List of Stage Appearances* (Jefferson, NC: McFarland, 1995), 97.

13. Ibid.

14. Jack Ryan, "Shirley Booth: Is She Really That Nice?," *Danville* (VA) *Register*, September 16, 1962.

15. "Revelry Sounds at Stage Door Canteen as Famous Unit Marks Third Birthday," *New York Times*, March 3, 1945.

16. "At the Theatre," *Berkshire Evening Eagle*, August 20, 1946.

17. Sam Zolotow, "'Land's End' Sees Its Termination," *New York Times*, December 13, 1946.

18. Arthur Laurents, *Original Story: A Memoir of Broadway and Hollywood* (New York: Knopf, 2000), 74.

19. Irene Mayer Selznick, *A Private View* (New York: Knopf, 1983), 293.

20. Thomas Congdon, "At Home with 'Hazel,'" *Saturday Evening Post*, September 22, 1962.

21. *Variety*, January 21, 1948.

22. Bill Henry, "By the Way with Bill Henry," *Los Angeles Times*, January 23, 1948.

23. *New York Times*, January 15, 1948.

24. "Eve Arden Set for 'Brooks,' in H'wood," *Variety*, June 16, 1948.

25. "Shirley Booth Happy Choice for Guilford Play," *Hartford Courant*, July 16, 1948.

26. Melvyn Douglas, *See You at the Movies*, 105.

27. Leonard Lyons, untitled column, *Washington Post*, November 30, 1948.

28. Richard L. Coe, "Comedy Tidbits brighten 'Stem,'" *Washington Post*, December 14, 1948.

Chapter 5

1. "'Hogan's Daughter Will Be Heard over Station WKPT," *Kingsport News*, June 20, 1949.

2. Val Adams, "Some Summer Shows: NBC Tries Its Hand at 'Package' Units with Only Indifferent Results," *New York Times*, July 31, 1949.

3. John Crosby, "Radio in Review," *Portsmouth Times*, July 13, 1949.

4. *Variety*, July 13, 1949.

5. Tennessee Williams, *Memoirs* (New York: New Directions, 2006), 90.

6. James Poling, "One Touched with Genius," *Collier's*, June 16, 1951.

7. Phyllis Battelle, "Eyes Hint Shirley Finds Life Interesting but Sad," *Elyria Chronicle-Telegram*, May 24, 1954.

8. Voss, 87.

9. Ralph Voss, e-mail to author, July 18, 2007.

10. Poling, "One Touched with Genius."

11. Mel Heimer, "My New York," *Valparaiso Vidette-Messenger*, July 2, 1951.

12. "The Trouper," *Time*, August 10, 1953.

13. Audrey Wood and Max Wilk, *Represented by Audrey Wood*, 225.

14. *Variety*, September 14, 1949.

15. *Variety*, October 26, 1949.

16. Phyllis Anderson, "Diary of a Production," *Theatre Arts*, November 1950.

17. Sam Zolotow, "Pemberton Keeps Comedy on Boards," *New York Times*, November 14, 1949.

18. Mark Barron, "Shirley Booth is Puzzled Star, Seldom Gets Fancy Clothes Role," *Bridgeport Post*, August 25, 1951.

19. Joan Lorring interview, Ronald Davis Oral History Collection on the Performing Arts, DeGolyer Library, Southern Methodist University, Dallas, Texas, A1980.0154.

20. "The Trouper."

21. "Actress," *New Yorker*, May 19, 1951.

22. Betty Smith and George Abbott, *A Tree Grows in Brooklyn* (New York: Harper, 1951), 23.

23. Poling, "One Touched with Genius."

24. Ibid.

25. Jay Kaye, "Shirley Booth: Broadway's Choice," *Coronet*, December 1953.

26. Phyllis Battelle, "Facing Reality Hard Task for Top Broadway Actress," *Charleston Gazette*, May 25, 1954.

27. Ibid.

28. Harry Gilroy, "Hollywood Can't Change Shirley Booth; Broadway's 'Favorite Aunt' Likes to Make Movies— But Strictly on Her Own Terms," *New York Times,* April 27, 1952.

29. Whitney Stine, *"I'd Love to Kiss You—": Conversations with Bette Davis* (New York: Pocket Books, 1990), 79.

30. Wood and Wilk, *Represented by Audrey Wood,* 228.

Chapter 6

1. Thomas M. Pryor, "Hollywood Memos: Telemeter Coin Box TV Test Successful; On the Set with Shirley Booth," *New York Times,* March 2, 1952.

2. Philip K. Scheuer, "Burt Breaks Mold When Typed," *Los Angeles Times,* December 14, 1952.

3. Charles D. Rice, "The Proper Miss Booth," *Los Angeles Times,* June 21, 1953.

4. Erskine Johnson, untitled column, *Lowell Sun,* April 20, 1952.

5. "The Trouper," *Time,* August 10, 1953.

6. Hedda Hopper, "Terry Cites Acting Sex-Appeal Views," *Los Angeles Times,* January 18, 1953.

7. Jay Kaye, "Shirley Booth: Broadway's Choice," *Coronet,* December 1953.

8. Rice, "The Proper Miss Booth."

9. Harold Clurman, *The Collected Works of Harold Clurman: Six Decades of Commentary on Theatre, Dance, Music, Film, Arts and Letters* (New York: Applause Books, 1994), 759.

10. Arthur Laurents, *Original Story By: A Memoir of Broadway and Hollywood* (New York: Knopf, 2000), 193.

11. James Poling, "One Touched with Genius," *Collier's,* June 16, 1951.

12. Joanne Kaufman, "Take Two Aspirin— And Get Onstage," *Wall Street Journal,* February 10, 2004.

13. Richard L. Coe, "Fame Sits Lightly on Shirley Booth," *Washington Post.* February 10, 1953.

14. "Shirley Booth Superb in 'Time of Cuckoo,'" *Los Angeles Times,* October 20, 1952.

15. Arthur Knight, "A Bouquet for Everybody," *Saturday Review,* December 27, 1952.

16. "Cannes Festival Cites Miss Booth," *New York Times,* April 30, 1953.

17. *Variety,* March 18, 1953.

18. Erskine Johnson, "In Hollywood," *Portsmouth Herald,* March 13, 1953.

19. Leonard Lyons, "Lyons Den," *Syracuse Post-Standard,* March 26, 1953.

20. Isaac Bickerstaff, "The Oscars— by TV," *Films in Review,* April 1953.

21. "Shirley Booth Gets Surprise in New York," *Los Angeles Times,* March 20, 1953.

22. Bickerstaff, "The Oscars— by TV."

23. "Shirley Booth Gets Surprise in New York."

24. Bickerstaff, "The Oscars— by TV."

25. Jack Gould, "Video Presentation of Film Awards Ceremonies Indicates Happy Marriage is Possible," *New York Times,* March 23, 1953.

26. Bob Zaiman, "The Human Touch," *Hartford Courant,* March 21, 1953.

27. Bob Thomas, "Shirley Booth Back Before Cameras," *Newport [RI] News,* October 21, 1953.

28. Erskine Johnson, untitled column, *Modesto Bee,* December 5, 1953.

29. Phyllis Battelle, "Facing Reality Hard Task for Top Broadway Actress," *Charleston Gazette,* May 25, 1954.

30. *Variety,* May 5, 1954.

31. Pressbook, *About Mrs. Leslie,* Paramount Pictures, 1954.

32. Gregory Katz, "Lunch with the FT: Theatre of Dreams," *Financial Times,* October 28, 2005.

33. Gilbert Millstein, "Wholesome First Lady," *New York Times,* April 4, 1954.

34. Walter F. Kerr, "Shirley Booth Only Steady Craft in 'Beautiful Sea,'" *Council Bluffs* (IA) *Nonpareil,* April 18, 1954.

35. *Variety,* April 14, 1954.

36. Dick Kleiner, "The Marquee," *Anniston Star,* July 5, 1954.

Chapter 7

1. Louella Parsons, "Shirley Booth Lines Up a Part," *Washington Post,* March 17, 1955.

2. Vernon Scott, "Shirley Booth Says She's No Slave to Actress Role," *San Mateo Times,* October 28, 1953.

3. Edwin Schallert, "Shirley Booth to Confer with Hal Wallis about Her Future Film Plans," *Los Angeles Times,* October 28, 1954.

4. Joyce Van Patten, telephone interview with the author, August 27, 2007.

5. Dorothy Kilgallen, "Adds an Office Party for Laughs," *Washington Post,* October 17, 1955.

6. Walter F. Kerr, "Theater: 'The Desk Set,'" *New York Herald-Tribune,* October 25, 1955.

7. Robert Coleman, "Shirley Booth Great in 'The Desk Set,'" *New York Daily Mirror,* October 25, 1955.

8. Van Patten interview.

9. John L. Scott, "Actress Shirley Booth Finally Gets Her Man in 'Desk Set,'" *Los Angeles Times,* July 15, 1956.

10. Elizabeth Wilson, telephone interview with the author, August 27, 2007.

11. Edwin Schallert, "Booth Triumphant in 'Desk Set' Bow," *Los Angeles Times,* July 17, 1956.

12. Van Patten interview.

13. "'Desk Set' Run to be Extended," *Los Angeles Times,* August 6, 1956.

14. Norma H. Goodhue, "Librarians Will Honor Miss Booth," *Los Angeles Times,* August 2, 1956.

15. Van Patten interview.

16. Wilson interview.

17. Ibid.

18. *Variety,* March 27, 1957.

19. Hal Humphrey, "Producer Likes His Live Plays," *Oakland Tribune,* July 18, 1957.

20. Edwin Schallert, "At Last, Shirley Booth Gets Comedy Film Role," *Los Angeles Times,* October 13, 1957.

21. Lydia Lane, "Girls Can Be Beautiful but Dull, Warns Shirley Booth," *Los Angeles Times,* June 16, 1957.

22. Edwin Schallert, "At Last, Shirley Booth Gets Comedy Film Role," *Los Angeles Times,* October 13, 1957.

23. Charles Winecoff, *Split Image: The Life of Anthony Perkins* (New York: Dutton, 1996), 149.

24. William Glover, "Tete-a-Tete with the Audience," *Oakland Tribune,* August 10, 1958.

25. Bosley Crowther, "The Screen: 'Hot Spell'; Film at Guild Deals with Marital Rift," *New York Times,* September 18, 1958.

26. *Films and Filming,* November 1958.

27. Playbill, *Miss Isobel.*

28. *Washington Post,* December 10, 1957.

29. Richard L. Coe, "Shirley's No Dumb 'Isobel,'" *Washington Post,* December 14, 1957.

30. Richard L. Coe, "Shirley Booth as 'Miss Isobel,'" *Washington Post,* December 10, 1957.

31. Van Patten, interview.

32. Glover, "Tete-a-Tete with the Audience."

33. Melvyn Douglas, *See You at the Movies: The Autobiography of Melvyn Douglas* (Lanham, MD: University Press of America, 1986), 104.

34. Carol Easton, *No Intermissions: The Life of Agnes de Mille* (Boston: Little, Brown, 1996), 367.

35. Douglas, *See You at the Movies,* 104.

36. Ethan Mordden, *Coming Up Roses: The Broadway Musical in the 1950s* (New York: Oxford University Press, 1998), 222.

37. Louella Parsons, "$400,000 for Inge Play," *San Antonio Light,* July 22, 1959.

38. Audrey Wood and Max Wilk, *Represented by Audrey Wood* (Garden City, NY: Doubleday, 1981), 232.

39. Millicent Adams, "Shirley Booth to Leave Play; Unhappy with Role," *Washington Post,* November 2, 1959.

40. William Inge, *A Loss of Roses: A New Play* (New York: Random House, 1960), foreword.

41. Ibid.

42. Richard L. Coe, "What Price Star System," *Washington Post,* November 3, 1959.

43. Dorothy Kilgallen, "Movie Producers Skip Cuba; New Grace Kelly Due," *Coshocton* (OH) *Tribune,* December 4, 1959.

44. Maurice Zolotow, "Playwright on the Eve: William Inge's Views of Critics, Actors and Collaborators," *New York Times,* November 22, 1959.

45. Jean-Pierre Aumont, *Sun and Shadow* (New York: Norton, 1977), 196.

Chapter 8

1. Hedda Hopper, "Shirley Booth Bans Sex, Violence," *Los Angeles Times,* February 17, 1963.

2. John P. Shanley, "TV Review: 'Steel Hour,'" *New York Times,* March 23, 1961.

3. Cecil Smith, "Little Sheba Comes Back," *Los Angeles Times,* March 19, 1961.

4. Shanley, "TV Review."

5. Bill Fiset, "About Television," *Oakland Tribune,* June 29, 1961.

6. Ted Key, "How Hazel Came to Life," *TV Guide,* January 13, 1962.

7. Harvey Pack, "Shirley Booth Is Still Going Strong as World's Richest Maid, Hazel," *Modesto Bee,* January 23, 1966.

8. "Solving the Servant Problem: Why a Great Lady of the Theater Took Over a Cartoon Character," *TV Guide,* October 7, 1961.

9. Thomas Congdon, "At Home with 'Hazel,'" *Saturday Evening Post,* September 22, 1962.

10. Kevin Minton, "Shirley Booth: A Tribute," *Classic Images,* June 1999.

11. "Solving the Servant Problem."

12. Ted Key, *The Hazel Jubilee: A Sixteen-Year Collection of Cartoons from the Saturday Evening Post* (New York: Dutton, 1959), introduction.

13. Isobel Ashe, "Hazel: She's Really Made It as Make-Believe Maid," *Appleton Post-Crescent,* October 24, 1965.

14. Cynthia Lowry, "Don DeFore: TV's First 'Neighbor,'" *Oakland Tribune,* April 12, 1964.

15. "Roughest Job in Television," *TV Guide,* October 6, 1962.

16. "Solving the Servant Problem."

17. Richard L. Coe, "Shirley's Back In Hit at Last," *Washington Post,* November 23, 1961.

18. Congdon, "At Home with 'Hazel.'"

19. *Variety,* October 4, 1961.

20. Jack Gould, "TV: 'Hazel' in Premiere; Shirley Booth Brings Warmth to Cartoon Character of Diversified Talents," *New York Times,* September 29, 1961.

21. Murray Schumach, "TV is New Pursuit to Shirley Booth," *New York Times,* July 28, 1961.

22. Bert Resnik, "Bert's Eye View," *Long Beach Independent Press-Telegram,* October 15, 1961.

23. Ibid.

24. Ibid.

25. Cynthia Lowry, "Shirley Booth Happy as 'Hazel,'" *San Antonio Light,* September 16, 1962.

26. Congdon, "At Home with 'Hazel.'"

27. Paul Henniger, "Come Back, Little Hazel," *Los Angeles Times,* June 24, 1962.

28. Aleene MacMinn, "Hazel's Mean Boss," *Los Angeles Times,* April 8, 1962.

29. "Roughest Job."

30. Rick du Brow, "Reviewer Heaps Praise on Emmy Awards Show," *Coshocton Tribune,* May 23, 1962.

31. Lawrence Laurent, "Award Ceremonies Can Be So Baffling," *Washington Post,* May 24, 1962.

32. Congdon, "At Home with 'Hazel.'"

33. Hedda Hopper, "Hazel Role another Miss Duffy Success," *Los Angeles Times,* February 6, 1962.

34. "Ed Gardner of Radio's 'Duffy's Tavern' Is Dead," *New York Times,* August 18, 1963.

35. "It's Good-By, Mr. B," *TV Guide*, August 14, 1965.

36. Margaret McManus, "Shirley Booth and 'Hazel' To Stay Together a While," *Syracuse Post-Standard*, October 18, 1964.

37. Ibid.

Chapter 9

1. Cecil Smith, "Hazel: How to Bow Out Gracefully," *Los Angeles Times*, March 28, 1965.

2. Isobel Ashe, "Hazel: She's Really Made It."

3. Cecil Smith, "'Sheba' Comes Back to Raves," *Los Angeles Times*, March 18, 1965.

4. Pack, "Still Going Strong."

5. Bob Noble, "Bob Noble Talks of Television," *Winnipeg Free Press*, February 14, 1965.

6. Harry Castleman and Walter J. Podrazic, *Harry and Wally's Favorite TV Shows* (New York: Prentice-Hall, 1989), 220.

7. *Variety*, September 15, 1965.

8. Walt Dutton, "Model Lynn Borden in Fashion," *Los Angeles Times*, February 12, 1966.

9. Ashe, "Hazel: She's Really Made It."

10. Cynthia Lowry, "Return to 'Sheba' Reassures 'Hazel,'" *Washington Post*, November 15, 1965.

11. *Variety*, September 15, 1965.

12. Pat Cardamone, e-mail to the author, August 30, 2007.

13. Cynthia Lowry, "Actress Shirley Booth Ends 5 Years as 'Hazel,'" *Appleton Post-Crescent*, September 22, 1966.

14. Margaret McManus, "Shirley Booth Won't Seek Roles," *Syracuse Post-Standard*, December 3, 1966.

15. Sheilah Graham, "Inside Hollywood," *Pasadena* (FL) *Independent Star-News*, August 28, 1966.

16. Lowry, "Actress Shirley Booth Ends 5 Years as 'Hazel.'"

17. Robert Musel, "Miss Booth Comes to Tea," *TV Guide*, December 3, 1966.

18. Arnold Hano, "Back from the Bobi Desert," *TV Guide*, May 12, 1973.

19. Lawrence Laurent, "Williams' Play Done Faithfully," *Washington Post*, December 10, 1966.

20. Bob Thomas, "Shirley Booth Shrugs Off Emmy Nomination for 'Glass Menagerie' Role," *Washington Post*, May 11, 1967.

21. Ibid.

22. Loring Mandel, *CBS Playhouse Presents: Do Not Go Gentle into That Good Night* (New York: CBS Television Network, 1967), 72.

23. Ibid., 91.

24. Ibid., 8.

25. Linda Gordon, "Shirley Booth Appears Despite Illness," *Syracuse Post-Standard*, July 31, 1968.

26. Louis Calta, "Shirley Booth Signs for Broadway After 10 Years," *New York Times*, January 6, 1970.

27. Ibid.

28. William Glover, "Shirley Returning to Stage, So She's Buying More Land," *Chicago Tribune*, March 1, 1970.

29. Dennis McGovern and Deborah Grace Winer, *Sing Out, Louise!: 150 Stars of the Musical Theatre Remember 50 Years on Broadway* (New York: Schirmer Books, 1993), 42.

30. Theodore Taylor, *Jule: The Story of Composer Jule Styne* (New York: Random House, 1979), 262.

31. Bob MacKenzie, "Shirley Booth — Warmth Comes Shining Through," *Los Angeles Times*, September 12, 1971.

32. Harold Clurman, *The Collected Works of Harold Clurman: Six Decades of Commentary on Theatre, Dance, Music, Film, Arts and Letters* (New York: Applause Books, 1994), 759.

33. MacKenzie, "Shirley Booth — Warmth Comes Shining Through."

34. Duston Harvey, "Acting Becoming Dull, Dead-Eyed, Says Star," *Stars and Stripes*, October 11, 1971.

35. MacKenzie, "Shirley Booth — Warmth Comes Shining Through."

36. Barbara Bladen, "The Marquee," *San Mateo Times*, September 6, 1971.

37. Rex Reed, "Dumb as a Mink-Eyed Fox," *Long Beach (CA) Independent Press-Telegram*, August 15, 1976.

38. Richard Plummer, "Shirley Booth Exceeds Material at Lakewood," *Kennebec Journal*, July 13, 1972.

Chapter 10

1. Lawrence Laurent, "Shirley Booth Offers 'A Touch of Grace,'" *Washington Post*, February 18, 1973.

2. Joan Crosby, "Young Comedy Writers are Saying Grace," *Eureka Times-Standard*, Feburary 11, 1973.

3. Ibid.

4. Dick Kleiner, "Shirley's 'Grace': Somebody I Wanted to Room With," *Eureka* (CA) *Times-Standard*, April 8, 1973.

5. Charlotte St. John, "Shirley Booth Says—'I Wouldn't Have Been a Good Mother' (But She Would Have Been a Marvelous Grandmother!)," *TV-Radio Show*, June 1973.

6. Saul Turteltaub, telephone interview with the author, September 15, 2007.

7. Arnold Hano, "Back from the Gobi Desert," *TV Guide*, May 12, 1973.

8. Turteltaub interview.

9. Hano, "Back from the Gobi Desert."

10. Robert C. Stewart, Jr., "'Grace' Is No Mistake for Rush," *San Antonio Light*, February 4, 1973.

11. Ibid.

12. *TV Guide*, March 17, 1973.

13. Clarence Petersen, "What's Troubling Grace and Herb?," *Chicago Tribune*, April 1, 1973.

14. Burt Prelutsky, "Impressions on TV Screen," *Los Angeles Times*, April 1, 1973.

15. *TV Guide*, June 2, 1973.

16. Bettelou Peterson, "Networks Still Undecided on Fall Schedule," *Chicago Tribune*, February 23, 1973.

17. Hano, "Back from the Gobi Desert."

18. "Shirley Booth's Long-Distance Duet with Santa," *Lumberton* (NC) *Robesonian,* December 8, 1974.

19. Ibid.

20. "People, Etc.," *Syracuse Herald-American,* July 20, 1975.

21. Thomas Congdon, "At Home with 'Hazel,'" *Saturday Evening Post,* September 22, 1962.

22. Enid Nemy, "Broadway," *New York Times,* August 31, 1984.

23. "Actress Shirley Booth Dies at Chatham Home," *Cape Cod Chronicle,* October 22, 1992.

24. Agnes Grehan, "TV Maid Hazel in Brave Battle for Her Health," *Globe,* undated clipping, circa 1988.

25. "Actress Shirley Booth Dies at Chatham Home."

26. William A. Henry III, "The Laureate of Longing," *Time,* July 23, 1984.

27. Dan Sullivan, "Sheba Does Come Back — to LATC," *Los Angeles Times*, April 27, 1987.

28. Burt A. Folkart, "Shirley Booth: TV's Hazel Won Oscars, Tonys, Emmys," *Los Angeles Times*, October 21, 1992.

29. Dick Van Patten, telephone interview with the author, September 9, 2007.

30. Julie Harris, letter to the author, September 19, 2007.

31. Bob MacKenzie, "Shirley Booth — Warmth Comes Shining Through," *Los Angeles Times*, September 9, 1971.

Bibliography

Books and Magazine Articles

Aumont, Jean-Pierre. *Sun and Shadow.* New York: Norton, 1977.

Bellamy, Ralph. *When the Smoke Hit the Fan.* Garden City, NY: Doubleday, 1979.

Berard, Jeannette, and Klaudia Englund, comps. *Radio Series Scripts, 1930–2001: A Catalog of the American Radio Archives Collection.* Jefferson, NC: McFarland, 2006.

Burrows, Abe. *Honest, Abe: Is There Really No Business Like Show Business?* Boston: Little, Brown, 1980.

Carroll, Carroll. *None of Your Business; Or, My Life with J. Walter Thompson (Confessions of a Renegade Radio Writer).* New York: Cowles, 1970.

Castleman, Harry, and Walter J. Podrazic. *Harry and Wally's Favorite TV Shows.* New York: Prentice-Hall, 1989.

Clurman, Harold. *The Collected Works of Harold Clurman: Six Decades of Commentary on Theatre, Dance, Music, Film, Arts and Letters.* New York: Applause Books, 1994.

Coleman, Lonnie. *Hot Spell.* New York: Avon, 1958.

Coughlan, Robert. "New Queen of the Drama." *Life,* December 1, 1952, pp. 128–130, 133–136, 141.

Delmar, Viña. *About Mrs. Leslie.* New York: Pocket Books, 1952.

Dick, Bernard F. *Hal Wallis: Producer to the Stars.* Lexington: University Press of Kentucky, 2004.

_____. *Engulfed: The Death of Paramount Pictures and the Birth of Corporate Hollywood.* Lexington: University Press of Kentucky, 2001.

Douglas, Melvyn. *See You at the Movies: The Autobiography of Melvyn Douglas.* Lanham, MD: University Press of America, 1986.

Dunning, John. *Tune In Yesterday: The Ultimate Encyclopedia of Old Time Radio, 1925–1976.* Englewood Cliffs, NJ: Prentice-Hall, 1976.

Easton, Carol. *No Intermissions: The Life of Agnes de Mille.* Boston: Little, Brown, 1996.

Eells, George. *Final Gig: The Man Behind the Murder.* San Diego: Harcourt Brace Jovanovich, 1991.

Fields, Joseph A., Jerome Chodorov, and Ruth McKenney. *My Sister Eileen: A Comedy.* New York: Random House, 1941.

The Flying Dutchman II: An Exposition of a New York City High School with Its Activities. Erasmus Hall High School, 1911.

Frankel, Doris. *Love Me Long: Comedy in Three Acts.* New York: Dramatists' Play Service, 1950.

Gardner, Ed. *Duffy's First Reader, By Archie.* New York: Bristol-Myers Company, 1943.

Gelbart, Larry. *Laughing Matters: On Writing* M*A*S*H, *Tootsie,* Oh, God!, *and a Few Other Funny Things.* New York: Random House, 1998.

Gordon, Eric A. *Mark the Music: The Life and Work of Marc Blitzstein.* New York: St. Martin's Press, 1989.

Gow, James, and Arnaud d'Usseau. *Tomorrow the World.* New York: Scribner's, 1943.

Havig, Alan R. *Fred Allen's Radio Comedy.* Philadelphia: Temple University Press, 1990.

Hayes, Richard K. *Kate Smith: A Biography, with a Discography, Filmography, and List of Stage Appearances.* Jefferson, NC: McFarland, 1995.

Jessel, George. *So Help Me: The Autobiography of George Jessel.* New York: Random House, 1943.

Kanin, Fay Mitchell. *Goodbye, My Fancy: A Comedy in Three Acts.* New York: Samuel French, 1950.

Kaye, Jay. "Shirley Booth: Broadway's Choice." *Coronet,* December 1953, pp. 48–52.

Key, Ted. *The Hazel Jubilee: A Sixteen-Year Collection of Cartoons from the Saturday Evening Post.* New York: Dutton, 1959.

Kobler, John. *Damned in Paradise: The Life of John Barrymore.* New York: Atheneum, 1977.

Laurents, Arthur. *Original Story: A Memoir of Broadway and Hollywood.* New York: Knopf, 2000.

Mandel, Loring. *CBS Playhouse Presents: Do Not Go Gentle Into That Good Night.* New York: CBS Television Network, 1967.

Maney, Richard. *Fanfare: The Confessions of a Press Agent.* New York: Harper, 1957.

McGovern, Dennis, and Deborah Grace Winer. *Sing Out, Louise!: 150 Stars of the Musical Theatre Remember 50 Years on Broadway.* New York: Schirmer Books, 1993.

Nadel, Norman. *A Pictorial History of the Theatre Guild*. New York: Crown, 1969.

Phelps, William Lyon. *The Twentieth Century Theatre: Observations on the Contemporary English and American Stage*. Freeport, NY: Books for Libraries Press, 1967, c.1918.

Poling, James. "One Touched with Genius." *Collier's*, June 16, 1951, pp. 23, 61–62.

Schaffner, Franklin J. *Worthington Miner*. Metuchen, NJ: Scarecrow Press, 1985.

Selznick, Irene Mayer. *A Private View*. New York: Knopf, 1983.

Smith, Betty, and George Abbott. *A Tree Grows in Brooklyn: A Musical Play*. New York: Harper and Brothers, 1951.

Taylor, Robert. *Fred Allen: His Life and Wit*. Boston: Little, Brown, 1989.

Taylor, Theodore. *Jule: The Story of Composer Jule Styne*. New York: Random House, 1979.

Terrace, Vincent. *Radio Program Openings and Closings, 1931–1972*. Jefferson, NC: McFarland, 2003.

"The Trouper." *Time*, August 10, 1953, pp. 58–64.

Voss, Ralph. *A Life of William Inge: The Strains of Triumph*. Lawrence: University Press of Kansas, 1989.

Williams, Tennessee. *Memoirs*. New York: New Directions, 2006.

Winecoff, Charles. *Split Image: The Life of Anthony Perkins*. New York: Dutton, 1996.

Wood, Audrey, and Max Wilk. *Represented by Audrey Wood*. Garden City, NY: Doubleday, 1981.

Young, Jordan R. *The Laugh Crafters: Comedy Writing in Radio and TV's Golden Age*. Beverly Hills, CA: Past Times, 1999.

Periodicals

The Hartford Courant
The Los Angeles Times
The New York Times
TV Guide
Variety

Websites

www.ancestry.com
www.findagrave.com
www.ibdb.com (The Internet Broadway Database)
www.newspaperarchive.com
www.radiogoldindex.com

Index

Page numbers in **_bold italics_** indicate photographs.